Kincentricity

Kincentricity

Connecting *to* Nature *with* American Indian Food Traditions

Enrique Salmón

Rizzoli
New York

New York · Paris · London · Milan

First published in the United States
of America in 2026 by
Rizzoli International Publications, Inc.
49 West 27th Street
New York, NY 10001
www.rizzoliusa.com

The information in this book is true and complete to the best of our knowledge. All recommendations are made without guarantee on the part of the author or Rizzoli International Publications. The author and publisher disclaim any liability in connection with the use of this information. In particular, ingesting wild plants is inherently risky. Plants can be easily mistaken and individuals vary in their physiological reactions to plants that are touched or consumed, and it is important for the reader to use judgment as to whether wild plants being harvested may have been treated by others with pesticides. Please do not attempt self-treatment of a medical problem without consulting a qualified health practitioner.

Publisher: Charles Miers
Editor: Stacee Gravelle Lawrence
Cover Design: Spencer Fuller/Faceout Studio
Text Design: Lauren Michelle Smith and Design per se
Production Manager: Maria Pia Gramaglia
Managing Editor: Lynn Scrabis

ISBN: 978-0-8478-7739-3
Library of Congress Control Number: 2026937151

Printed in China
2026 2027 2028 2029 / 10 9 8 7 6 5 4 3 2 1

The authorized representative in the EU for product safety and compliance is
Mondadori Libri S.p.A.,
via Gian Battista Vico 42, Milan, Italy, 20123

www.mondadori.it

Visit us online:
Instagram: @RizzoliBooks
Facebook.com/RizzoliNewYork
Youtube.com/user/RizzoliNY

Cover images: Shutterstock/Olga Korneeva, mamita, Morphart Creation, Hein Nouwens

FSC
www.fsc.org
MIX
Paper | Supporting responsible forestry
FSC® C104723

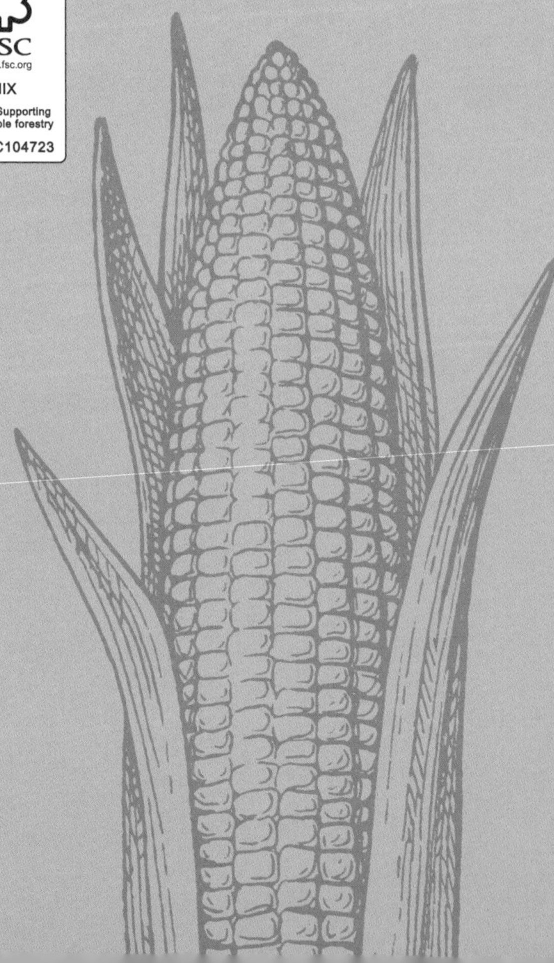

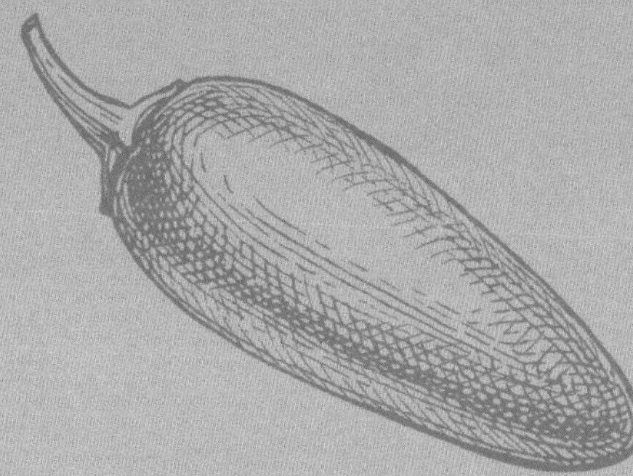

For my aunts—Anna, Christina, Trini, Nic, Georgia, Alicia, and Vera.

For my grandmother Maria and for my mother, Esperidiona, always.

Your lineage of recipes, dishes, laughter, and wisdom continues to inspire and make me smile.

Contents

1. Kincentric Ecology 8
2. Indigenous Gardens 24
3. From the Fields 36
   - Beans 42
   - Corn 49
   - Chiles 61
   - Squash and Pumpkins 66
4. Berries and Fruits 72
   - Blackberries 74
   - Blueberries 78
   - Currants 79
   - Huckleberries 82
   - Strawberries 85
   - Cranberries 86
   - Prickly Pear 90
   - Saguaro 94
5. Nuts and Seeds 98
   - Acorns 100
   - Bay Laurel 105
   - Black Walnut 107
   - Butternut 111
   - Mesquite 115
   - Piñon 119
   - Wild Rice 123
6. Tubers, Roots, and Corms 128
   - Groundnut 131
   - Wapato 134
   - Nahavita 138
   - Timpsila 140
7. Edible Greens 144
   - Cattail 148
   - Goosefoot 152
   - Epazote 156
   - Fiddleheads 158
   - Purslane 163
   - Stinging Nettle 165
   - Watercress 169
   - Wild Onions 172

GLOSSARY 176
FURTHER READING AND REFERENCES 182
ACKNOWLEDGMENTS 186
PHOTOGRAPHY CREDITS 190
INDEX 196

1

Kincentric Ecology: Sharing Breath with Our Relatives

Basaseachi Waterfall in Copper Canyon, part of the Sierra Madre Occidental in Mexico and part of the homeland of the Rarámuri.

An artist's rendering of Tarahumara men playing a dice game, using a board made of cavities poked directly into the ground.

KI-ANIYA, THE TIME BEFORE THERE WAS TIME

The friends Tobacco and Drinking Gourd were at the gambling place, slamming the ends of long marked sticks against the flat angle stone and moving the pebbles from circle to circle in the clay playing platform. Their mutual friend, Corn Husk, showed up to tell them about a *tesguinada*, a ritual corn beer–drinking gathering hosted by Rarámuri communities all around the Sierra Tarahumara. The three friends sought out *tesguinadas* because they provided a time for the friends to "become beautifully drunk." Unfortunately, the three friends did not heed the advice of the leaders to not get *too* drunk. They began to gamble again, and unsurprisingly they were not doing well, losing their bets. Soon they began to gamble their belongings, their goats, and even considered gambling their children. At this point Onorúame, the Creator, interceded and transformed the friends into the vegetal forms we see around us today: tobacco, drinking gourd, and corn husk.

Among my people, the Rarámuri, we consider it good to drink corn beer—Onorúame enjoys and is enlivened by the smell of our beer-laden burps. When Onorúame is pleased and entertained, he has more energy to bring the rains for the people's crops. People also smoke at *tesguinadas*, as the smoke helps our thoughts and prayers to be understood by the spirits. This is why it is good to smoke and drink at *tesguinadas* and to become (mildly) drunk.

Tesguino cooking in pots in El Limón, Nayarit State, Mexico, circa 1937.

Rarámuri people during a sacred pascol *dance.*

This story illustrates the human traits sometimes bestowed on plants by the Rarámuri, but also offers a cultural example of a particular tradition: applying behavioral expectations we consider proper for humans to stories involving plants, by way of instruction for the listener. In addition, tobacco, smoke, and fire also carry additional weight in Rarámuri ritual and prayer. The Rarámuri only smoke at night so as not to confuse the creator, who might mistake smoke he can see in the daytime for clouds. If this happened, he might not produce real clouds for making rain. Both smoke from tobacco and from pine resin incense are therefore employed as healing agents. Smoke is interpreted as one visible manifestation of the breath that permeates all life: what the Rarámuri have termed *iwígara*.

The Indigenous peoples of North America view ourselves as an integral part of the life and environment within which we live. This concept encompasses many ideas and ways of thinking, some unique to the Rarámuri, some shared by many Indigenous cultures. Rituals and ceremonies, the language—and therefore even our thoughts—are influenced by the lands, animals, and winds with which we live. *Iwígara* is the total interconnectedness and integration of all life in the Sierra Madres, physical and spiritual. To say *iwígara* to a Rarámuri calls on that person to recognize and respect life in all its forms. To a Rarámuri, invoking that term makes them recall the stories related to the beginning of Rarámuri life, our origins, and our relationships to animals, plants, the place that nurtures us, and the entities to which the Rarámuri look for guidance.

This is just one example of how Indigenous languages can express abstract concepts related to the natural world very differently than English. The closest way I've been able to translate *iwígara* into a concept with English words is to first explain that we see all forms of life as our relatives, or "kin," and then extrapolate from there to get the term "kincentric ecology" to refer to a worldview where all life-forms are inherently understood to be interconnected, part of the same living planet. The term "kincentric ecology" would be meaningless to Indigenous language speakers—they have no need of it, as they already express this concept in traditional terms. The concept of *iwígara* as a perception of self and culture intertwined in the web of life already exists for the Rarámuri, and is reinforced in us from a young age.

A way to delve deeper into the concept of *iwígara* is to examine how it is reflected in a traditional ritual, *Yúmari*. The nearest translation in English for *Yúmari* is probably "blessing." *Yúmari* songs often make references to *sewa'ra*, flowers. In one specific *Yúmari* song, reference is made to *sumati okilivea*, the beautiful lily. *Yúmari* dances and songs are performed during the growing season to both bless and heal people as well as animals and the land. During *Yúmari* ceremonies, the women are asked to dance—the only time they do in Rarámuri culture. The women dance in an *iwí* (rotating circle), while two male singers and chanters dance within it. The songs ask that the land be nourished and that the land nourish the people. The land is nourished by the results of the ceremony, which brings rain. As the songs are performed, the *iwí* continues to turn. The *iwí* represents the fertility of the land. *Iwí* can convey other meanings, however. It translates roughly into "the idea of binding with a lasso." But it also means to unite, to join, to connect. Another meaning of *iwí* is to breathe, inhale/exhale, or respire. *Iwí* also makes reference to the Rarámuri concept of the soul. It is understood that the soul sustains the body—with the breath of life. Everything that is affected by the air has a soul. Plants, animals, humans, stones, the land—all share the same breath. When humans and animals die, we believe their souls become butterflies that visit the living. The butterflies also travel to the Milky Way, where souls of the ancestors reside.

Iwí is also the word used to identify a specific caterpillar that weaves its cocoons on the madrone tree (*Arbutus* sp.). The implication is that *iwí* encompasses a whole morphophysiological process of change, death, birth, and rebirth. *Iwí* is the soul or essence of life everywhere. *Iwí* is of course the prefix to *iwígara*. *Iwígara* channels the idea that all life, spiritual and physical, is interconnected in a continual cycle. We are all related to, and play a role in, the complexity of the universe. Kincentric ecology, then, is a physical process and manifestation of *iwígara*.

In a similar example of how pervasive this idea of connectedness is to Indigenous peoples, the Rarámuri term *numat'ɪ*, or "things of the natural world," is for relatives in a more literal sense. Non-Christianized Rarámuri believe that there have been at least two previous worlds and that we are currently occupying the third. In the world prior to our current one, humans were part plant. Specifically, it's said the Rarámuri owe their emergence into the world to corn. It is believed that the Rarámuri emerged from ears of corn after a great flood and the destruction of a previous world. And when the Rarámuri emerged into this world, many other plants followed. They live today as humans of a different form. Tobacco, drinking gourd, corn husk, peyote, datura, maize, morning glory, brazilwood, coyotes, crows, bears, and deer are all humans—from the previous world. Rarámuri feel related to these life-forms much as Euroamericans feel related to their human cousins and siblings.

We still venerate corn as a staple food whether eaten raw, made into tortillas, used in soups, or as tamales. As a medicine, corn meal itself is sprinkled onto patients as a blessing. We make a medicine from tassels and other plants that's used to cure dysentery and treat kidney problems. Similar worldviews exist among Pueblo peoples such as the Hopi, Jemez, Zia, and Laguna, who all understand that there were up to four previous worlds and that animals and plants played a role in helping the people emerge into this one. Not all Indigenous peoples of North America believe that there were previous worlds, but many creation stories across the continent tell of specific plants and animals that helped the people emerge, brought the first light, created the shape of the landscape, and breathed life into the first people.

For Indigenous people the natural world is not one of separation or fear, it is a world of wonder and of familiarity. The human niche is only one of myriad united niches that work together to encourage a kincentric process. If one aspect of this interwoven mosaic is removed, the integrity of the weave is threatened and all other aspects are weakened. A certain attachment results from knowing that some of your relatives are the life-forms that share your place with you. This belief influences one's sense of identity, thought, language, and how we interact with everything around us.

A collection of diverse ears collected from a Rarámuri farmer near Creel in Chihuahua, Mexico.

KINCENTRICALLY MANAGING THE LAND

Over the centuries, methods of land use developed by Indigenous people adhered to a kincentric understanding. Horticultural and agricultural techniques included selective coppicing, pruning, and harvesting, gathering, cultivation, transplanting, vegetative propagation, sowing, controlled burning, and weeding. Some plant populations and individual plant species were intentionally selected "in accordance with ecological principles in order to increase population abundance, diversity, growth, longevity, yield, and quality to meet cultural needs." As an example, my people select some corn varieties for their ability to produce naturally occurring sugars, which enhances their fermentation qualities in making corn beer. With regards to kincentric ecology, this is a sound practice because the corn beer is a necessary element in keeping the Creator strong and bringing the rain. Another example involves the practice of many Indigenous agriculturalists who intentionally move or encourage individual species of edible chenopods from their natural habitat to the edges of agricultural fields. The greens come from fields where the breath, spirit, or energy of the field is considered strong. In translation, this means that the population of the greens is abundant.

An archaeological site along the Menominee River, in Michigan's Upper Peninsula, that provides evidence of the Menominee tribe engaging in intensive farming techniques based on a raised ridge field system to grow corn, beans, squash, and other crops; the site was in use for over six hundred years, constructed initially around the year 1000 CE.

The concept of kincentric ecology is at the heart of many Indigenous land management philosophies. It guides agriculture and foraging techniques, as well as the practice of medicine. Using plants for healing as well as for food creates a strong relationship between people and the natural world, and Indigenous reliance on local landscapes has created a worldview wherein people see themselves very much as participants in their natural community, not separate from it. Most Indigenous peoples understand that they were placed here as caretakers of the land; they understand intrinsically that their job is to aid in keeping it healthy, which in turn works to provide for its inhabitants.

Caretaking translates to practices such as transplanting edible greens among corn and bean fields. The greens become readily harvestable for the people as they walk through the fields tending to the other crops and, in return, the greens thrive and become more abundant by benefitting from the irrigation engineered to nurture the corn and beans. Caretaking also means that only the longest pine needles, the straightest Indian hemp branches, or the smoothest cedar bark is collected for making baskets—not taking everything all at once and then discarding a lot of it. There is little waste in Indigenous systems. We know from centuries of experience how selective collecting can enhance new growth, just as pruning does for fruit trees. Traditional harvesting of these basketmaking materials is also purposefully periodic, for example. Caregiving, in terms of land, is a method of benefitting from land while enhancing it. The materials we use for our own purposes are carefully managed. This is due largely to the collection philosophy influenced by kincentric ecology: always thinking about preserving the population of any given plant so it will thrive the following year and for years to come, instead of short-sightedly taking more than what we truly need today.

As previously mentioned, part of the traditional management regimen for ensuring that ample basketmaking materials will be available involves controlled burning. In California, burning is employed in the management of other plants as well. An overgrown understory of oak groves on a savanna with enough mature oak trees will be burned to retard growth of oak saplings and other trees and plants that would compete with the existing oaks, and simultaneously removes underbrush that could act as fuel for a devastating and uncontrollable fire—all while transforming the savanna into a healthy, open ecosystem. This results in higher yields of acorns because the oaks can soak up ample nutrients and moisture without competition, and better harvests of fruit-producing shrubs such as chokecherry and manzanita because periodic burns encourage these species to sprout new growth via rhizomes.

As non-native people become more interested in discovering how they can connect to local landscapes, the overharvesting of useful plants has become a concern in places where American Indians have traditionally practiced kincentric gathering. Thanks to good land management, certain areas support bountiful populations of medicinal and useful plants, and that bounty attracts the eye of new foragers who are not always as careful in their harvesting practices. These concerns intensify also where arable land is cherished for large-scale farming and where the pressures of logging and other contemporary resource issues make sustainable gathering tenuous. Therefore, wild edible and medicinal plants must be treated with extra respect. When collecting wild onions for example, Native collectors often select the middle-sized bulbs, leaving the larger and smaller ones in the ground, thus promoting a second harvest—the old ones will go to seed while the young ones have room to grow to maturity. In addition, many Indigenous collectors still use digging sticks to harvest bulbs such as timpsila. The use of digging sticks disturbs the soil only as much as necessary to retrieve the bulb; the less soil is exposed to oxidation and moisture loss, the better. This method encourages further growth of the plants and decreases competitive perennials, which cannot take root unless open patches of disturbed soil are present. A symbiotic relationship exists between Indigenous gatherers of onions and other edible tubers and those plants.

How deeply embedded the concept of kincentric ecology is in the minds of Native peoples is difficult to quantify and document. Through conversations and careful observation, however, it is possible to begin to understand that it's an entire philosophy.

For example, an elder Rarámuri consultant often allows me to accompany him on his plant-collecting forays into the mountains near the community of Norogachi in Chihuahua, Mexico. He prefers to collect some of his medicinal plants from a particular *rincón*, or corner, of a large arroyo. He collects from other "favorite" locations as well—he claims each of them has the best plants, in turn. While walking to this *rincón* one afternoon, we passed by several plants of the very same species that we were intending to harvest that day, but he waited until we reached the actual *rincón* to begin gathering. Because he had been tending that area, we were able to collect a bushel with little impact on the overall population. When questioned as to why we did not just collect the plants that we had passed earlier on the trail, he asserted that "those plants are not right for harvest because they are in the wrong place." In hindsight, I realized that the populations of plants that we had passed over were much smaller in number in comparison to those that were eventually harvested; taking from there could have easily decimated the colony.

Indigenous peoples have a basic understanding that harvesting threatened populations is not an ecologically sound practice. Yet, my friend would not explain the situation in these basic terms. He suggested something even more profound: that the *iwígara* in these low-population areas is "weak" and must, therefore, be allowed to strengthen itself before the plants there will be of any nutritional or medicinal use. In further conversation, he explained that collecting the plants in the *rincón* was good because thinning them out a bit would actually help strengthen the *iwígara* of the unharvested plants in that area. He mentioned that their roots had become entangled, crowded, thus weakening their breath. In addition, he mentioned that the plants did like to be near each other because they share their breaths, but they do not like to have to compete for breath, which is not the same thing. Experience told him which populations were best for harvesting.

Indigenous land management in North America represents a tradition of conservation that relies on a deeply embedded reciprocal relationship with nature in which ideas that reflect kincentricity become affirmations of caretaking responsibilities and therefore an assurance of sustainable subsistence and harvesting. It is a realization that our homelands are places of nurturing, full of relatives with whom all breath is shared.

EFFECTS OF KINCENTRIC ECOLOGICAL PRACTICES ON ECOSYSTEMS

A central premise of this book is that kincentricity has a direct and positive influence and impact on Indigenous land management practices. These influences directly affect the choices Indigenous land managers make when interacting with the land, and affect as well the following pivotal land-management practices.

Seed Saving

The plethora and variety of food plants that fed American Indians prior to European contact was a direct result of seed saving. Indigenous

A Pomo woman using a specialized seed beater to gather them into a burden basket, circa 1924.

agriculturalists and agroforesters selected for and sometimes intentionally hybridized specific crops and plants based on cultural tastes as well as on adaptability to regional climates. For example, it is widely understood now that maize (*Zea mays*), what European colonists began referring to as corn, was first hybridized from the kernel-producing grass teosinte. This happened about nine thousand years ago somewhere near the Río Balsas region of southern Mexico. Gradually maize began to migrate north as Indigenous traders spread this food product along established trade routes. By 3550 BCE, corn had reached the Tehuacan Valley of Pueblo, Mexico. By 2400 BCE, it is found in the Tamaulipas region. Around 2000 BCE, corn is being grown in the arid Southwest. And approximately one thousand years ago, corn begins to be raised by Indigenous farmers in the New England area as well—acknowledged to be the most northerly climate where maize can be successfully grown. During the gradual migration of corn, Indigenous agriculturalists continued selecting for plants that were best able to adapt to their local climates.

The Río Balsas region of southern Mexico where corn was first developed is a hot, tropical region where the growing season is nearly year-round. In the American Southwest, Ancestral Puebloan farmers live in a high-altitude desert region that is arid and often experiences cold nights and sometimes freezing temperatures during the winter months, with a correspondingly shorter growing season of perhaps about 120 days. For the Penobscot farmers of New England to be able to raise corn during an even shorter growing season that lasted only about ninety days is evidence of how much selective

*An ear of the "sacred corn" of the Abenaki (*Zea mays *var.* tunicata*), whose ancestral homeland covered today's New England and into southern Canada. It was cultivated for centuries; each kernel is covered by an individual husk, and so it came to symbolize resilience.*

breeding must have taken place in the interim. Penobscot and other New England farmers selected seed cobs from plants with ears that emerged earliest (normally on the lower portions of the stalks). By the time of European contact, Indigenous farmers in New England were raising corn that could be planted, flower, be pollinated, fruit, and reach maturity within just seventy days, including flint corn, popcorn, sweet corn, different colors of corn, and flour corn. The Abenaki were known for growing a variety in the oxbows of today's Connecticut River that grew to only three feet tall and produced just one ear per stalk, each about four inches long.

Puebloan farmers had to adapt to very different growing conditions. On the high-altitude Colorado Plateau, unexpected late-spring frosts and snow could abruptly kill young corn plants that had been already sprouted after being planted in late March. Due to arid conditions in the region, the soil does not retain much moisture at the surface and life-giving monsoon rains do not arrive until around the middle of July. They nevertheless bred a variety of corn that could sprout and reach maturity in these difficult conditions. During the gradual migration and regional hybridization of corn, Indigenous chefs were also selecting for variation in the cooking and palatableness of corn.

Dry Land Farming

To practice agriculture in very dry areas, crops of corn, squash, and melons are often planted in areas where floodwaters (when they arrive) will spread out at the mouth of an arroyo (gully). This is the most common method used by the Tohono O'odham now, and also in pre-Columbian times, and they are known as *ak-chin* fields. They are designed to catch water due to natural changes in floodplain slope gradients; fields were historically placed just downstream of where floodwaters and their detritus were deposited. The term *ak-chin* means "mouth of a wash." The floodwaters are divided into irrigation channels by a series of brush weirs strategically placed above the fields, so other flood-washed detritus is also caught and held, to enrich the soil. This water-control system is rebuilt annually. The system overcomes the two most limiting factors to food production in the desert: water scarcity and low fertility. In addition, it encourages oxygenated irrigation, soil health, and encourages species diversity as it retains some plants that may reseed later and the creation of microhabitats.

A Pueblo man irrigating wheat in New Mexico, circa 1899. The irrigation channel at his feet is in stark contrast to the dry desert mesas in the background.

Pruning and Coppicing

Similar to non-native gardeners who periodically deadhead rose bushes, or when people who grow fruit trees will selectively cut branches to shape their trees to encourage healthy fruit production, Indigenous gathers and harvesters will selectively beat and also cut away unwanted parts of certain trees and large shrubs in order to maintain the health of certain plants and to promote new growth. Indigenous pruning prevents disease in trees and shrubs, encourages desired growth, creates space for the sunlight to reach the ground, and encourages the movement of nutrients to desired parts of a plant. Indigenous peoples often practice pruning on shrubs and large herbaceous plants, however, by cutting them all the way back to ground level. Indigenous peoples have employed this practice for centuries. It is often reserved for plants needed for basketry materials, where annual coppicing encourages plants that will be used for basket making to grow straight. Coppicing has the added benefit of creating and encouraging diverse habitats for wildlife.

Land Management with Fire

Indigenous peoples have used low-intensity burns for millennia as a way to return nutrients to the soil, invite the propagation of specific plants, to encourage useful herbaceous plants, and to decrease competition for nutrients and moisture for food-producing hardwoods such as maples, walnuts, and oaks. The burns were and are carefully planned in order to prevent out-of-control and catastrophic fires. Today, in the Sierra Madres of Chihuahua, Mexico, my people still set periodic and seasonal fires for the same reasons. This kind of burning is different than the practice of slash-and-burn agriculture, which eventually depletes the nutrients of the soils. In North America, controlled burns removing undergrowth in forested areas to stop it from choking plants seen as particularly useful. There are several benefits to these burns. Certain plants, such as wild tobacco and lodgepole pines, for example, actually require fire in order to reproduce. Other plants, such as echinacea, bluestem grass, and camas, benefit from a reduction in competitive species and in the nutrient cycling that results from controlled burns. The practice encourages grasses, and therefore brush forms that attract small mammals and ungulates. Other benefits of controlled periodic burning include the control of insect pests that can destroy entire forests, improved growth of desired plants, and even the creation of habitats for animal species. For many Indigenous communities, periodic burning is performed as a part of an annual renewal or other ceremony as a way to honor our responsibility as caretakers of our homelands.

Controlled fires set the agroforestry stage for selective harvesting of medicinal, edible, and utilitarian plants as well as for a mosaic of agricultural areas that afforded perennial and annual crops. The concept of a mosaic is significant here. Before contact, many of the forests throughout North America resembled more of a patchwork of mixed hardwoods and some conifers interspersed with meadows. For centuries, Native agroforesters managed more open woodlands that encouraged spaces for useful plants. Shade-tolerant plants such as ferns, spruces, and beech would grow into too-dense undergrowth, and so were intentionally controlled through fire. With more sunlight able to reach forest floors, crops of oaks, maples, nut-bearing trees, and fruit-bearing shrubs were maintained.

In many cases, useful plants were selectively planted, particularly in what is today New England. At one point in my academic career, I was a part of a professor exchange between my small college in Colorado and a college in western Massachusetts. During that semester, I co-taught an ethnobotany class with a botany professor. One day my co-instructor led the class outside through the local woods near the campus. The woods were part of the larger property of the campus and were therefore not very strictly managed. The floor of the woods was relatively overgrown with a tangle of shrubs, small saplings of mixed conifers and beeches, ferns, and other

Some of the earliest illustrations and descriptions of the Willamette Valley by white explorers, like this painting by Henry Warre in 1845, depict landscapes of grasslands interspersed with occasional oak and conifer stands—evidence of the Kalapuya using fire to manage the land, particularly to create areas to drive deer during hunts, to clear underbrush from under oak and hazel trees, and to stimulate root production in camas prairies.

plants that I do not recall. We were still able to walk through the woods without too much difficulty. At one point he asked us all to stop and line up in a particular place. He asked us to look past the line of students, and into the woods to the right. Then he asked us to repeat this by looking to the left. He asked us if we noticed anything different in the two vantage points. It took a few seconds before one of the students realized that all the maple trees were growing in a straight line. The point of the lesson was to demonstrate how Indigenous forest managers had, at one point, intentionally planted the maple trees in a pattern to control what grew around and beneath them, and to force controlled burns to ignite in a predictable way. My co-instructor told us that there had been a time where a person could gallop a horse through most of New England's woods as a result of Indigenous agroforestry practices, which kept much of the ground relatively clear. Today, a person would risk life and limb trying to ride a horse through most North American forests for the tangle of underbrush.

THE RELATIONSHIP BETWEEN HUMANS AND THE NATURAL WORLD

When ecologists, land managers, environmentalists, and conservationists speak and write about endangered species and their potential loss, they rarely mention the parallel loss of human cultures that have worked for centuries to maintain and enhance their habitats. Cultures such as the Rarámuri represent a group of people that maintain and nurture their place through their traditional land management practices. They maintain the environmental integrity of the Sierra Tarahumara region, which would quickly decline in terms of overall ecological health, we believe, if the Rarámuri culture were to disappear. Fortunately, the Rarámuri culture remains viable despite modern encroachment. Our educational system ensures that the beliefs and traditional land practices are being transferred between elders and children, which in turn ensures the integrity of the Sierra Madres.

Indigenous cultures of North America include human communities in their cultural equations of nature. To Indigenous peoples, humans are on an equal standing with the rest of the natural world, not above it; they are kindred, relations. With the mindset of humans being just one example of the complex life-forms that inhabit the planet, and fully dependent on all the others, it follows that Indigenous land-management techniques would all aim at enhancing and preserving the ecosystems with which Indigenous people have lived for centuries—a practice I've termed kincentric ecology. Indigenous land management systems reflect the kincentric relationship that Indigenous cultures maintain with their natural resources.

In addition, Indigenous people believe that the complex interactions that inevitably result from this relationship enhance and preserve the larger ecosystem in their homelands. It is inherently understood that human practices such as burning and pruning promote new growth in shrubs, trees, and grasses; that this attracts animals such as birds to sprouting trees and shrubs, and mammals such as deer and elk to grasslands. If humans maintain the land, we can be sustained by its abundant nuts, seeds, vegetables, fruits, and meats.

The natural world is referred to in various ways by Indigenous languages, all of which are telling in terms of worldview. The Yoeme of Sonora, Mexico and Southern Arizona use the terms *huya ania* to describe natural areas outside the boundaries of their villages; the term roughly translates to mean "nurturing life." The Rarámuri use the idea of *gawi wachi*, the "place of nurturing," to describe the Sierra Madre Mountains. The Mid-Columbia River Indians use the Sahaptin term *tiic'm*, which means "the land." All these terms make reference to the complex flow of life with which they and their ancestors have lived interdependently for centuries. Nearly all Indigenous cultures share a set of structures—expressions, metaphors, or concepts—that describe their links to the natural world.

Indigenous peoples believe that they live interdependently with all forms of life. Their spiritual, physical, social, and mental health depends very much on their ability to live harmoniously with the natural world. Indigenous identity, language, land base, beliefs, and history are personifications of culture that regulate and manifest the health of the human as well as the natural world. It is understood that a person who harms the natural world also harms himself.

History, identity, language, land base, and beliefs connect, secure, and regulate the human–nature relationship. To Indigenous people, history does not lie in a linear past. History is continuous and, more importantly, contextual. Cultural history is intertwined with the origins of humans and the origins of nature in equal measure. For many cultures, their origins are a result of relationships with animals or plants. The Abenaki believe they were created from ash trees. The Lenape say that humans sprang from a "great tree." The Mayans and Rarámuri believe they came from corn. The Hopi owe their emergence into this world to a spider, a spruce tree, a pine, and a stalk of bamboo, which functioned as ladders through the *Sípàapu* into the Fourth World.

The land base is often a central subject in nearly all Indigenous creation stories. They often mention how their people emerged, in one way or another, from the land. The land base, however, is therefore also the land to which they claim a relationship. It may be the land on which they now live, or a historical, or even mythical place. Nevertheless, the life-forms that occupy the cultural land base are direct relatives of the human culture.

The concepts of identity and language are connected to Indigenous peoples' concepts of self as well. Words shape thought, and thought is an expression of the spirit. Many Indigenous people feel that both humans and other life-forms are part spirit and part matter. Both are manifestations of the interdependency of humans and nature. Self-identity is a result of a developed relationship to the environment as it is perceived by the culture. Cultural perception stems of course from patterns of language and thought. The human/nature relationship intertwines both the land and cultural histories.

To all Indigenous cultures, cultural beliefs form and explain the human/nature relationship. Beliefs help a person recognize an internal link to the natural world and responsibility in ensuring its survival. No person is truly connected to the natural world or to culture without maintaining physical, social, spiritual, and mental health. Together, these elements key to being human form the breath of life. Breath is the matter and energy, which Indigenous people believe moves in *all* living things. Maintaining a balanced and pure human breath therefore also ensures the purity and health of the breath of the natural world.

With the awareness that our breath is shared by all surrounding life, that our emergence into this world was possibly caused by some of the life-forms seen daily in our own environment, and that we are responsible for its mutual survival, it becomes apparent that it is related to you, that it shares a kinship with you and with all humans, just a family or tribe does. A reciprocal relationship has been fostered with the realization that humans affect nature and nature affects humans. This awareness influences all Indigenous interactions with the environment. It is these interactions, these cultural practices of living *with* a place, not in it, not on it, that are manifestations of kincentric ecology.

2

Indigenous Gardens

Indigenous "gardens" are places where people have come for centuries to collect medicinal and other useful plants. Before ethnobotany, agroecology, and sustainability became recognized terms in the popular environmental media and among the population, herbalist and wise woman Phyllis Hogan had been practicing these disciplines and helping to maintain and manage traditional specific locations around the San Francisco Peaks in northern Arizona where Navajo, Hopi, Havasupai, and other Indigenous peoples collect and manage culturally significant plants. Around the flanks of the San Francisco Peaks, near the Little Colorado River, and in other various locations around the Colorado Plateau, there are places that Hogan refers to as "gardens." And while educators and nongovernmental organizations (NGOs) were still trying to figure out how to include Native youth in local ethnoecological projects and educational programs, Hogan was already training the next generation of traditional "gardeners."

Sípàapu, *in the Colorado Plateau, a spring and Hopi sacred site, believed to be the original place of the people's emergence. It is fed by the Little Colorado River, now threatened by private landowners, utility companies, and governmental organizations that have diverted the water for other purposes.*

The San Francisco Peaks in Arizona, sacred to Indigenous nations, and to the Diné (Navajo), is known as Dookó'oslíid, *the western boundary of their homeland. The peaks connect cosmology to the physical world; healers visit to collect soil and materials for medicine bundles and to renew spiritual powers.*

Some of these gardens are guarded by individuals, while others are stewarded by extended families and even clan groups. Many plants are endemic to these gardens, meaning they can only be found growing at that specific location. In the process of collecting the plants, Indigenous people have "cultivated" the gardens with intentional pruning, coppicing, planting, and even small-scale burning. These human-induced impacts serve to attract more understory plants, small and large mammals, and certain local and migratory birds. In other words, the gardeners have enhanced the diversity of the landscape. During her many years of building up trust with local Native knowledge holders, Hogan has become privy to many of these locations where plants are collected. She guards her knowledge jealously, further adding to the trust of the Native people that she has earned.

The typical Western concept of a garden often involves a conception of a space that is enclosed in one way another—think of a walled garden, a secret garden. The demarcation between the garden and that which is not part of the garden can be as obvious as a fence, or even just an arbitrary and visible property line where a private green space ends and a city sidewalk begins. Gardens can be defined as everything from a small plot in an individual's backyard to an entire city park. In all of these examples, the modern idea of a garden is related to the idea of instituting and maintaining some kind of human control over the area inside the garden, taming nature to fit into an aesthetic ideal. An Indigenous garden, however, ignores any attempt to set a boundary and actually *encourages* influences from outside the recognized space. These influences may arrive from below the ground, from any of the cardinal directions, or even from the cosmos above.

Early attempts to describe Indigenous concepts of "gardens" date back to the first decades of the twentieth century, when anthropologists such as Bronislaw Malinowski and Franz Boas were acknowledging "cultivation" and Indigenous land management practices that they experienced in the Trobriand Islands and in the Pacific Northwest. More recently, ethnobotanists such as Sandra Peacock and Nancy Turner note the reports of early researchers describing what they assumed were naturally occurring areas where Indigenous gatherers collected edible tubers and other useful plants. The descendants of these tribal members, however, describe it differently:

> *their ancestors developed and maintained root gardens through: weeding out grasses and sedges, transplanting and replanting of propagules (parts of living plants that can be replanted) with desired properties, selective harvesting of optimal sized roots, and enhancing soils via tilling and removal of rocks and debris.*

Bronislaw Malinowski on the Trobriand Islands in 1918.

Furthermore, Peacock and Turner describe that these "garden" areas are often "owned" by family groups and specific clans. Ownership is based on lineage, tenure on a specific area, and sustainable stewardship of the collecting area. This notion of ownership is unlike what occurs in non-native economic systems. There is no correlation to the land as a commodity. Ownership here implies responsibility for the ongoing and sustainable stewardship of the area. Failure to comply to these culturally sanctioned rules of responsible care of the plant relatives often results in family or clan loss of access to the area.

In British Columbia Gitksan and Witsuwent'en communities host annual "big house" gatherings and feasts. The annual activities during these feasts include meetings of the community elders, the hereditary chiefs who make decisions regarding which family units and clans should continue to have access to plant gathering areas. According to Antonia Mills, who spent years living with these communities, "the chiefs are

Top: *A field of wild yellow glacier lily (*Erythronium grandiflorum*), an important root for food for the Secwepemc peoples of the Pacific Northwest, growing in the East Kootenays of British Columbia.* Below: *Important food plants to members of the Secwepemc in particular include (left to right) balsamroot (*Balsamorhiza sagittata*), spring beauty (*Claytonia lanceolata*), and water parsnip (*Sium suave*).* Opposite: *Additional food plants include (clockwise from top left) wapato (*Sagittaria latifolia*), wild mint (*Mentha arvensis*), Northern California black walnut (*Juglans hindsii*), and Saskatoon serviceberry (*Amelanchier alnifolia*).*

A bridge constructed by the Wet'suwet'en people of British Columbia that crosses the Bulkley River in Hagwilget. Photo taken in 1872.

responsible for seeing that the relations between all . . . beings are in balance."

Researcher Gabriel Valle offers another perspective with regard to gardens and community responsibility. It is one where an entire community exists in continual resistance as they work to create a social justice path into the future by growing food gardens with "convivial labor," defined by Valle as acts of care by diverse gardeners that connect people through alternative food systems in a place with stark income inequality. During his research Valle spent time with Latino, Asian, and other home gardeners in the Washington/Alma neighborhoods of San Jose, California. All these gardens are individually located in the backyards and front yards, with citrus trees towering over modest houses, beans growing up chain-link fences, and yerba buena growing around foundations. Valle describes their efforts as a form of community resistance in the face of economic, political, and social pressures that result from trying to eke out a living in Silicon Valley. In the introduction of Valle's enlightening book, *Gardening at the Margins*, he states that:

> *home gardeners are doing far more than "growing tomatoes." They are fertilizing the soil with thoughts and values for future movements to come. They are growing food to strengthen relationships with each other and the land, they are sharing food to restore their bodies and communities, and they are generating new knowledge and propagating ancient ways of knowing to find escapes from the biopolitics of industrial capitalism.*

Sprouting from the merger of new and ancient knowledge in San Jose is an expanded social construction of health. A decolonization of food and health is emerging with a new logic that ancestral immigrant foods, free from modern Western influences, are inherently healthy. When we decolonize our foods we realize how simple it is to find a foundation for a healthy diet. At the same time, we redefinine the practice of gardening. It becomes something akin to milpa-based agriculture. Scattered throughout Latin America, milpas are small agricultural plots that have been cleared from local forests in order to make room for locally grown vegetables. From these milpas emerge heirloom and traditional foods (*comidas*). The word *comidas* refers to more than just food, however—the idea of nourishment is also wrapped up with a social exchange that can become a "source of solidarity and conviviality" as well as sources of health and wellness.

When we look at the translation of *comida* in the light of it revealing a cultural relationship to more than just sustenance, we realize the word has roots including a conception of having a relationship to the land, and to self-determination and autonomy. The home gardeners of the Washington/Alma neighborhoods of San Jose are negotiating new ecologies and ways of life to break free from the constraints of Western epistemologies that project a "dichotomy between humans and nature creating space for Indigenous practices and narratives that have survived colonization and that preserve and adapt traditional environmental knowledge."

The places where foods and medicines are traditionally collected are much more than naturally occurring abundant outdoor native pantries or medicine cabinets. They are places where we come in intimate and direct contact with our plant relatives. The plant relatives live here, we live here, and therefore that makes them our garden-kin. These are places of story. They are often the places where Indigenous peoples pass on legends of how plant relatives helped us to emerge into this world, helped us solve a problem, or perhaps were present as witnesses when specific events occurred involving members from our human—or also our more-than-human—community. There are stories of Coyote fooling Bear with some chokecherries, and where the people emerged from corn after an earth-covering deluge, to name just two examples. Stories are included throughout this book not as only entertainment, but to engage you, the reader, and help you to relate your own story to the plants.

These plant food stories are essential because they often are the only manner through which we can understand how Indigenous peoples relate to and make choices with regard to sustainable land management. Encoded in many of the stories is ecological knowledge, so it is through these stories that Indigenous peoples learn and are reminded about how the land is managed and must be cared for, just as if it were a big garden. In our modern and contemporary gardens we prune many of the plants in order to encourage certain growth of fruits, berries, and flowers. We amend the soil in order to retain and add nutrients. We carefully rid the space of invasive

An Indigenous woman walking through a milpa, a small plot for vegetable gardening, in Mexico.

Vesper Meadow, in Southern Oregon, is a success story about an interagency effort between the local tribes Latgawa, Takelma, Shasta, and Klamath and U.S. government agencies to restore a traditional Indigenous garden in constant use for the past 5,000 years but degraded with the advent of the forest industry. A private conservation buyer purchased 1,000 acres of the traditional site in 2018. Today, culturally significant species flourishing again include serviceberry, brodiaea, oceanspray, yamhap, Klamath plum, yarrow, nettle leaf horsemint, camas, and willow.

species and plants that might compete for precious moisture, nutrients, shade, and sunlight. We even shape the space to encourage pollinating insects and birds, useful wild plants, and sometimes small animals. On a (much) larger scale, this is exactly what American Indians had been doing with nearly the entire North American continent prior to the arrival of Europeans.

Story is the central avenue along which American Indians and people from many other cultures and ethnic groups reproduce and transfer ecological and plant knowledge. As I was growing up it was through story and other forms of oral literature and narrative that I learned most of what I know about ancestral ecological knowledge and plants.

Up until a couple of decades ago, if you had asked me to explain where I learned the wealth of ecological and cultural knowledge unique to my tribe, I would not be able to tell you specifically. It's not as though my grandparents, my mom, and other relatives sat me down at prearranged times in order for me to learn "traditional stuff." My grandfather introduced me to certain agriculturally related plants while we shooed away crows and other critters from the corn, beans, and chilis that grew in his fields. Sometimes I would help him rid the field of weeds using an old rusted hoe. The handle was gray with age—as if the years of being worked in the sun had faded the natural color of the wood. There was a fracture in the handle that had been repaired with pieces of old stained cotton material and wire. There was no telling how old the tool was. I never asked my grandfather as he rarely spoke while we worked, except to give orders and motion with his dark-skinned arm to where I should be working. We would sit in the shade of a large fig tree for breaks. During these lapses in the work I learned how corn and chile were our parents and protectors. He told me about the beginning of the world as he whittled on a piece of wood he had picked up somewhere. He taught me to respect the trees as relatives when he caught my cousins and me swinging from the rubbery limbs of his huge fig. I gained most of my plant knowledge from many of my immediate relatives. It is difficult now to brew a cup of some native tea or medicinal herb without picturing the specific time someone in my family introduced me to that particular remedy. These memories, these introductions all came in the form of story.

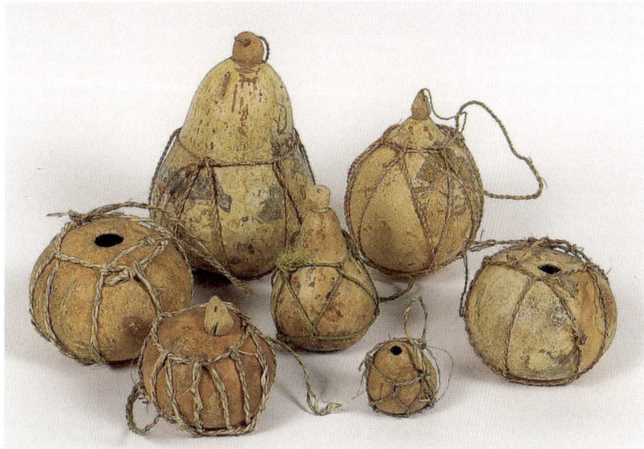

Rarámuri vessels made from gourds, with agave-fiber carrying nets.

When you pause to consider what stories really do for us, it does not take long to recognize that story is all that we are, regardless of culture or nationality. We are all part of multiple versions of "us"—families, faiths, cultures, communities, organizations, and nations in which we participate with others through shared story. Story in one form or another is what your people, tribe, movement, community, or organization has used to relate its shared purposes, goals, vision. Stories help us to acknowledge the challenges that our communities face, the choices we must make, and the hope to which "we" can aspire. These stories are often urgent, requiring us to drop other things and to pay attention. They are rooted in the values we celebrate in our shared story and act as contradiction to those values that require action.

A storyteller figurine by Seferina Ortiz of the Cochiti Pueblo in New Mexico, late twentieth century.

Stories communicate our values through the language of our emotions. And it is what we feel—our hopes, our cares, our obligations—not simply what we know that can inspire us to hold onto or revitalize our ancestral knowledge. Stories teach us how to act. They inspire us to act. When Martin Luther King Jr. spoke at the Lincoln Memorial in 1963 he did not present a five-year plan or a strategy. He told a story about his dream. Our ability to empathetically identify with a protagonist allows us to enter into the story, feel what s/he feels, see things through his or her eyes. And the moral, revealed through the resolution, brings understanding. From stories we learn how to manage ourselves, how to face difficult choices, unfamiliar situations, and uncertain outcomes because each of us is the protagonist in our own story, facing everyday challenges, authoring our own choices, and learning from the outcomes. Because stories allow us to express our values not as abstract principles, but as lived cultural experience, they have the power to move others. In addition, stories are specific: they evoke a very particular time, place, setting, mood, color, sound, texture, taste. The more you can communicate this specificity, the more your story will engage others.

Why am I going on so much about story? Story is at the core of resilient communities. It comprises the matter, substance, and the adhesive of human cultural capital. As humans we hunger for community and places we can connect to on a personal, ecological, and spiritual level. It is the rare individual in this modern industrialized society who will be born, raised, and die in the same place. Those who can make this claim understand what it means to be a part of a place. They know the seasons that shift, the tastes, smells, and winds of their homelands. They can return to where events on the land took place, and discern what grows where and when. They are able to predict weather patterns and water flows, and figure out where best to construct a house or plant a garden. Their tacit knowledge of landscapes and ecological systems may not be discernible on the surface, however.

These knowledge-keeping people are important. They hold the future of human resilience. Where are these people and their supporting communities? What lessons do they have for the rest of us that long for the kind of intrinsic connections and understanding that they hold? How do they grow and collect their foods? What foods do they rely on for sustenance? Every

Members of the Esselen tribe in California's Big Sur region hold a ceremony on recently returned ancestral land for the first time since 1770.

human reflection and story of a deep relationship to place is a living example of our social legacy, reorganization, and natural and cultural capital.

All humans think in our primary language, which is also a nuanced reflection of how the people in our culture express their knowledge of the world. The structures of our languages are also reflections of our worldviews. The reality is that our modern foodways are causing a host of nutrition-related diseases never experienced by our ancestors. How the modern agriculture industry describes getting food to market—from the terms they use to the practices they invent to make that economy profitable—is directly related to higher and higher degrees of environmental and ecological destruction. But how Indigenous peoples talk about and think about and raise our foods has always reflected a way to live healthily and sustainably.

3

From *the* Fields: Beans, Corn, Chiles, Squash

Corn sprouting from sandy ground in Hopi cornfields in northeastern Arizona. The spacing is vastly different from the tight rows used in commercial agriculture.

Indigenous elders and a growing number of young Indigenous farmers are managers of stores of complex knowledge about how humans have for centuries—and could continue to—maintain responsible and sustainable relationships with local habitats. Unfortunately, more often than not historians, conservationists, environmentalists, ethnoecologists, and even native people relegate this knowledge to categories that sound unscientific, such as "traditional knowledge," "the sacred," and "the old ways." When this knowledge is categorized in a biased way that makes it sound unsophisticated, it becomes stagnant, metaphorically pickled and sucked of what is in fact intrinsically valuable content.

Once a student of mine asked a Hopi elder why he could not simply write down or make a verbal recording of his knowledge; he told the student that his kind of knowledge is alive, that it has its own energy and spirit, so to put it into a book or audio recording would kill it. His specific kind of knowledge must be kept alive through oral traditions and through its active use. And as an Indigenous scholar myself, when considering how I might best transmit American Indian ecological understandings for non-native scholars and scientists, with emphasis on underscoring how they are in every way equal to Western ecological knowledge and practices, I struggle with the issue of living knowledge the most.

In current examples of Western academic articles and journals that reference native ecological knowledge, even those written by some of the most respected researchers and scholars, most times when the text mentions how an Indigenous person played a role in the study, or shows a how native elder instructs a Western fieldworker to impart deep ecological understanding, it's palpably described in an almost tongue-in-cheek way. I have yet to see Indigenous ecological knowledge consistently be given the same gravitas as Western science.

A Southern Paiute pecking, a form of petroglyph, showing mountain sheep in the Delamar Valley of southern Nevada. The valley is marked by many peckings, indicating its ceremonial importance. Now a desert, it has been occupied by the Paiute people for 40,000 years and was formerly a major seasonal basin for water; the alluvial plains and aboveground flow created wetlands and supported irrigated farming communities as well as large fauna. The Southern Paiute have long recognized what modern science has only recently confirmed: that a large aquifer runs underneath the land as well. Its spiritual elders, Puha'gants, traveled to certain portals in the valley periodically that were said to allow movement to an alternate dimension, likely a partial reference to the caves and underground rivers of the complex geological and hydrological system, part of which has since been obscured by the creation of Hoover Dam and Lake Mead.

I believe one explanation for this lack of Western respect for American Indian science and ecological knowledge is simply because American Indian knowledge is inherently unstandardized, making it difficult to categorize in pat academic ways. Every American Indian nation customizes its knowledge to suit its immediate environment, and across a wide and geologically varied continent, this means homogeneity of approach is impossible. Native understanding of the immediate environment is both deep and nuanced. For example, there is no single American Indian ecological practice for sustainably collecting willow braces for basketry. Prescribed burns along the West Coast differ necessarily from prescribed burns in the Rocky Mountains. I have often joked to my students that it would be very difficult for a traditional Apache to survive in Vermont. This is because American Indian ecological knowledge and practice is geographically local and adaptive. To many Western minds, this comes across as unscientific or fragmented tradition, a misunderstanding of what it really is: a reason for the centuries-long resilience of some American Indian communities.

All resilient systems, especially human systems, move through periodic phases of stabilization and conservation. These are periods where there is cultural growth and perhaps levels of social stratification. This is also when a community generates or accumulates cultural memory of past ecological successes and applies that knowledge to current and planned ecological relationships.

The elder's reluctance to write down or record his knowledge is, perhaps paradoxically to Western readers, an example of keeping that hard-earned long-term memory alive and of ensuring American Indian communities remain resilient: if you know you have to pass that knowledge on in person or it will be lost, you're more motivated to make sure you pass it on. He views his knowledge as alive, imbued with its own spirit and energy, because it has been reproduced, regenerated, and recalled among untold numbers of living members of every generation.

A variety of Hopi corn grown from 800-year-old seeds found in a cave in Glen Canyon; when planted, about one-fifth of the seeds sprouted.

As another example of what a struggle it can be to translate Indigenous knowledge and practice for Western science to understand and appreciate, take a Hopi elder's knowledge of how to plant blue corn. Of course it is not only that single individual's knowledge; he is but one point in a continuum that has been developing a practical and kincentric relationship with a specific landscape over millennia. Hopi blue corn has been planted and raised on the Colorado Plateau for nearly two thousand years. In the Hopi timeline, they have been raising blue corn since Spider Woman introduced it to the Hopi during their emergence into this world, which they call the Fourth World. During that time, Hopi ancestors have developed a collective cultural library of best practices regarding how to raise corn in a very arid habitat. They have created a linguistic domain related to how they talk about corn. They continue to engage in ceremony and ritual connected to their reverence for this staple grain, and Hopi artists reflect their culture's relationship to corn in pottery, jewelry, song, and ceremonial regalia.

An image of a corn dancer, or Qao Kachina, *by Narron Lomayaktewa, from Hopi Pueblo, circa 1965.*

Kachinas of the Powamu *ceremony, 1893.*

There is hardly anything in Hopi culture that is not somehow related to or connected to corn.

The knowledge of the corn, beans, and squashes introduced in this chapter is therefore not static guidance. It is in constant flux as Native agriculturalists shape, retune, and adjust their practices to meet shifting rainfall patterns, changes in soil types, and the hybridization of new varieties. This kind of practical and practiced knowledge that's assumed to continue adapting for resilience, therefore, cannot be interrupted by being captured in one moment in time as any sort of final "reference" in a book or a video. It remains alive and vibrant—it is continually used. It is argued about in the kivas, sung about at corn dances, and opinions are shaped when Indigenous chefs grind corn kernels and adjust recipes in their contemporary cuisines. Similarly, the fishing knowledge of the Haida, who occupy coastal areas of British Columbia needs to be continually used and reframed as, over time, Haida culture adapts to environmental changes along the costal ranges and forest of the Pacific Northwest. In order to ensure their annual harvest of plant resources, Miwok basket makers in California have had to learn how to shift gathering and management patterns. These examples of adaptation lead to the next essential elements of resilience and cultural invention.

A carved wooden Haida fish hook from British Columbia.

Remember that "resilience" is simply a term to describe how effectively American Indian cultural and social systems adapt organically over space and time. One would be remiss to approach an American Indian elder or holder of cultural knowledge and ask them to describe why their cultural systems are resilient. The elder would not have a reference point from which to begin to translate the concept, because by definition American Indians have always considered resilience a baseline for life. Nevertheless, resilience exists only because external forces and shocks compel us change our human systems. Like all systems both human and nonhuman, American Indian systems have experienced myriad external changes. Our oral traditions are forms of historical texts. And they describe how our ancestors dealt with many kinds of geomorphic forces, invasions from other tribes, diaspora, and forced relocation due to changes in the land and climate. During the past five hundred years these shocking forces have been multiplied, and have led to near-extinction of the Indigenous populations of North America. Those of us who are still here *are* here due to what resilience theory describes as "phases of cultural invention."

Beans

***MUN* (HOPI), *MUNÍ* (YAQUI), *MUNIKI* (RARÁMURI), *AMA'CA* (HIDATSA)**
PHASEOLUS VULGARIS, P. COCCINEUS, P. ACUTIFOLIUS, P. ANGUSTISSIMUS

PLANT FAMILY: *Fabaceae*
PARTS USED: *Pods, leaves, stems*
SEASON: *Summer, fall*

Top: *Common runner beans.* Above: *The Powamu Altar of Albuquerque, New Mexico.*

February gets cold on the high Colorado Plateau of northern Arizona. Hopi communities are situated here, across three mesas. February for the Hopi is also known as the time of *Powamuya*. During this time the annual *Powamu*, or bean dances, are celebrated. *Powamuya* is the time of the Hopi ceremonial calendar when the *katsinam*, or rain and earth spirits, return to the Hopi mesas in order to help the people prepare for the coming growing season and to oversee the initiation of young Hopi into a Kiva Society. Kivas are subterranean structures where different spiritual societies meet in order to perform ceremonies and to hold meetings. The *Powamu* ceremonies involve several rituals spread over sixteen days, and they honor fertility as well as germination.

During *Powamu*, beans are sprouted inside different kivas. The sprouting beans honor the coming growing season and are seen as a good omen for the success of the harvest. On the final day of the ceremonies, many *katsinam* gather and give away gifts to those in attendance. The gifts include lightning sticks, dancing sticks, arrows, rattles, moccasins, kachina dolls, and sprouted beans.

My people call beans *muni-ki*. Among the Yaqui the word is *muní*. The Hopi word for beans is *mun*. The similarity in nomenclature is because the three languages represent branches of the Uto-Axtecan linguistic family tree. The Lakota refer to beans as *oh-min'-nee-chah*. The Hidatsa, neighbors to the Lakoat, call beans, *ama'ca*. The Onondaga word for bean is, *hsahet*, while the Cherokee call beans *thuya*. Nearly every Indigenous language in the Western Hemisphere has a word for beans—a reflection of the ubiquity of *Phaseolus sp.* across North and South America.

After corn, beans are the second-most-consumed traditional food among American Indians today.

IDENTIFICATION

Today, when we are talking about beans that the typical home cook would have boiling in a pot on the kitchen stove, we are most likely referring to one of two types. There is *Phaseolus vulgaris* and *P. coccineus*. *P. vulgaris* is an erect, herbaceous bush that grows between eighteen inches and five feet tall. The bushes have many pubescent, willowy branches. The compound leaves are trifoliate with ovate leaflets and the flowers are often white to pink and pea-shaped, and grow in clusters from between the leaf axils. The pods are elongate, containing from three to ten beans. The pods are most often green, but do come in several colors. The beans inside the pods also come in different shapes and colors, but normally take a kidney shape and are about half an inch long. *Phaseolus vulgaris* is the species name for a category of beans that includes a number of cultivars and varieties including Anasazi beans, appaloosa, black turtle, bolita, cranberry, kidney, pink, pinto, white, and yellow eye.

The other variety of beans are called runner, or pole, beans, *Phaseolus coccineus*. They are sometimes called broad beans or butter beans, due to their large size and softness once they are cooked, though the beans in the pod are quite hard and often an inch long or sometimes larger. This is a perennial climbing vine growing up to fifteen feet long. Unlike *P. vulgaris*, it has a tuberous taproot. The thicker stems tend to be prostrate for most of the length of the plant and and rise up toward the terminus of the vine. The trifoliate leaves emerge at the end of long petioles. The leaflets are between two and a half to seven inches long and one and a half to four inches across. The terminal flowers appear in pairs and come in white, purple, and red. Each flower produces a single pod that is slender, and can be green, yellow, black, or purple in color. Some are even striped. The pods can be knife-shaped, cylindrical, flat, or straight. Each is one-half to one inch wide and up to eight inches in length. The pods will contain four to twelve large kidney-shaped seeds with colors ranging from white, red, green, tan, and purple to gray or black. Cultivars of *P. coccineus* include aeron purple star bean, black runner, butler, Hammond's dwarf, painted lady, and scarlet runner.

All of these varieties of *P. vulgaris* and *P. coccineus* originated from wild relatives such as the slim leaf bean, *P. angustissimus* and *P. maculatus*. Both are tiny wild beans found on hillsides of mixed deciduous forests. These beans, at one time, were a single species, but diverged about one hundred thousand years ago into Andean and a Central American species. About eight thousand to ten thousand years ago the wild species were hybridized into the beans that we are familiar with today. However, some beans experienced local adaptation and phenotypical changes as the gene pool was traded throughout the different ecosystems of the Americas.

The Sonoran Desert of southern Arizona and northwestern Mexico is an incredible culturally and biologically diverse region of North America. At the borderlands that divide Arizona from Mexico live the Tohono O'odham. Among the tall saguaro cacti, greasewood bushes, ocotillo, and mesquite trees, the O'odham continue to raise tepary beans, *Phaseolus acutifolius*. Tepary bean

plants are normally small shrubs that grow up to about a foot in height and spread to around 20 inches in diameter. The leaves are shaped into three narrow, pointed lobes (trifoliate). The skinny pods can reach three inches long, and hold between seven and ten small beans inside. The beans are oval-shaped and are about the size of a lentil, and come in different colors, from white, brown, black, and beige to mottled. It is likely that tepary beans were hybridized from their close wild relative, the slim leaf bean.

CULINARY USE

Nearly every week I will cook up a pot of beans. Normally I cook pinto beans, but sometimes I will cook the big, beefy, sweet runner beans or perhaps some small, earthy-tasting tepary beans. Or perhaps some yellow beans. Maybe I will do the pinto-like beans that are white with splotches of black and brown that resemble little black-and-white goats. There are any number of beans to choose from—and they all taste good. Across native North America, dried beans

Nutritional Values

Native peoples did not consume beans for their medicinal properties. However, recent studies are confirming that the ancestral diets of many American Indians that included beans played an important role in preventing nutrition-related disease, especially adult onset type 2 diabetes. Beans are high in fiber, complex carbohydrates, low-fat soluble and insoluble fibers, and mucilages. Together these compounds help to control glucose and insulin levels and help any regular eater of beans to avoid obesity and high cholesterol. Leguminous fibers found in beans have a special effect on postprandial glucose levels—the glucose levels in the bloodstream after a meal. Consistent, sudden rises in postprandial glucose levels can spur diabetes. After meals, glucose levels generally rise as we digest carbohydrates and starches that are transformed into sugars. Fiber-rich meals can control postprandial levels, but leguminous fibers seem to control these levels particularly well, because bean fiber in particular slows glucose absorption in the gut, regulating glucose levels over a longer period of time compared to, say, white bread. The mucilaginous bean coats basically slow down the digestion process. Beans are also high in proteins and complex carbohydrates. And a final benefit of eating beans is the trace of chromium found in their outer coats: chromium deficiency has been found to cause insulin resistance.

are cooked and eaten plain or with different spices and additional ingredients. They are main characters in soups and stews. They can also be mashed to make a thick soup base. The Cherokee will add them to hickory-nut soup; they also mash cooked beans and make them into bread. Many tribes enjoy cooking beans in combination with fresh or dried corn. Many American dishes that are cooked and eaten today have their origins in American Indian cuisine, including the cracked-corn and bean dish we call succotash. Many people still enjoy sweetened baked beans. Tex-Mex cuisine, like so many Southwestern meals, would feel empty without the ever-present side of *frijoles*.

WHEN, WHERE, AND HOW TO GATHER IN KINCENTRIC ECOLOGY

Except for the difficult-to-find wild relatives of beans, beans have to be planted and tended to yield a harvest large enough to consume. Traditional Native farmers do not plant their domesticated foods in straight rows as modern farmers and even gardeners have become accustomed to, however. For the most part Native farmers will plant beans in small mounds that are distanced from each other by about three feet. In some cases, beans are planted among other crops such as corn and squashes. Many have heard of the "three sisters" approach, where beans are planted near young sprouting corn to encourage the bean plant to climb up the stalk of the growing corn plant while the large leaves of a squash plant shade the soil and decrease evaporation. This, however, only works for pole beans. Native farmers will often plant bush beans around the edges of their cornfields or in separate fields. My people, the Rarámuri, plant a field of beans adjacent to a field of corn.

In one of the most important accounts of Indigenous agriculture in North America, Hidatsa farmer Maxi'diwiac, or Buffalo Bird Woman (who lived from ca. 1839–1932), was chronicled by an ethnographer, Gilbert Wilson, who established a connection with her son, Edward Goodbird. She described her particular

The "three sisters" planting method.

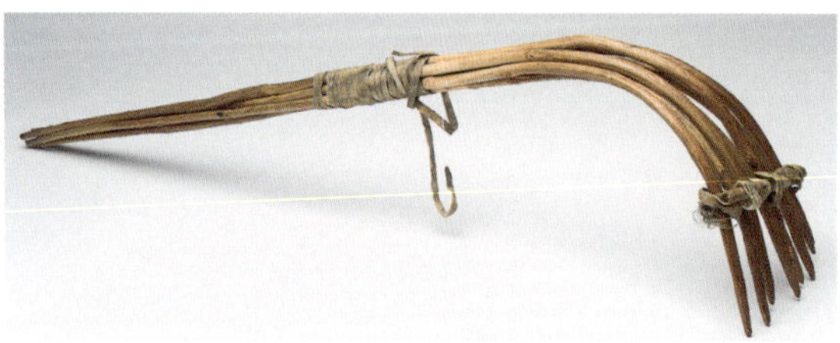

A Hidatsa rake, circa 1905–1918, made of ash and bound with hide. Originally rakes were made of antlers, and these later wooden rakes often have a number of tines equivalent to the number that would be found on an antler.

technique for planting beans. She would dig into the soil where she planned to build up a mound, then loosen the soil with her gardening tool. The small mounds, measuring about fourteen inches across and situated about four feet from each other, are built up with the loose soil to a height of about seven inches. She planted beans in threes around the sides of the mounds. This is done by simply pressing the beans into the soil to a depth of about two inches. A traditional, successful method for sowing that is efficient and does not disturb the soil more than necessary.

The young, immature pods of *P. vulgaris* and *P. coccineus* can be harvested and eaten while the beans inside are still soft, but the adventurous gardener should not wait too long as the skins of these kinds of beans can quickly become very fibrous. Most American Indians wait until the pods have actually dried on the bush or vine, late in the summer or early fall, before harvesting them. Then, the entire plant is collected and piled on top of blankets or tarps among the other harvested bean plants. The harvested plants are allowed to dry fully, then they are shaken or beaten with brooms or sticks, causing the dried beans to separate from the pods. The beans are collected and stored for later use.

Tepary beans (*P. acutifolius*) grown by Tohono O'odham farmers in the Sonoran Desert have been hybridized to thrive in very hot and arid conditions: they can even survive on seasonal monsoon rain alone. Their leaflets track the movement of the sun, thereby reducing heat load on the plant, and their roots extend much deeper into the soil than their domesticated

*Tepary beans (*Phaseolus acutifolius*), native to the desert and semi-arid regions of North and Central America, thrive in harsh conditions and have become of interest to farmers as climate change causes more frequent droughts and higher temperatures.*

Tepary beans being grown in a traditional dryland farming formation and without irrigation at Texas A&M University, where breeders are working on making more commercial varieties available while monitoring how they perform year over year with variable levels of rainfall.

relatives. The wild relatives of tepary beans can be found growing along the edges of high-altitude sandy washes in the Sonoran Desert. The O'odham employ a unique farming technique that takes advantage of the tepary's wild ecological taste: known as *ak-chin* (mouth of the wash). Because the tepary beans respond to summer monsoon rains and use water freely, which allows them to maintain a high photosynthetic rate, the plants complete their reproductive cycle rapidly to finish the life cycle before drought. *Ak-chin* fields are placed at the mouth of desert washes where stormwaters naturally spread out because of changes in floodplain slope gradients; fields were historically placed just downstream of where floodwaters and their detritus were deposited. The floodwaters are broken by a series of berms that are strategically placed above the fields, or, today, often as concentric rows of berms formed by the farmers. The waters and detritus flow into the ruts between the berms, slowing absorption and harnessing any nutrients that flowed along with the water. This system overcomes the two most limiting factors to food production in the desert: water scarcity and low fertility. In addition, the gurgling floodwaters also create an oxygenated environment for the plants' roots.

A Simple Pot of Beans

INGREDIENTS:

- 4-5 quarts (or more) water
- 1 lb. dried beans (pinto or a similar variety)
- 1 ½ tsp. baking soda
- ½ c. white onions, chopped
- 1 clove garlic, finely chopped
- 2 tbsp. cooking oil (olive oil recommended)
- 1 bay leaf
- 1 tsp. salt
- 1 tsp. ground black pepper
- 1 tsp. dried Mexican oregano (*Lippia graveolens*)
- 1 ½ tsp. dried cilantro
- 1 dried leaf of epazote
- 2 chiltepin peppers or 1 jalapeño (optional), diced

Cooking beans may appear to be a simple process: put the dried beans into a pot of boiling water and cook them until they're soft. However, if a person wants the cooked beans to taste good and to be edible, a little culinary skill is required. The recipe below calls for a pound of dried pinto beans, but any variety of bean similar in size to pintos will work. This includes the ones mentioned previously: anasazi, appaloosa, black turtle, bolita, cranberry, kidney, pink, pinto, runner, white, and yellow eye. Follow this old recipe and you will end up with a pot of beans that can be eaten immediately or saved for use over the next several days in other dishes that call for cooked beans. I like to add cooked beans later to a red chili recipe. Finally, this recipe uses very specific herbs, but any variety of herbs can be used, to taste.

Spread out the dried beans on a large, clean surface and sort through them to remove any little dirt clods, stones, or broken beans. Rinse the beans in a colander. Add the beans to a large pot and fill it with fresh water up to about a thumb's length over the top of the beans. Add the baking soda. This next step can be accomplished two different ways: 1) the beans can be soaked overnight, or 2) the beans can be brought to a boil. If the first method is chosen, skip this next part. If the latter method is chosen, allow the water to boil for a minute, then turn off the heat. Allow the beans to rest and cool for an hour.

People often ask about the baking soda. It creates an alkaline brine solution that helps to break down the pectins in the beans. Pectin is what causes beans to maintain their hardness. This process is also referred to as nixtamalization—it can also be used on dried corn kernels, helping to soften the kernels as well as to release important nutrients.

After the beans have either soaked overnight or rested for an hour after boiling them, drain and rinse the beans. Return them to the pot.

Refill the pot with fresh water as before, covering the beans to about the length of your thumb. While the water is coming to a boil, add the remaining ingredients. The chiltepins or jalapeño are optional, but do add nice flavor and a little heat.

How long to boil the beans depends on their age and dryness. Simmer them uncovered anywhere between 40 and 90 minutes. Begin tasting the beans after about 35 minutes to be sure that they are not getting too soft. Serves 6 to 8.

Corn

MAIZE, SUNU

ZEA MAYS

PLANT FAMILY: *Poaceae*
PARTS USED: *Ears, leaves, pollen, silks, fungus, husk*
SEASON: *Summer, fall*

For centuries, we said "corn is mother, corn is life." Today, however, the international commodification of corn, and along with it corn genetically modified to contain terminator genes, processed corn products, and even corn-based materials found in paint has diminished and removed the close relationship that humans used to have with corn. On the Colorado Plateau in northern Arizona, however, corn still holds its revered place.

Everyone in attendance early in the morning for the first corn roast near the Hopi Second Mesa in northern Arizona is reminded of this. The sandy dirt is dug away, revealing the metal

Corn came in many colors before being genetically modified to yellow.

The Hopi Second Mesa in Northern Arizona, in 1944; a challenging environment for growing corn without specialized agricultural techniques and knowledge.

cover that has been placed over a deep roasting pit. When the cover is lifted, steam shoots from the pit, releasing the sweet, musky scent of ears of corn that have been roasting below ground all night. Young men kneel down and then climb into the deep pit, pulling up and tossing ears of hot corn from inside. The elder offers a prayer while presenting a large ear of steaming corn first to the east, and then to the other cardinal directions. After that, everyone can eat.

Corn plays a central role in the foodways and cultures of American Indians throughout the Americas—except for some tribes from the Pacific Northwest, along the West Coast, and others farther north where it cannot grow. Even tribal peoples whose nomadic lifestyles precluded them from engaging in agriculture still maintain some kind of relationship with and reverence for corn.

Corn is the only American Indian food plant that needs humans in order to survive. If humans were to suddenly disappear, corn, as we are familiar with it, would only grow perhaps one more year. This is because humans cultivated corn, and it is humans who continue to plant its seeds. According to paleoethnobotanists, corn was first hybridized from a wild grass relative of *Zea mays* called teosinte, *Zea luxurians*, about nine thousand years ago. Some think that it was somehow also crossed with another grass relative called tripsacum, *Tripsacum dactyloides*. It is possible that other relatives such as *Zea perennis* or *Z. diploperennis* got involved as well. Archeobotanical evidence suggests that this purposeful mutuation occurred somewhere in what today is southern Mexico, perhaps near the Río Balsas region of the Mexican state of Michoacan.

My guess is that a group of Indigenous women were responsible for the creation of the new, spectacular food. Native women have always been responsible for feeding the community. To this day, it is largely Native women revitalizing ancestral foodways, trading heirloom seeds, and fighting for food sovereignty rights. But, according to many tribal stories, corn has always been with us. Some of us believe that we are literal children of corn. Our relationship with corn has been so long and extensive that we have developed hundreds of varieties of corn in different colors, sizes, and for differing culinary uses.

The practice of growing and eating corn spread from southern Mexico throughout the Americas. When Europeans made first contact with Taíno people in the Greater Antilles, they also made their first contact with corn. The Taíno called it *mahis*, which would become the alternate English word for corn: maize.

My people, the Rarámuri, believe we emerged into this world from ears of corn after a huge, cleansing deluge. Hopi beliefs suggest that they were asked by the Creator to choose from certain ears of corn after they emerged into this, the

*Teosinte (*Zea luxurians*), domesticated corn's wild ancestor.*

*Eastern gamagrass (*Tripsacum dactyloides*), likely used to hybridize the first domesticated corn.*

Fourth World. The Hopi also maintain spiritual figures known as corn maidens.

Other tribes have similar beliefs centered around corn. The Abenaki believe that First Mother brought corn to the people. The Menominee believe that the people received the gift of corn in a dream. To the Navajo, corn is one of the four first sacred plants—each represents a cardinal direction, and corn represents the north.

There is also a Cheyenne legend of how corn came to the people. The story tells of a time when the Cheyenne were hungry. They could not find buffalo or other game to hunt. Even the edible plants were scarce. Two young men, both wearing buffalo robes and who had painted their bodies yellow, entered into a cave where there was a spring. In the cave, sitting next to the spring, was an old woman. She was cooking buffalo meat in one pot. In another pot was a food that the young men had never seen before. The woman fed the two young men with the buffalo and with the contents from the second pot. Afterward, she revealed that the second food was corn. She told the young men to leave, but first gave them some corn kernels and instructed them on how to plant them. She also told them that after they left, the buffalo would return. The young men returned to their village, and thousands of buffalo began to spring forth from the cave. The young men taught their people how to grow the corn. For several seasons, the people experienced an abundance of both buffalo and corn. One hunting season years later, when the corn was almost ready to harvest, the people left in order to follow a very large herd of buffalo. They returned to their village to discover that all of their corn had been stolen. There was not one cob or kernel left. They tried to find the thieves, but were not successful. Without any cobs to save for kernels the next year, the Cheyenne could no longer grow their corn. From that moment on, they would only get corn by trade.

Corn is indeed central to American Indian beliefs, identity, culture, and foods. It is more than a food. It is also a medicine, used in crafts, and in construction. In addition, we feel that we are directly related to it. It is often a significant part of ceremony, and even traditional arts.

IDENTIFICATION

Corn is in the Poaceae plant family, which means that corn is actually a large grass. This family of plants includes the grass on your neighbor's front lawn, bamboo, and grains such as wheat, rye, oat, and rice. Corn is a true annual since it must be planted by humans every year. Like other grasses, corn has a hollow stem that produces leaves arranged alternately. Corn flowers, or tassels, form at the top of the plant, appearing like a small mop. Most grass flowers are hermaphrodites. Corn's, however, are not. The pollen must be distributed by wind, insects, or—to best guarantee fertilization—humans, from the flowers down to the silk emerging from the tops of the newly forming ears. Each silk strand links directly to one kernel on the eventual cob.

Since *Zea mays* was first hybridized by Indigenous Americans thousands of years ago, the species has branched into hundreds of varieties made distinct by color, size, number of rows, and their ability to grow in specific conditions. However, corn can be categorized into six major types of corn: dent, flint, pod, sweet, flour, and popcorn. Each category has a distinctive shape, size, and color.

Corn's flowering tassels help identify it as a member of the grass family Poaceae.

CULINARY USE

American Indians have developed so many ways to cook and eat corn that I could never enumerate them all here. But native peoples roast corn, separate the kernels from the cob to roast something called chicos, grind roasted corn into atole and pinole, add roasted corn to soups, stews, and make roasted and ground corn into a thin bread the Hopi call *piki*. Some people ferment corn into beer, turn corn flour into tortillas, tamales, cornbread, and mush. The Navajo make blue corn flour into small, round dumplings called marbles. When I go backpacking or on day hikes, I like to bring a pouch of corn that has been soaked in salt and slowly parched into a centuries-old version of corn nuts. On Sunday mornings, I still like to whip up a batch of blue cornmeal pancakes served with real maple

Atole, a beverage made with corn, milk, and cinnamon.

Hopi piki *bread, made with blue corn, as served in a modern restaurant in Santa Fe.*

Cuitlacoche, a delicacy made with corn and corn smut.

syrup. There is an edible gray tar-like fungus or mushroom, *Ustilago maydis*, that grows on ripening ears of corn. Many people refer to it by its Nahuatl name, *cuitlacoche*. Others simply call it corn smut. It forms when moisture from rain seeps down in between the protective husks on ears of corn. The moisture causes the fungus to grow among the kernels. In many parts of Central America and the American Southwest, *cuitlacoche* is considered a delicacy. In some farmers markets in Mexico the fungus can fetch the price of three dollars for a small bucket. It is cleaned and cooked with spices, garlic, and onion and then added to quesadillas or tacos, and stuffed in chicken.

Corn silk is also of value; it's collected during the growth period from the tops of the emerging ears. The silk is steeped into a decoction and then taken for bladder and urinary tract infections, to treat kidney stones, and even to stop bedwetting. The same decoction is used to treat a weak heart, diabetes, high blood pressure, and taken as a general tonic.

Dried corn cobs can be soaked in water and rubbed on the skin to treat poison ivy. The Tewa use blue cornmeal mixed with water to treat muscle pains and sore throats. Cornmeal is also used to treat diaper rash, rheumatism, and eczema.

A corn husk doll from the Wampanoag people. Many tribes of the Oneida Nation didn't draw faces on their dolls, due to a story that the Great Spirit told corn she could be made into a doll; she was originally given such a beautiful face that she grew vain and constantly looked at her own reflection in pools and lakes. The Great Spirit gave her a warning, but when she did not heed it, she looked at herself again and found that the Great Spirit had taken her face away completely.

Many tribal peoples roll a smoking mixture into dried corn husk for ceremonial use. The husks are also used for wrapping tamales as well as for making children's dolls. Husks are also braided and used to make ceremonial masks, sleeping mats, baskets, and sometimes footwear. Every part of the corn plant is used in ceremony in one way or another.

WHEN, WHERE, AND HOW TO GATHER IN KINCENTRIC ECOLOGY

I enjoy growing one of my people's forty-one varieties of corn every year. Many tribes who rely on corn as a staple will conduct up to three separate plantings. There is often an early planting, which takes place toward the end of March. Then there will be a second planting about a month later, and a final planting at the beginning of summer. Planting dates are often determined by phases of the sun and moon.

Southwestern tribes such as the Hopi, Tewa, Zuni, and Navajo will plant their seeds deep into the sandy soils of the Colorado Plateau. They also plant several seeds into each location so that when the stalks grow to maturity, they will support each other in the region's windy conditions. Further north, in locations such as New England or the northern Great Plains, native farmers normally wait until around May to plant their corn crops.

Most American Indian corn is produced with the intent of grinding it into flour. Therefore, the cobs are left on the stalks well into the fall. You know corn is ready to be harvested by feeling the ends of the cobs: if it feels pointy, it needs to

Minataree Green Corn Dance, *a lithograph by Blackbear Bosin (1921–1980).*

continue growing. If it feels rounded or blunt, the cob is ready for picking, roasting, and eating. However, some tribes, such as the Cherokee, collect and eat green corn in early July. The consumption of green corn is more than a reflection of a unique Indigenous dish—it is actually a part of a ceremony of renewal for the Cherokee and other Southwestern Indigenous nations. The ceremony consists of several days of dance, drumming, ritual cleansing, and the eating of the young corn. The focus is on forgiving debts, putting aside grudges, and especially strengthening community.

Ancestral and contemporary Indigenous approaches to growing and consuming corn provide ideal examples of kincentric ecology. Santa Clara scholar Gregory Cajete refers to this as Native Science. In its most simplistic explanation, Native Science is a collected inheritance of our Indigenous experience with the natural world. Another way to consider Native Science is as a map of a Native paradigm of reality drawn from the experiences of thousands of human generations that have given rise to a diversity of technologies for hunting, fishing, gathering, agriculture, cultural expression, healing, being, and of course, eating.

This Native paradigm includes the basic question, "What is the nature of our relationship to our landscapes?" At a very basic level, we eat our landscapes. We eat what sprouted from it, what we coaxed into growing from it, and what ran around on top of it and swam in the nearby waters. We also cooked the landscape. Cooking is a very conscious and deliberate act—always cultural, social, political. Through our choices, we support certain processes over others. When we choose to eat in a traditional way, we support and reaffirm intricate contextualized and collective cultural experiences that strengthen community and identity. Eating in a kincentric way can also be thought of as a personal choice to engage in a daily ritual, a culturally derived performance. If culture is, in part, performing certain acts that are recognized as traditions, then part of how we recall our lines for this ongoing performance happens each time we prepare an old family recipe. So many traditional foods are a result of our longtime and direct relationship to landscapes. Therefore, to be able to continue practicing our traditions, it is essential to preserve the knowledge of how to manage our landscapes sustainably. Together, the food and landscapes remember how they should be cooked. I suggest that a path toward better Native health is for people to relearn how to cook and also how to eat their landscapes.

To this day, in the Sonoran Desert of southern Arizona and across the border into the Mexican state of Sonora Tohono O'odham, farmers practice the *ak-chin* kincentric ecological agriculture discussed above. When floodwaters are broken up by a series of brush weirs strategically placed above the fields, other flood-washed detritus drops out of the waters to enrich the soil. This water-control and irrigation system is rebuilt annually. The system overcomes the two most limiting factors to food production in the desert: water scarcity and low fertility. The O'odham have also hybridized a variety of corn that sprouts and reaches maturity in just ninety days—most corn varieties need at least 120 days of full sunlight to reach maturity. Growing such a fast-maturing corn permits O'odham farmers to take full advantage of a growing season that is fed by late-summer monsoon rains.

Further north, in the arid, high elevations of the Colorado Plateau, the Hopi have developed another method of raising corn in a region of low precipitation: dry land farming. This a reference to how the Hopi, and other American Indian agricultural systems in the Southwest rely on only the rain that falls from the sky in order to irrigate their crops. It is a farming technique that has existed in the Southwest for several thousands of years and relies partly on a culturally sanctioned selection of corn varieties that can sprout and reach maturity with very little moisture. The Hopi grow nineteen varieties of corn, all of which are uniquely significant to their culture and endemically suited to the arid Colorado Plateau of northeastern Arizona.

The ancestral Hopi corn planting technique requires a simple digging stick, taking long strides to mark adequate space between where the corn is planted, and singing. To the Hopi, corn is more than a mere source of calories. The corn plants are perceived as children, and by extension the fields are seen as the source of all life—not just an agricultural patch of land. The plants and the fields where they are raised are acknowledged to be alive, and must be respected and sung to. From my work with Hopi farmers, I've recognized that the linguistic metaphors that the Hopi use when they talk about corn plants are the same as when they speak about female children. Also, among the Hopi, there are many references to spiritual beings known as Corn Mothers and Corn Maidens. Corn, therefore, is a female entity. This is further exemplified when the Hopi farmers invite some of the women who work at Crow

A Hopi corn grinding maiden kachina doll by Eldon Kewanyama of Hopi Pueblo, 1965.

A Zuni digging stick from Ojo Caliente.

Canyon to participate in a dance in honor of the corn that is planted.

Though it may seem like a simple implement, a digging stick for planting corn is in fact indicative of a deep ecological relationship with a landscape that receives only six inches of rain a year. Planting with a stick to create a small hole (as opposed to tilling) does not disturb the topsoil in the constant winds of the Colorado Plateau, which would pull away precious moisture. Additionally, the topsoils are also not exposed to oxidation, which could hasten the degradation of essential nutrients. Another factor in successful corn planting in a harsh environment is choosing where to plant their fields: Hopi fields are normally found surrounding the base of one of the three mesas that comprise the Hopi homeland, but the fields are not located directly on the flat base of the mesas: they are planted just at the end of a slight slope so that moisture from any rains or snowfalls will trickle along the downward slope and accumulate where the cornfields are planted.

Hopi knowledge of corn is also not static. It is in constant flux as Hopi agriculturalists retune and adjust their practices to meet shifting rainfall patterns, changes in soil composition, and the hybridization of new varieties. This kind of practical and practiced knowledge, then, cannot be captured as a permanent and final record in a book or a video. The knowledge remains alive and vibrant since it is continually used and revised. Planting techniques are argued about in the kivas, sung about at corn dances, and opinions are shaped when Hopi cooks grind the resulting kernels and adjust the character of the crop in a variety of Hopi dishes.

The general assumption regarding the lifestyles of pre-contact Plains Indian cultures is that they were all nomads. In the regions north of the Rio Grande River up to what today is southern Canada and east of the Rocky Mountains all the way to the Mississippi, Plains Indian peoples did follow and harvest from the vast herds of buffalo that roamed the Great Plains. So it's rare that these peoples are accredited as having developed any form of sophisticated agriculture. Fortunately for those interested in the various approaches to American Indian agriculture, anthropologist Gilbert L. Wilson took it upon himself to document the annual planting and harvesting cycle of Hidatsa gardener Maxi'diwiac, aka Buffalo Bird Woman, between 1906 and 1918. Several local varieties of corn were among the many Indigenous ancestral foods that Buffalo Bird Woman planted in the northern plains of North Dakota.

We learn from Wilson's work that Maxi'diwiac raised hard white corn, a "soft" flour corn, blue corn, red corn, and other varieties of multicolored corn. There was a corn called *ma'ikadicake* in the Hidatsa language that was a sort of "gummy corn" of different colors that would wrinkle and become rough when dry and would be roasted as a green corn or later dried and ground and made into "corn balls." Wilson also documented how the Hidatsa processed corn in many different ways—they would parch it, roast it, soak it with lye to make it into hominy, make corn cakes, boil it, and cook corn mush.

Maxi'diwiac's primary method for determining when to plant corn was to wait until about two months after people planted sunflower seeds. This normally would be around the month of May in her area. She built short, eight-to-nine-inch-wide hills spaced several feet from each other. Using her fingers, she loosened the soil in the small hills and planted six to eight seeds in each hill, pressing the seeds about half an inch into the soil. She would complete the process by patting down the tops of the hills with her palms. With the corn mounds spread so far apart, they would not have to compete for the scant moisture and few nutrients in the soil. She also wanted to ensure that would be enough room among the planted hills to scoop soil up and over the root systems of the corn as they developed, to keep them from drying out. Maxi'diwiac did not plant her corn in straight rows, but in hexagonally shaped patterns with a hill at each point of the hexagon's "corners" and one in the center.

Beans were then planted between the corn mounds, as well as squashes at the edges of the field. During the months while the corn was growing, Maxi'diwiac and her community hoed weeds and scared away magpies, crows, and other critters such as gophers that might eat the young corn plants. During normal years, the corn would be harvested at around the beginning of September.

All three of these examples of planting and raising corn reflect some of the approaches that Native farmers have taken to grow corn sustainably, and also to work in step with what their local landscapes can offer by adapting to a hyper-local climate. The Hopi method of planting corn twelve to eighteen inches deep in the soil would not work in Maxi'diwiac's plains landscape, for example. Nor would Maxi'diwiac need to identify locations among washes where she would have had to take advantage of seasonal floods to bring moisture and nutrients to her fields. Kincentric agroecological knowledge and practices have evolved over sometimes thousands of years as resilient Indigenous peoples listen and adapt to their landscapes' dynamic natural cycles.

Nutritional Values

Except in times of famine, drought, and other lean periods, historic Indigenous foods did serve us well. But who today has time to go catch a salmon for dinner, hunt a buffalo, to trek out to collect wild tubers and edible greens, or to raise a field of ancestral crops? Fortunately, these and other similar foods are increasingly becoming available through more and more retail channels. Modern humans must have a paradigm shift in how we consider and think about food and health, for how we "think" about something can affect our actions around it.

From my conversations with Native peoples, I realize that food and nutrition are only two strands in the complex woven tapestry of interconnected knowledge that comprises what Santa Clara Pueblo native scholar Gregory Cajete calls Native Science. We may have mainly continued to use corn silk because our ancestors recognized it had "medicinal benefits," but today we can identify and quantify that it contains phytochemicals that are diuretics, antioxidants, and that help reduce inflammation. The chemicals in it are also antilithiatic and uricosuric. The phytochemicals include flavonoids, alkaloids, phenols, steroids, glycosides, terpenoids, glycosides, and tannins. What we absorbed and repeated as tradition is in fact valuable knowledge that we can now, perhaps, apply in a more targeted way for specific conditions—and if we had ceased to keep our traditions alive, in the modern era we may never have taken the time to analyze the reason behind the medicinal "traditional" uses.

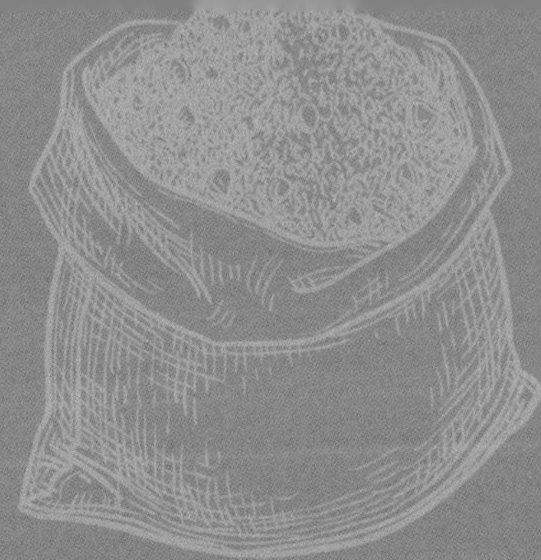

Hopi Sumiviki (Someviki)

INGREDIENTS:

- 14 dried corn husks
- ½ c. sprouted red beans, ground
- 1 ½ c. blue cornmeal
- 3 tbsp. culinary ash or 1 tsp. baking soda
- 1 c. boiling water

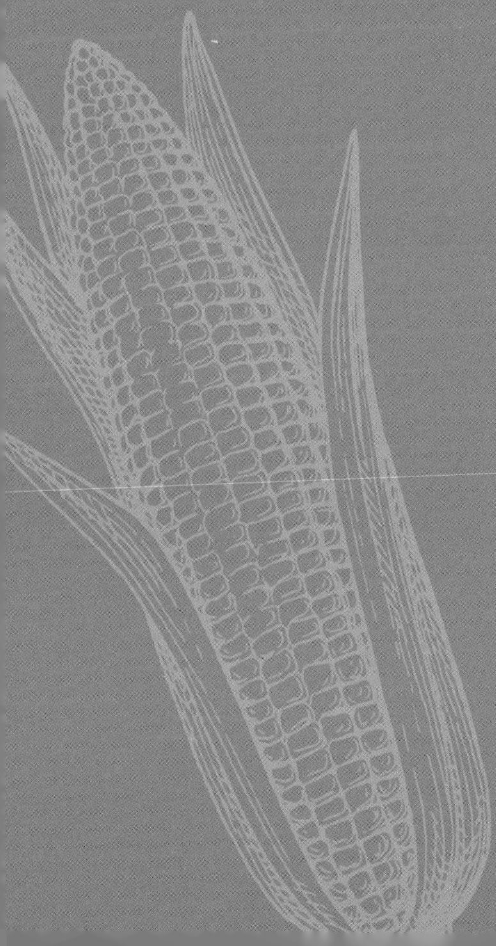

The ways that people have invented to eat corn are as varied as the landscapes and cultures that feed and raise it. It seems that nearly every Indigenous community that grows corn reserves specific recipes for ceremonies and special occasions. The Hopi make small, tamale-like semisweet corn cakes wrapped in a corn husk, called *sumiviki* or *someviki*. They're served during kachina and social dances, and are enjoyed during celebrations such as family gatherings, birthdays, and when special guests arrive.

Nixtamalization, the process of soaking and cooking dried corn kernels in an alkaline solution to break down the tough outer hulls, is part of the process of preparing *sumiviki*. Culinary ash derived from greasewood (*Sarcobatus vermiculatus*) or juniper (*Juniperus sp.*) is also included in the recipe, which adds a unique flavor to the corn mix and serves to draw out essential nutrients, including niacin. The culinary ash also softens the cornmeal to help in the digestive process. If culinary ash is difficult to find, substitute baking soda.

Most *sumiviki* are sweetened in one way or another; the method I learned uses sprouted beans that have been ground into a paste. Sugar, honey, or agave syrup can be substituted for the sprouted bean paste, but I enjoy the added protein that comes with the little bit of extra effort.

If you plan to include the sprouted bean paste in your *sumiviki*, you will need to plan a few days in advance. Rinse the beans and store them in a safe location on a baking sheet between wet cheesecloth or another clean cotton cloth. Keep the cloth and beans wet until they have sprouted (usually takes 2 to 3 days). Add the sprouted beans to a food processor with a couple tablespoons of water. Mix until you have a smooth paste; set aside.

Rinse and then soak the corn husks to make them pliable enough to roll and fold without splitting. When they are soft, tear or cut 3 or 4 of the soaked corn husks lengthwise into narrow strips about ¼ inch wide.

Mix the ash or baking soda into the boiling water. Then pour the ash mixture through a fine-mesh strainer and add it to the cornmeal. Mix until combined. This will change the color of the cornmeal to a bluish gray. Add the sprouted bean paste to the cornmeal. If the mixture seems runny, add some more cornmeal. The batter should be just smooth enough to evenly spread onto the cornhusks, but not too thick or lumpy.

Using a spoon or a flat spatula, place about ¼ cup of the mixture onto the center of a cornhusk, then spread it lengthwise along the husk. Fold the sides of the husk over the batter, and then fold over both ends to encase the filling completely. Use one of the thin corn husk strips to tie the *sumiviki* in place around its middle. *Sumiviki* are normally about 2 inches long and 1/12 inches wide.

Steam the sumiviki in a steamer basket over boiling water for about 15 minutes, or boil them gently in a covered pot. The *sumiviki* can be eaten as they are, without additional seasoning, but I like to pour some red chili sauce over them. Makes 10 *sumiviki*.

Chiles

CAPSICUM ANNUUM, C. FRUTESCENS

PLANT FAMILY: *Solanaceae*
PARTS USED: *Fruits, leaves*
SEASON: *Summer, fall*

In North America, and in the southwestern United States in particular, people are both particular about and proud of different varieties of chile peppers. Some people believe that whatever variety they grow is the best one—the ultimate example of hot pepperiness perhaps—to the point of getting defensive. Other people try very hard to avoid the fruit, unable to handle spicy food. Most people can tell some kind of story about eating peppers that surprised them, in a pleasant way or not. Mention roasted green chiles to any native

Chiles have been hybridized into many unique varieties.

of the Southwest, whether Hispano, Indigenous, or Anglo, and then brace for reactions as varied as claiming they're actual ambrosia to disdainful anecdotes relayed as serious, soulful warnings. Some American Indians claim the food has mystical and medicinal properties.

I was talking with an Indigenous farmer from Bolivia who now grows food at Tesuque Pueblo in New Mexico. When I asked whether he was growing chiles, his eyebrows shot up—I had his full attention. His normally serious demeanor shifted to one of credulity coupled with a knowing smirk. "Enrique," he said in his richly accented English, "I have something for you that you will love." Later, when we returned to his office near the pueblo's civic buildings, he produced a small bottle. The screw-on lid kept a rubber stopper in place in the neck. I could see an orange-red liquid through the glass. He handed me the bottle very carefully—clearly he considered it a precious gift. I opened the bottle and began moving it to my nose to smell what was inside. He quickly cautioned me to be careful. The elixir assaulted my sinuses and eyes immediately, but at the same time I discerned a pleasantly pungent undertone. He began reciting the many medical uses for this oil, from curing a cold or flu to using it as an antibiotic. I knew immediately, however, exactly what I was going to do with it: I used it (sparingly) to enhance the flavors of my home-cooked pinto beans, omelets, and tortilla soup.

Chile peppers are regularly eaten by Indigenous peoples throughout the Americas. Today these mildly irritating, addictive, and powerful plants are grown throughout South and North America at commercial farm scale, but also very commonly in people's home gardens, and in pots on apartment balconies from Massachusetts to San Francisco. Cultural identity by region is often tied to the ability to tolerate chiles of various degrees of "hotness." Capsaicin is the chemical in chiles that makes them register a sensation of heat on the tongue, and it varies widely in concentration among chile varieties. When it touches the skin, it triggers receptors that trick the brain into thinking that area being impacted by the capsaicin is burning. Some cultures associate the ability to eat hot chilis as a sign of manliness. In the Sierra Madres of Chihuahua, Mexico, where my people come from, we are wary of anyone who does not like or refuses to eat chiles—to us, only evil sorcerers wouldn't eat chiles.

Chiles were not always a traditional food or spice in North America; they were introduced when Spanish colonists began moving north from the Valley of Mexico during the sixteenth century. Chiles are native to places farther south—Bolivia, the highlands of Peru, the Tehuacan Valley of Mexico, and other tropical areas of Central and South America. The only variety of chile that existed north of the tropics before its human introduction was the chiltepin (*Capsicum annuum* var. *glabriusculum*) and its close varietal cousin, the pequin chile (*Capsicum annuum* 'Pequin'). Both are tiny red peppers that in maturity grow erect on small bushes in the wild. The fruits of pequin are about the size of a pinky fingernail. The round little fruits of chiltepin grow to about a quarter inch in diameter. My grandmother used to grow these tiny balls of fire in our fields. She would grind about two of them up to add to a pot of beans or a stew. That was enough to change a bland pot of beans into a mouth-stimulating dish. Like other chiles, one has to be careful when

Chiltepin peppers are the only variety native to North America; all others migrated from Central and South America.

handling chiltepins and pequins. An errant touch to one's lips, eyes, or nose can result in irritation for about an hour or so due to the irritant, capsaicin, found to varying degrees in all chiles.

IDENTIFICATION

Capsicum annuum is the botanical name for a genus that includes about 200 different kinds of commonly known peppers such as cayenne, jalapeño, bell pepper, Anaheim, and paprika. Peppers are perennial plants in their native habitats; vegetable gardeners north of the Mexican border probably recognize them as being frost-tender, but by bringing them inside in the colder months, stripping the stems of all leaves, and reducing watering significantly to induce artificial dormancy, it's possible to overwinter them and then plant them out again when the weather warms the following spring. I have a chile variety named Chile de Diablo growing in my backyard in Northern California. It grows as a small tree and somehow manages to remain alive even through the hard frosts that sometimes occur in our region.

Most varieties of *C. annuum* grow as a large woody herb or small shrub with lance-shaped leaves that form alternately. The plant produces single off-white or yellowish flowers. The fruits are green at first and mature to yellow, orange, or red, depending on the variety.

CULINARY USE

Chile peppers are loaded with antioxidants such as vitamins A and C, flavonoids, beta-carotene, alpha-carotene, and lutein. The principal active phytochemical is the alkaloid capsaicin. This chemical protects it from some pests, and capsaicin and oleoresin together create the heat and burning sensation humans detect when chiles are consumed. Capsaicin, however, is also an analgesic, diuretic, anti-inflammatory, and antimicrobial. Chile consumption is considered good as a general tonic for overall wellness and for lifting a person's spirits.

There are numerous ways to consume peppers. I typically grow several varieties of chile peppers in my garden every year. One of my favorite ways to prepare them is to simply roast the large, milder green chiles over coals until they are nearly all black. I shake them up inside a paper bag until the blistered skin peels mostly away. I remove the last of the peels and eat them fresh. Roasted peppers can also be saved for adding to scrambled eggs, soups, stews, posole, and many other dishes. Some varieties of peppers, such as the hotter jalapeños, are usually chopped and served raw. Larger varieties can be stuffed and baked, roasted, pickled, boiled, and dried. Some varieties of chile are best when picked after they have turned fully red, then left to dry on the plant. They can then be stored in decorative strings or ground into a powder to be added to soups and stews or used as a condiment.

Peppers are probably most appreciated for their central role in seasoning sauces.

WHEN, WHERE, AND HOW TO COLLECT IN KINCENTRIC ECOLOGY

Chile peppers are grown throughout North America but thrive in hot, dry regions. However, I have witnessed friends and colleagues growing habaneros and Scotch bonnets in New England and in Washington state. The peppers can be harvested when green or left on the plant to turn color and mature. The mature peppers should be collected before fall rains begin.

Chile peppers were first domesticated separately in different parts of the Americas beginning about 6,000 years ago, in central Mexico, parts of the Amazon region, and in Bolivia and Peru. Sometime during the evolutionary history of chiles, humans developed a taste for them and a kincentric relationship was born. Chiles are self-pollinating, making them easy to domesticate and hybridize, which is likely why hundreds of varieties have been cultivated today.

It is likely that the first human uses of chile peppers were for medicinal purposes. Mayan and Aztec records indicate chile peppers being used to treat toothaches, coughs, and sore throats. Chiles were also used for ceremonial purposes by early Mayan and Aztec cultures. According to Mayan mythology, the sun fell in love with a girl on Earth. Her father, not happy with the relationship, aimed a blowgun at the sun, but not before the sun filled the blowgun with dried chile powder. When the father took a deep inhale as he prepared to blow the dart, he inhaled the fiery powder and died, but he did still manage to shoot the dart. The chile-infused dart hit the sun, and this explains why the sun is hot.

In a Zuni story, two warrior twins, Ahaiyuta and Matsailema, buried their mean and cantankerous grandmother in the ground. A chile plant grew from her grave; it produced fruits that could be helpful, but that would also deliver a bite.

Finally, the Cora of Nayarit, Mexico, believe that the Creator sent individuals to earth to act as caretakers of specific food plants, animals, and other parts of the natural world. Narama was brought to earth to act as the nurturer of salt, mezcal, and chile peppers. During a fiesta where all of the nurturers were gathering together, Narama arrived encrusted in salt. He climbed up onto the center of the table everyone was gathered around and shook himself, so that all the food that had been placed onto the table was sprinkled with his salt. Unbeknownst to anyone, his testicles had been transformed into dried chile peppers. His movement caused the chile pods to burst their spicy contents down and onto the food as well. Everyone was initially annoyed with Narama—until he encouraged them to taste the now-salt-and-chile-flavored food. After a few bites, they were grateful.

All of these beliefs reveal a deep love of chile peppers among Indigenous cultures in the Americas. Even among the Hopi of northern Arizona list a hot chile pepper kachina among their pantheon of kachinas. Still, the amount of acreage Indigenous farmers devote to raising chile peppers is relatively small when compared to other traditional crops such as corn, beans, squashes, fruit orchards, and other pre-Columbian foods. Most Indigenous farmers take great care to ensure that one or two of the many varieties of chile peppers, from mild green Anaheims to fiery habaneros, are planted every year.

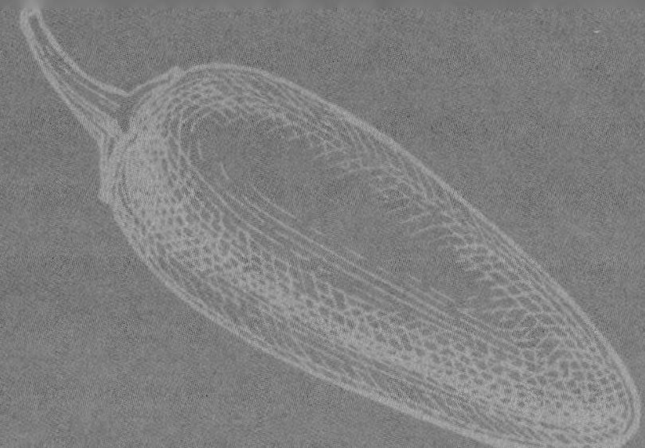

Aunt Vera's Salsa

INGREDIENTS:

- 3 fresh jalapeños, chopped
- 4 medium, red heirloom tomatoes, chopped
- 1 white or yellow onion, finely chopped
- 1 clove of garlic, minced
- 3 tbsp. chopped cilantro
- 1 small leaf of dried epazote, crushed
- 2 tbsp. apple cider vinegar
- 1 tsp. lime juice
- ½ tsp. cumin
- salt and pepper, to taste

My mother's youngest sister is Vera. Although every cook in the family can conjure up a quick salsa, there was always something special about Aunt Vera's salsa—I believe it's because of the epazote and cumin she adds. This is a fresh salsa, meaning that none of the ingredients are cooked. This recipe calls for jalapeños, which makes it fairly spicy. I normally do not bother to separate out the seeds and the inner light-colored membrane of the peppers, but it is acceptable to in order to decrease some of the heat.

Combine all the ingredients in a molcajete or large mortar and pestle, or a food processor using the pulse feature. Crush and mix the ingredients to the desired consistency. Serve with your favorite chips, or just pour the salsa over any meat or bean dish for extra flavor.

Squash and Pumpkins

***ASKUTASQUASH* (NARRAGANSETT), *BACHI-KI, SITO-BACHI* (RARÁMURI), *PATNGA* (HOPI), *NAAYIZI* (NAVAJO)**
***CUCURBITA PEPO* & *CUCURBITA* SP.**

PLANT FAMILY: *Cucurbitaceae*
PARTS USED: *Inner meat, leaves*
SEASON: *Summer, fall*

Indigenous peoples use and cultivate many varities of summer and winter squashes.

Every fall, with expectation, I hungrily watched my mother pour some olive oil into one of our large cast-iron skillets in preparation for making one of my favorite seasonal dishes: *calabacitas*. After the oil heated up, she added onions minced on our old cutting board. Next came chopped garlic. She would allow that mixture to slowly sweat; I have such a potent memory of the aroma wafting through our little kitchen. It seemed as if she did this purposefully, in order to whet my appetite. While the onions and garlic were simmering, she would mince some cilantro and Mexican oregano (*Lippia graveolens*) and toss that into the mix. Next she added yellow summer squash that she normally cut into narrow discs. The squash cooked for about a minute or two, and then my mom added some cooked pinto beans as well as some sweet corn shucked straight from a fresh cob. By this time, my hunger would really be raging. But Mom had to add a couple more ingredients before it was ready: chopped tomato, chopped jalapeño peppers, and then finally some salt and black pepper. The calabacitas recipe above is only one of many dishes that can be made from the wide variety of squashes and pumpkins grown by American Indians.

During the second half of the summer in the American Southwest, both American Indian and Hispano families eagerly await the blossoms that create constellations of yellow stars among their fields of summer squashes and pumpkins. Their prevalence are indicators of how large the upcoming harvest of pumpkins and squashes will be. My family often grew yellow summer squash (often referred to as banana squash). Every year, as I raise summer squash in my own garden, I remember how as a little boy I was fascinated by the beetles that sometimes infested the plants. They resembled little gray, armored tanks. Now I know that these are squash vine borers, and that they severely damage squash plants. My grandmother encouraged me to pick the beetles off the vines in order to protect the plants—and our harvest—from destruction. I would oblige her because I knew it would help conserve the yellow blossoms for one of my favorite dishes from her kitchen: squash blossom quesadillas.

For millennia, squash has been one of the most important food sources in the Southwest. Squash blossom iconography is prevalent in Indian art from the region, dating back to pre-Columbian artifacts. This highlights the cultural significance of squash and squash blossoms to the indigenous peoples of the American Southwest. For example, the potters from Tesuque, Hopi, and other Pueblos are noted for their use of stylized squash blossoms in their finished glazes. Squash blossom necklaces are particularly famous exports of native Southwestern silversmiths.

A silver necklace with squash blossom iconography, c. 1900–1920, from the Diné (Navajo) Nation.

A Hopi squash-head kachina, carved by Pariscilla Auguh of the Hopi Pueblo, circa 1979.

Squash and pumpkins are not unique to the Americas, however. There are around 825 species of cucurbits grown around the world. In North America, the genus Cucurbita around ten thousand years ago originated somewhere in what today is Mexico. Since then, this genus has grown to twenty-five wild and cultivated species diverse in fruit color, size, and shape. One of the first species to be cultivated was *Cucurbita pepo*. *C. pepo* has formed the basis for most of the squashes and pumpkins grown by native peoples from Mexico up to Montana.

The word "squash" is derived from the Narragansett word *askutasquash*. My people, the Rarámuri, use the words *bachi-ki* and *sito-bachi* to describe pumpkins and squashes, respectively. We call pumpkin seeds *bachi-raka*. The Hopi call pumpkins and squash *patnga* and pumpkin seeds *patangsivosi*. They refer to dried squash as *saaviki*. The Navajo call pumpkin *naayiziztossoi* and squash *naayizi*. And the list could continue several pages more if I were to

Cushaw squash, a traditional variety.

list the names from each tribe in North America, but the point is that they have always been an important food source, and accordingly have received as many unique names as there are unique varities. Today, we refer to squashes and pumpkins with terms that describe their shape, origin, and whether or not it is a summer or winter squash. This designation is important as it determines how and when the fruits are grown, collected, stored, and eaten.

IDENTIFICATION

Cucurbits are generally easy to recognize. The plants are vine-like with sprawling, prostrate stems emanating from a shrub-like central plant. Sometimes the vines climb using tendrils to catch onto nearby fences, ladders, or even other plants. The large, palmate leaves are arranged alternately on the stems. They are pinnately lobed and grow small, thin spines on the petioles. Winter squash varieties are hard-shelled and are produced in a variety of shapes and sizes. Some farmers have even managed to produce 900-pound squashes and 1,800-pound pumpkins.

The soft-skinned summer squashes include varieties such as straight-neck, crooked-neck, baby acorn, chayote, zucchini, pattypan, and scallopini. The hard-skinned winter squashes and pumpkins include acorn, butternut, delicata, golden nugget pumpkins, carnival, spaghetti, sugarloaf, and turban. The different cucrcurbits from North America include *Cucurbita pepo*, which can include winter squashes, summer squashes, pumpkins, and ornamental gourds. There is also *C. mixta* which are winter squashes, pumpkins, and cushaws. *C. moschata* is a winter squash and pumpkin. Finally, there is *C. maxima*, which is a winter squash in Peru, but also a turban squash and pumpkin. The different species are distinguished by their skin hardness and stem shapes.

Squash and pumpkin plants will produce an abundance of large, mustard-yellow star-shaped blossoms beginning about midsummer and into the early fall. Not all of the blossoms will produce fruits—only the female blossoms will result in a pumpkin or squash. That means male blossoms can be harvested for eating separately, and are often considered a delicacy. Be careful not to overharvest the male blossoms, however, as some are required for pollination of the female blossoms. The male blossoms can be identified by the tall stamens rising from the center of the flower; male blossoms also have longer stems than the females and are straight, without an obvious baby fruit forming at its base. The stems can be up to seven inches long.

CULINARY USE

Squashes and pumpkins are, of course, cultivated and used primarily as food. The softer shelled summer squashes are normally sliced and then fried, sautéed, boiled, roasted, or baked. They are frequently added to soups and stews. The thicker- and harder-shelled winter squashes and pumpkins are often stored in a cool, dry place to be consumed later into the fall or winter. In the Southwest Pueblos, people store the harvest in the back corners of their adobe structures. The Navajo will dig a nearby pit lined with stones where they will store their harvest of pumpkins and other vegetables. Winter squash can simply be cut in half to harvest and to save seeds for the following year's crop.

Calabacitas.

Sometimes the whole or halved pumpkins are baked on coals in open pits or slow baked in closed pits. Many Native peoples will cut the fruits into discs so that they can be dried in the sun, on racks.

The seeds of winter squash are also eaten throughout the Americas, often roasted and eaten as a snack. They can also be baked, hulled, or ground into a kind of marzipan. Sometimes the paste is mixed into pinole for an interesting take on the dish. Pumpkin seeds were once an ingredient for the Mexican drink horchata, which today is more often made with rice. Many Hopi and other Pueblo Indian cooks still season their *piki* stones with the oils of pumpkin seeds before making *piki* bread. The nutrient-rich blossoms are eaten directly with soups and stews, dried for later use, or mixed with cornmeal, mesquite, and meats. In addition, many do not realize that young pumpkin and squash leaves make excellent and tasty greens when steamed, sautéed, or boiled.

Squash and pumpkin leaves have traditionally been ingested to treat upset stomachs. The seeds of *C. pepo* are eaten by many Native peoples to treat intestinal worms, as a diuretic, and as a kidney aid. The Zuni use the seeds of a summer squash called gray squash as an ingredient in what they call schumaakwe cakes. The other ingredients include evening primrose (*Oenothera triloba*), lobelia (*Lobelia cardinalis*), and western snakeroot (*Ageratina occidentalis*). The mixture is applied externally for rheumatism and swelling. The Zuni also make a poultice of the blossoms and seeds to treat scratches from cactus. The Cheyenne take an infusion of pumpkin rinds to treat rheumatism, arthritis, as a laxative, to treat fevers, as a kidney aid, and for earaches.

The flesh of squash and pumpkins are an excellent source of nutrients. They are full of carotenoids, lutein, soluble and insoluble fiber, potassium, vitamins C and E, riboflavin, B vitamins, thiamine, and magnesium. *Cucurbita* sp. seeds are a source of phytosterols, palmitic, stearic, oleic, linoleic, linolenic, and gadoleic fatty acids, polysaccharides, peptides, violaxanthin, auroxanthin epimers, flavoxanthin, and many other phytochemical compounds. The seeds also contain a chemical called squalene that is effective in the treatment of certain types of cancer. Finally, the seeds contain cucurbitosides that are phenolic glycosides. Together, the constituents of *C. pepo* are anticancer, anti-inflammatory, antimicrobial, known to improve urinary function, are anti-ulcer, antioxidant, and anti-hyperglycemic. Squash and pumpkin blossoms contain vitamin C and a mix of beneficial B and A vitamins as well as folate. They also contain nutritious minerals such as iron, magnesium, potassium, selenium, and phosphorus.

WHEN, WHERE, AND HOW TO COLLECT IN KINCENTRIC ECOLOGY

Summer squashes are typically ready for harvest from middle to late summer and into the early fall. Winter squashes are grown to be harvested later in the fall, once the shells are hard enough to withstand a little pressure from a pressed fingernail. The seeds are often scooped from the insides of winter squash before cooking. They will be intertwined with stringy flesh and pulp. I often lay the seeds and stringy pulp out on paper towels or newsprint in an area protected from insects. They will dry in a couple of days, making it much easier to separate the seeds from the pulp. When collecting squash or pumpkin leaves for consumption, be careful of the spines situated on the stems. It is also important to split open the thick, hollow petiole and to then pull up toward the top of the leaf in order to remove the hard veins from the leaves before cooking.

Although both the female and male blossoms are technically edible, only male blossoms should be harvested early; females need to mature into pumpkins and squashes. Harvest of the male blossoms can begin once they reach a deep yellow color. They can be harvested by hand, but be mindful to wear gloves, as the stems are often covered by hundreds of tiny prickly hairs. My grandmother used to send me out to where our squash was growing armed with just a kitchen knife. These days, I collect squash blossoms with metal store-bought clippers.

Calabacitas

INGREDIENTS:

- 2 tbsp. olive oil (or vegetable oil)
- 1 medium yellow onion, chopped
- 2 cloves of garlic, minced
- 3 summer squashes, cut in half lengthwise and sliced into ¼-inch half moons
- 1 c. cooked pinto beans
- 1 c. fresh corn
- 1 c. fresh tomato, chopped
- 1 tbsp. chopped fresh cilantro
- 1 ½ tsp. dried Mexican oregano (*Lippia graveolens*)
- 1 medium jalapeño, chopped
- Salt and pepper, to taste

There are as many calabacitas recipes as there are Mexican families who make this savory and sometimes spicy summer treat. Some include both yellow and green summer squashes, some, just the yellow summer squash. Some recipes include pork or chicken, others leave out the tomatoes, and still others smother the dish in cheese. What all the different approaches to making calabacitas have in common is summer squash.

Calabacitas translates into English as "little squashes." Typically the dish is made with yellow summer squash, green summer squashes (zucchini), or both. The little scallop squashes and others can be substituted, but the dish just doesn't come out quite the same. This recipe calls for jalapeños, but they can be omitted to avoid heat. This dish is often served as a side dish, but it also makes a great main dish.

Heat the oil in a large skillet over medium heat. Add the onion and garlic and sauté for about a minute. Add the squash and cook until they begin to get soft. This normally takes about 5 to 8 minutes. Add the pinto beans, corn, tomato, cilantro, and oregano. Cook for another 2 minutes so that all the flavors combine. Add the jalapeño and cook for about 30 seconds. Add salt and pepper to taste.

Serves 4.

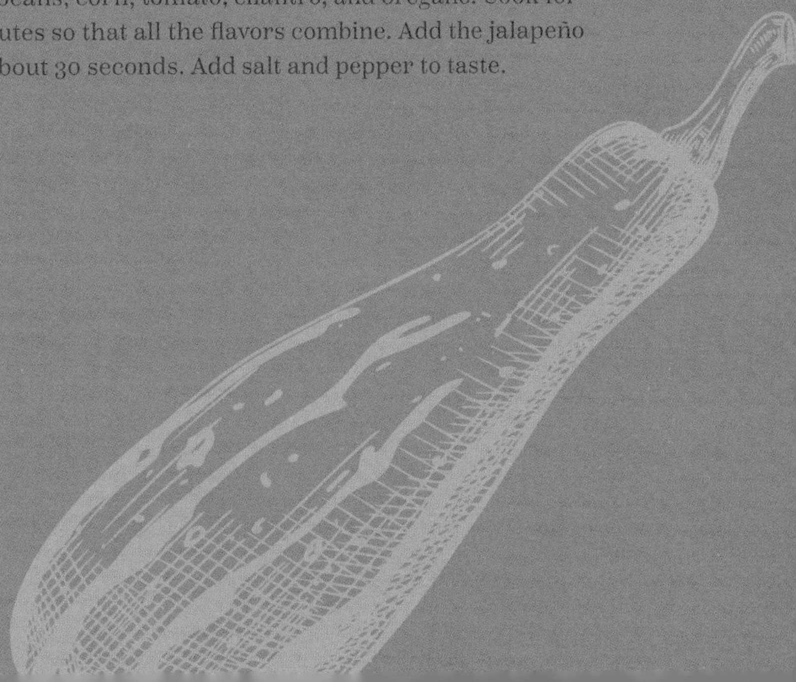

4

Berries *and* Fruits

Berries are juicy, sweet, and sometimes sour, but always associated with handfuls of happiness. In every Indigenous landscape across North America, berries bring flavor and nutrition to local Native nations. They're so entwined with the Indigenous cultures that berries appear in stories related to the creation, bring a focus to tricker's mischief in local legends, and even trigger specific seasonal celebrations.

Toyon berries, an important food source for the Chumash peoples of what is today Central and Southern California.

Whatever the specific relationship that any given Indigenous nation has with the berries local to their ancestral homelands, something that is shared across all Indigenous homelands, no matter how different, is a kincentric ecological land management practice that ensures that the berry population will continue to flourish. Methods of management certainly include those that have already been mentioned in previous chapters, such as periodic prescribed burning, careful pruning, seasonal coppicing, and culturally sanctioned gathering in a way that prevents overharvesting. One commonality among all Indigenous nations and methods of practicing kincentric ecology is the simple recognition that the berries are gifts. We, as caretakers of our homelands, are charged with the responsibility to carefully manage these gifts; not only for ourselves, but also for our nonhuman relatives.

There is not enough space here to detail every edible berry from across Native North America, of course, so I have selected six different berries that are key to Indigenous diets across the continent.

Rubus allegheniensis, *a blackberry native to eastern North America.*

Blackberries

***RUBUS* SP.**

PLANT FAMILY: *Rosaceae*
PARTS USED: *Fruit, leaves, stems*
SEASON: *Summer to fall*

At least once a year, out in my garden, I will be forced to dig up an errant blackberry vine. I usually find them sprouting underneath the bay laurel tree growing in the corner of my property or trying weasel their way toward sunlight among some large squash leaves. I am not sure how the blackberry plants arrived in my yard, but the most likely culprits are the many birds that visit my garden. I am guessing that they drop seeds that they picked up from a plant growing somewhere else in my neighborhood. I have even spied blue jays burying peanuts and acorns in the soft soil of my planting beds. I recently realized that there was an oak tree sapling growing in a potted jade plant sitting on my front porch. Nothing surprises me anymore when it comes to birds

One day, during the late summer when blackberries are fully ripe, Coyote went down to a creek to drink some of its cool water. Looking around, he noticed nearby bushes full of ripe blackberries. Coyote did not know that this spot was one of Bear's cherished berry-picking places, or that Bear would chase off anyone who tried to eat his berries. So when Coyote moved close to the bushes, Bear, who was behind them, suddenly reared up to his full height from the other side of the bush. Bear roared and tried to swat his huge claws at Coyote. Coyote, scared for his life, bolted away from the bushes with Bear right on his tail. Coyote, being small and more agile, managed to get away from Bear. He ran up a tall hill and finally came to rest in the shade of an oak tree.

While he was resting under the tree, Coyote noticed Raven looking down at him from one of the oak branches. Raven asked Coyote why he looked so tired. Coyote told Raven about Bear chasing him away from the blackberries.

Raven said, "He won't share any of those blackberries with anyone. It's not fair for the rest of us who like berries."

Coyote, always thinking mischievously, said, "You know, we should do something about that. Do you want to help me get back at Bear and get some of those berries?"

Raven agreed, and the two of them hatched a plan.

Over the next couple of days, Raven and Coyote watched as Bear gorged himself on blackberries. They noticed that after Bear had his fill, he would drink from the creek and then lie down for a little nap.

Finally, on the third day, as Bear settled in for his nap, Coyote strolled down to the blackberry bushes and began to eat them, noisily. Raven was coasting in the air above the scene. After eating a good amount of berries Coyote whooped loudly, jolting Bear from his nap. Bear began to chase Coyote through the woods. Just before Bear was able to get Coyote's tail with one of his claws, Coyote jumped up into the air as high as he could. Raven swooped down and caught Coyote, then circled around and dropped Coyote onto Bear's back. Coyote reached around Bear's fat belly and hung on while Bear bucked, jumped, and circled around, doing anything he could to shake Coyote off. All the while Raven kept swooping in and pecking at Bear's head.

Finally, when Bear was exhausted, he flopped down onto the ground near the blackberry bushes. Coyote jumped off Bear's back, walked over to one of the blackberry bushes, and began to eat. Raven also flew over onto a blackberry branch and began to help himself. Still spent from the wrestling match, Bear could only watch as Raven and Coyote ate his berries. Raven and Coyote ate only a few berries, however, then brought some over and placed them in front of Bear's nose as it rested on the ground.

Coyote said, "All we wanted was a few berries. There are so many bushes and berries—there is enough for everyone."

Bear considered this. The next day, Coyote and Raven went back over to the blackberry bushes near the creek and carefully began to eat some berries.

Bear at first reared up in his habitual way, but instead of charging at Coyote and Raven he said, "I thought about what you said. There really are plenty of berries for everyone—as long as we share and each of us takes only take what we need."

This Chumash story about Bear, Coyote, Raven, and the blackberries teaches a kincentric ecological approach to Indigenous maintenance of local ecosystems for berry production. The reasons for managing landscapes to encourage high berry production are not always culturally narcissistic. The flowers of berry plants attract and feed important pollinators. The young, tender shoots of many berries provide forage for deer and other forest dwellers. Many nations found that low-level burning encourages berry production as well: a burn removes competing shrubs and herbaceous plants, so managing the forest floor for berry production increases the overall health of the forest and surrounding ecosystems while attracting animals tribes may also want to hunt.

Pemmican cakes, a Native American energy bar, are made with a base of dried berries, dried meat, nuts, and honey.

sneaking seeds into my garden. Nevertheless, if I didn't make the effort to uproot the invading blackberries, it would not be long before a section of my garden would be transformed into a nearly impenetrable bramble of dark green leaves protected by bloodletting thorns. The birds would be happy, of course. I could leave one of the plants, with the best intention of maintaining and containing its size with constant pruning, but I know these blackberries are the invasive species, *Rubus armeniacus*, Himalayan blackberry, not a native American variety. If one of the species of blackberry native to North America was growing in my yard, I would gladly welcome it; these have long been a favorite forage food for American Indians. And, in addition, wild native species offer more beneficial polyphenols, anthocyanins, and other phytochemical compounds. Domesticated varieties are bred to contain more water (for plumper berries), which leaches away the beneficial compounds. Also, wild berries produce more beneficial compounds that help them to fight off natural diseases, insects, and to outcompete other plants.

IDENTIFICATION

Blackberries often get confused with another of its rose family relatives, the raspberry. One way to tell the difference is that when a raspberry fruit is picked the torus, the cone-shaped core around which the fruit grows, stays on the plant, leaving the characteristic hollow inside raspberry fruits. By contrast, when a blackberry is picked, the torus stays inside the fruit. Blackberries are a perennial plant, and they produce several stems, or canes, from a central root system. A single stem can reach over twenty feet long and often grows in an entangled way with several other stems, creating thickets, or brambles. The stems produce large, palmately compound leaves of between three to five leaflets. The stems also produce thousands of short, curved, sharp prickles or spikes. These are sharp and strong enough to rip through denim and into leather gloves. White to pink flowers emerge in late spring and early summer on short racemes. Each flower is about an inch to an inch and a half across in diameter, with five petals each.

CULINARY USE

The sweet fruit that we commonly think of as one single "berry" on a blackberry plant is actually an aggregate of small fruits, called duplets. It is a common forage food for native peoples across Native America. They are eaten directly, ground with wild game meat to make pemmican cakes, or dried and stored for later consumption. But blackberries are more than a sweet treat. They are useful in the treatment of cancer, dysentery, diarrhea, whooping cough, colitis, toothache, anemia, psoriasis, sore throat, mouth ulcer, hemorrhoids, and even minor bleeding.

Many Indigenous nations in eastern America use an infusion of blackberry roots, sometimes mixed with the leaves, to treat diarrhea and rheumatism. The same infusion is used by the Iroquois for colds and cough. The Menominee use an infusion of the roots to wash sore eyes. The Cherokee also drink a decoction of the bark of blackberry stems for urinary tract infections. Abenaki herbalist Judy Dow points out that not only are blackberries good food and medicine, their canes are also good for weaving baskets—once the thorns have been removed.

WHEN, WHERE, AND HOW TO GATHER IN KINCENTRIC ECOLOGY

Blackberries are one of the most widely distributed plants worldwide. There are around 375 different species, subspecies, and hybrids of Rubus, and they happily occupy a diversity of habitats from the arid lands in the American Southwest to the windy, damp coastal bluffs of California and the frigid forests of Alaska. Rubus represents a genus of berries that are extremely successful at adapting to local habitats. Their seeds and root systems can stay dormant for several seasons, until the conditions are right for them to sprout. They can easily adapt to low light or direct light, changing soils, and availability of moisture. The seed coats are durable, which has aided their dispersal by birds throughout North America. A large percentage of these species are native to North America, and some species are so unique that they can only be found in a single state, such as *Rubus aculiferus*, also called thorny dewberry, which grows only in Vermont, or *Rubus aliceae*, also called roadside blackberry or Santa Fe raspberry, a rare species endemic to a single small county in north-central New Mexico.

The common names of blackberries sometimes reflect the habitats and regions to which they are endemic or where they were first identified by Western botanists. These include blackberries such as *Rubus allegheniensis* (common blackberry), *Rubus andrewsianus* (Andrew's blackberry, endemic to New England), *R. ithacanus* (the Ithaca blackberry, found in the north-central states of New York and Pennsylvania), *R. lawrencei* (Adirondack blackberry, found in the eponymous mountain range), *R. noveboracus* (New York blackberry, found only in New York and Pennsylvania). Then there is *R. ortivus* (Mt. Desert Island blackberry, found in Maine); *R. stipulatus* (Big Horseshoe Lake Blackberry, found in several north-central states), *R. trux* (Lookout Mountain Blackberry, found only West Virginia, Georgia, Tennessee and Kentucky). And finally, there's *R. uvidus* (Kalamazoo dewberry, found only in Michigan, Wisconsin, Ohio, and Pennsylvania), and *R. ursinus* (Pacific blackberry, found only in California, Oregon, Washington, Idaho, Montana, and north into British Columbia).

Blueberries

***VACCINIUM ANGUSTIFOLIUM* (LOWBUSH BLUEBERRY), *V. CORYMBOSUM* (HIGHBUSH BLUEBERRY)**

PLANT FAMILY: *Ericaceae*
PARTS USED: *Ripe berries*
SEASON: *Midsummer*

Blueberries are truly one of nature's power foods. American Indians across North America have recognized this and used them in a variety of nutritious recipes and as a treatment for various ailments for centuries.

It was one of those warm, humid July days high up on a shoulder of the Mad River Valley in Vermont. I was at Knoll Farm helping to facilitate a retreat on a 250-acre acre working farm that also hosts what are called "whole thinking retreats." In order to keep the farm a designated working farm, the stewards of the land raise Icelandic sheep and blueberries. They asked if some of us who there as a part of the retreat wanted to help collect the blueberries ripening on the bushes that covered about a quarter acre of a gently rising hillside. I grabbed a bucket, found a row of bushes, and began picking the blue-gray little balls of juicy deliciousness. With about every five or six berries that I picked, I would pause to allow one of them to find its way into my smiling mouth. I felt like a ten-year-old again.

It's amazing that blueberry flowers can be pure white, when the ultimate berries are so purple as to be almost black.

IDENTIFICATION

There are thirty-five different varieties of blueberry species indigenous to North America. Their size and growth habit varies a bit with species and growing conditions, but wild and native blueberries are normally small shrubs that grow upright from between six inches up to around three feet. Domesticated varieties can reach up to twelve feet tall. The foliage is typically deciduous, but some are evergreen. The leaves are ovate to lanceolate, between a half inch to three inches in length and between a half inch to one and a half inches wide. The bell-shaped flowers dangle from the branches in groups of greenish-white, pale pink, or red. The berries of the wild, lowbush variety tend to be small and pea-sized. Most people are familiar with the larger berries that grow on the cultivated high-bush variety, which reach about half an inch. Both varieties have a flared crown at the end of the fruit. All blueberries begin as a small pale-green fruit, then become reddish-purple, and finally ripen into a dark purple berry covered by a light coating of powdery wax.

CULINARY USE

One of my favorite uses for blueberries is to simply pick them off the bushes and eat them raw. Some native peoples, such as the Micmac, dry the blueberries and add them later to soups and stews. Dried berries can also be mixed with dried meats to form a pemmican-like cake. Blueberries can also be canned, made into jam, crushed, filtered and cooked down into syrup, and juiced. Additionally, the Iroquois ceremonially consume blueberries in order to ensure good health and fortune for the coming summer and fall. The Iroquois also make a decoction of the berries to treat itchy skin rashes and to improve night vision.

WHEN, WHERE, AND HOW TO GATHER IN KINCENTRIC ECOLOGY

Blueberries are typically a midsummer fruit. Harvesting times vary by growing conditions such as elevation, latitude, whether they're growing on a south- or west-facing slope, etc. In the Northeast, peak harvesting generally happens in July. Blueberries grow well in open areas of full sun where their feet stay damp, but not overly soggy. During pre-Columbian times, native peoples maintained their favorite blueberry collecting areas and bushes with selective and periodic pruning and coppicing of the bushes and by clearing away competing plants and shrubs. Ripened berries are relatively hardy and can withstand harvesting by hand. Just don't be too clumsy or overly ambitious with piling berries too deep in buckets or baskets. Berries are considered overripe if the inside of the fruit easily squeezes out when you're pulling it off the bush.

Currants

GOOSEBERRY, WAX CURRANT, BLACK CURRANT, BUFFALO CURRANT

***RIBES* SP., *R. AMERICANUM* (BLACK CURRANTS), *R. AUREUM* (GOLDEN CURRANTS)**

PLANT FAMILY: *Grossulariaceae*

PARTS USED: *Leaves, berries, woody stems, roots*

SEASON: *Spring to summer*

The creamy yellow flowers later surprise by turning into jet-black currants.

When I lived in Colorado, one of my favorite times of year was late summer to early fall. This was the time of year when berries ripened at the higher elevations. Armed with any kind of bucket and thoughts of a sweet-tart syrup that I would soon be pouring onto pancakes, my friends and I would venture up to about 10,000 feet, to our favorite stands of black currant bushes. For American Indians, annual berry picking forays are both a communal event and a necessary subsistence practice. It is a time for families, relatives, and clans to tell stories and be social. It is also time to gather a nutritious food and source of medicine for the coming winter. Some cultures even mark the changes in season by the ripening of certain berries. Black currants, for example, mark the end of summer and the beginning of fall in the intermountain west.

IDENTIFICATION

Currant shrubs grow between four and eight feet tall. Their multiple branches are erect. The leaves are simple, alternate, lobed, and about three inches wide. The leaves are dark green and slightly hairy underneath. In May, black currant bushes sprout clusters of small white, tubular, five-petaled flowers. The flowers of golden currants are likewise golden. Later in the summer, small greenish smooth berries are produced in drooping clusters. Between August and September, the fruits of black currants turn from red to a purple so deep it's nearly black. Golden currant berries ripen from green to yellow to red, and then finally turn purple.

Gooseberry bushes tend to be wide and spread out, growing up to about five feet tall. The thick

Gooseberries are remarkable for their striped and hairy appearance.

branches contain sharp spines that emerge from the base of the leaves. The spines stand alone or in groups of two or three. The large leaves are rounded with three to five lobes. Sprouting from the groups of leaves are solitary greenish to pinkish bell-shaped flowers. Gooseberry bushes normally produce small hairy greenish fruits although there are varieties that are yellowish, white, red, and dark purple to black.

CULINARY USE

There are several species of currants native to North America. Some argue that currants should be separated taxonomically from gooseberries. Nevertheless, they are still both referred to as species of Ribes. The difference is that gooseberries have spiny branches and solitary flowers while the foliage of currants do not have any spines and the flowers are clustered. Although the common names for many Ribes fruits is "currant," these are not to be confused with the dried European currants found in scones, cakes, and puddings. That berry is actually a dried, raisin-like variety of grape known as the Zante currant, *Vitis vinifera*.

For the most part currants are a delightful food for American Indians. The Lakota eat black currant berries, *Ribes americanum*, raw or dry them for later use in soups, stews, cakes, and as an important ingredient in pemmican. The berries of golden currants are also eaten. The Lakota also eat Missouri gooseberries, *R. missouriense*, in a similar fashion. Tribes throughout the western half of the continent eat the berries of *Ribes* sp. The berries are also made into jams, preserves, and syrups. But currants afford other uses as well.

Different varieties of gooseberry are eaten by tribes from across North America in much the same way as are black currants.

The Cheyenne and Navajo are known to make arrow shafts from the woody stems of black currants and gooseberries. The roots of gooseberry are also pounded with cedar (*Juniperus* sp.) and rose roots and woven into cordage.

Missouri gooseberries, Ribes missouriense.

WHEN, WHERE, AND HOW TO COLLECT IN KINCENTRIC ECOLOGY

North American currants often form open thickets at the edges of shaded woods in the higher elevations of evergreen and mixed deciduous forests. Currants grow from New England south to Delaware and West Virginia, and east to Indiana, Iowa, Nebraska, and throughout the intermountain west from the Canadian border to New Mexico. Varieties of golden currant such as *R. aureum-gracillimum* are endemic to California. The yellow-flowered and black-berried clove currant, *R. aureum-villosum*, is endemic to the central United States from western Texas north to Montana and eastward to New York and Vermont. Different varieties of gooseberries are found throughout North America and as far north as the Arctic Circle. Care should be taken when harvesting the leaves, stems, and berries of gooseberry as the spines are sharp and stout.

Huckleberries

VACCINIUM PARVIFOLIUM, V. OVATUM, GAYLUSSACIA BACCATA

PLANT FAMILY: *Ericaceae*
PARTS USED: *Fruit, leaves, twigs, bark*
SEASON: *Spring*

Vaccinium parvifolium*, the red huckleberry.*

A basket plaque woven with rabbitbrush, wild currant, and yucca fiber from the Second Mesa of Hopi Reservation, Navajo County, Arizona.

There was a period when I was facilitating retreats for college graduates whose studies focused on environmental and climate studies. During the summer, the organization that hired me to lead these retreats would bring about eighteen students to a lodge situated on the southwestern slope of Mt. Hood, east of Portland, Oregon. The large main windows of this old lodge faced a slope of the mountain that was really a long stretch of meadow edged by different varieties of conifers. If you craned your neck enough, you could see the snow-capped peak.

I was in the habit of waking early in order to go outside and practice some tai chi and yoga in the early dawn light. One morning, as I was standing on the large porch of the lodge after having completed my exercises, I noticed a shadow moving among the huckleberry bushes growing in the open meadow. While I was trying to figure out what I was seeing, the shadow stood up and faced me. It was a large black bear, still chewing on a bunch of huckleberries. I felt blessed.

Huckleberries are considered sacred food for the Yakima. They believe that huckleberries originated from the eyes of the Creator. In this legend, the Creator takes out his own eyes and plants them in the ground, like seeds. The veins become the plants' roots and sprout to create huckleberries. Huckleberries are a popular plant among many American Indian communities. The berries of the plant are enjoyed fresh, dried, and as jam, providing great nutritional value. The leaves can be used to make a tea to treat a variety of internal

Huckleberries growing between tall pines near Dewey Lake in the Washington State wilderness.

and external ailments. Many American Indians have also been known to utilize the berries as a fish bait—as they are small, circular, and red, they resemble salmon eggs.

IDENTIFICATION

Red huckleberry (*Vaccinium parvifolium*) is native to California, however it is also commonly found in Oregon, Washington, and other regions along the Pacific coast. Evergreen huckleberry, also known as green huckleberry and California huckleberry (*Vaccinium ovatum*), shares the same geographic distribution with red huckleberry. Both plants prefer to propagate in dry, open areas of mixed forests and are in bloom in the months of March through May. Red huckleberries can be found in coastal forests, coniferous forests, and canyons as well.

Evergreen huckleberry shrubs can be found in similar ecosystems, and at higher elevations. Huckleberry shrubs hold bright green leaves and grow to about six feet tall and six feet wide. Occasionally, the shrub can grow up to twelve feet tall. The leaves of both red and evergreen huckleberries are small and oval-shaped. The berries of red huckleberry resemble blueberries but are bright red, while the berries of evergreen huckleberry are dark blue. The flowers of both plants are small, light-pink, and bell-shaped. The stems of the plant are typically green, however during some times of year they can present as red. The shrub itself is known to be commonly found growing atop decaying logs and stumps.

The eastern relatives of Vaccinium, *Gaylussicia* sp., are similar in appearance. Today the most common species of Gaylussicia is black huckleberry (*Gaylussacia baccata*). It is a shorter shrub, normally growing only up to three feet. The shrubs are many-branched and often grow in colonies from the upper Midwest, down the Appalachians, and into the Southeast. Like Vaccinium, black huckleberry can be found in open forested areas. The leaves are also small and have small dots of resin underneath. The orange-to-red bell-shaped flowers dangle down in groups of three to seven, then turn into dark blue berries.

CULINARY USE

Huckleberries are most commonly eaten fresh. Members of the Hesquiat and other Pacific Northwest nations enjoy eating the berries raw with fish oil. Most other Indigenous eaters eat the berries fresh, but they can also be dried or mashed into cakes, jams, jellies, pies, and mixed into pemmican.

WHEN, WHERE, AND HOW TO COLLECT IN KINCENTRIC ECOLOGY

Huckleberries, either the Vaccinium or Gaylussacia genera, are good indicators of a forest's health. In the West, the presence of Vaccinium means there will be a healthy stand of mixed pine/deciduous trees nearby, while in the East, Gaylussacia are components of healthy oak forests. Huckleberries require a daily dose of sunlight in order to grow, so you'll most likely find them by searching at the edges of forest meadows and often on south-facing hillsides. When I was greeted that morning by the bear on the side of Mt. Hood, I was also witness to the results of forest management. The meadow where the bear was feasting on huckleberries, and other similar meadows, provide just the right amount of sunlight for huckleberries and their frequent companion plants such as serviceberry, Indian hemp, and camas root. Indigenous peoples in the Pacific Northwest employ periodic burning, pruning, and coppicing in order to ensure health of huckleberries and other useful plants.

You will not find huckleberries in areas that receive little shade, however, as intense heat can kill the underground rhizomes that work to create colonies of the shrubs. It is for these reasons that Indigenous maintenance of huckleberry and other berry stands is beneficial to entire forest ecosystems. If the forests are permitted to overgrow, berry production decreases. Alternatively, if forests are overharvested, berry colonies will overproduce, but soon reach ecological climax and face sudden collapse. Fire management and culturally sanctioned use of the forests have played an important role in the survival of huckleberry stands.

To collect the berries, simply comb the berries off a branch with your fingers. Indigenous people sometimes carved hollow, rough, wet planks to hold them and would later separate any remaining leaves. The Karuk of Northern California will pluck off the entire tip of any branch holding a clump of huckleberries—it is a way of simultaneously collecting the berries and pruning the bushes.

Strawberries

WOODLAND STRAWBERRY, WILD STRAWBERRY

FRAGARIA VESCA, F. VIRGINIANA

PLANT FAMILY: *Rosaceae*
PARTS USED: *Fruit, root, leaves*
SEASON: *Summer to fall*

For many years, the native peoples of California had ceased to have roundhouse ceremonies and annual festivals of thanks and renewal. Before World War II, the communities were still rebuilding from two centuries of near-genocide. During the war, many of the remaining inhabitants moved away from their original homes to find work in the orchards, in the hop fields, or to help with the industrial war machine. After the war, the Kashia Pomo community, in an effort to create harmony with outsiders, decided to ignore tradition and to open their roundhouse ceremonies to nonnative visitors. At the same time, they began to celebrate their annual strawberry dances again.

For many American Indian communities, strawberries represent annual spring renewal. Some Algonquin-speaking tribes feel that strawberries are symbols of thanksgiving. Every year the annual Kanatsiohareke Mohawk Strawberry Festival is celebrated with a pow-wow, food, music, crafts, and storytelling at the Kanatsiohareke Mohawk Community in Fonda, New York. Strawberries are also part of the pantheon of Navajo sacred life medicines, so the enthusiasm for this early-summer fruit reaches across the continent.

The Cherokee believe that strawberries are a love medicine and were originally given to us by the Creator in order to reunite a couple after they had been quarreling. Their story tells of how, after First Man and First Woman had been quarreling, First Woman left her husband and headed east, toward the Sun. First Man was very sad and began to follow his wife. The Creator looked down upon First Man with pity and asked if he was still angry with First Woman. After he said that he was no longer upset with her, the Creator told First Man that he would help him get his wife back. The Creator caused huckleberries to ripen along the path that First Woman was following, hoping she would slow her pace as she stopped to collect them. But she was not interested in these. The Creator tried other berries: blackberries, serviceberries, and even other kinds of sweet fruits. None tempted her to stop. Finally the Creator invented a new kind of bright-red berry and placed it in her path. Intrigued, she finally stopped to eat some of these new berries. As she was eating, she glanced west. This caused her to think of her husband and to realize that she missed him. She gathered more strawberries to bring to him and began to head back home. First Man and First Woman met each other on the trail and were happily reunited while sharing the newly created strawberries.

Wild strawberries, Fragaria vesca.

IDENTIFICATION

Woodland strawberry resembles the hybridized garden-variety strawberry that many people purchase from local nurseries, except on a much smaller scale. Wild strawberry is an herbaceous perennial that normally spreads through short rhizomes. The plant grows up to four inches tall. The thin green trifoliate leaves typically grow in sets of three and are about three inches long and an inch and a half wide. The individual leaves are serrated. Strawberry plants produce small white flowers with five petals and a yellow center. The fruit of the wild strawberry is much smaller than that of the hybridized or store-bought variety.

CULINARY USE

Many American Indian tribes across North America consider strawberry to be an important fruit, since it is one of the first to ripen in the spring. But eating those wonderfully tart and sweet berries raw is not the only way they're consumed. The Navajo believe strawberry is good medicine because it is shaped like a heart. When it is eaten or juiced, we believe it revitalizes us. Strawberry juice is often drunk as a general tonic and to relieve arthritis as well. Many native people make a decoction or infusion of the leaves and roots to treat diarrhea and dysentery, inflamed bowel, and gout. The leaves are dried and powdered and then applied to open wounds as a poultice with disinfectant properties, as well as to soothe sores on the skin.

WHEN, WHERE, AND HOW TO COLLECT IN KINCENTRIC ECOLOGY

Look for strawberries in cool, moist, shaded areas near the edges and open areas of forests. Strawberries grow throughout North America. When collecting the leaves, it's important that you do not gather so many that it will harm the entire plant. When gathering the roots, be sure to leave some of the root system in the ground rather than yanking out an entire plant, to enable future growth.

Cranberries

VACCINIUM MICROCARPON, V. MACROCARPON, V. OXYCOCCOS

PLANT FAMILY: *Ericaceae*
PARTS USED: *Fruit, root, leaves*
SEASON: *Summer to fall*

Ask an Indigenous person, perhaps someone from the Northeast, to choose a plant that epitomizes persistence. There is a good chance they will name cranberries: they keep finding their way into our cultures and kitchens. For centuries, cranberries have been used as a key ingredient in pemmican recipes. Once Europeans arrived, we introduced cranberries at the fabled first Thanksgiving. They are now a regular part of granola and energy bar recipes, and still make their annual presence on our dinner tables toward the end of November. The Wampanoag of the Northeast still celebrate Cranberry Day on the second Tuesday of every October, and consider it one of their most important annual festivals.

IDENTIFICATION

The cranberry is a low-growing, vine-like, woody perennial. It has small oval evergreen leaves that are arranged alternately on fine vine-like

In the wild, cranberries often grow in wet areas alongside species that like similar habitats, such as mosses.

The flowers of Vaccinium macrocarpon.

shoots; these root at intervals as they crawl along the ground. The plant often forms a dense mat. The leaves are dark green on top, and pale underneath. One to four flower buds form on short, upright shoots that appear between May and July. The flowers shoot up from the tips of stems. They appear as small, pale, rose-colored flowers and have petals that are bent backward, causing them to often be described as shooting stars or cranes—hence the early colonist name for the plant, craneberry. The bright-red berries ripen in late summer to early October.

CULINARY USE

Cranberries have first and foremost always been a food plant. Cree, Penobscot, Passamaquoddy, and other Algonquin-speaking peoples eat the berries fresh, include them in stews, and dry them for winter storage. If they're consumed in season, they're often mashed in with wild game meats, or used to sweeten and flavor pemmican cakes. The juice of the berries is also used as a dye for blankets, rugs, clothing, and even porcupine quills. An infusion of the twigs and leaves are used to treat inflamed lungs as well as to relieve nausea.

Berries are tasty sources of numerous phytochemicals, antioxidants, polyphenols, and anthocyanins. Cranberries are nutrient-rich, being loaded with vitamin C, fiber, and potassium. The plant and its berries are rich sources of polyphenols that display antibacterial, antiviral, antimutagenic, anticarcinogenic, antitumorigenic, antiangiogenic, antiinflammatory, and antioxidant properties. Cranberries also contain flavonols, A-type procyanidins, anthocyanins, benzoic acid, ursolic acid, phenolic acids, and terpenes. Due to these phytochemicals, cranberries demonstrate the ability to fight urinary tract and other infections.

WHEN, WHERE, AND HOW TO COLLECT IN KINCENTRIC ECOLOGY

Cranberry plants are found in scrub-shrub swamps and bogs, and marshy shores of ponds and lakes of northeastern North America. The plants are shade intolerant. Therefore the plants

The natural cranberry bogs of the Gay Head cliffs on the western end of Martha's Vineyard, where the Wampanoag tribe still holds an annual Cranberry Day harvest celebration the second Tuesday in October.

do well where they are exposed to warm and sunny weather. Old stands will be found in bogs among the peat where there is a conifer overstory. Cranberries are best harvested by hand during the late summer to early fall, though the evolutionary quirk that makes this berry float has led to today's commercial method of harvesting by flooding bogs and skimming the berries off the surface of the water. Early commercial growers of cranberries learned this method from eastern Indians who collected the berries by hand after first diverting water and flooding the cranberry bogs. It is a sustainable method of harvesting cranberries that continues into today.

Wóžapi

INGREDIENTS:

- 4 c. water
- 8 oz. fresh cranberries, chokecherries, or a mix of different berries
- 2 oz. rosehips, seeded and dried
- 3 oz. maple syrup or honey

Wóžapi is a traditional Lakota sauce made of stewed berries that can be sweetened with honey or maple syrup as a dessert, or used as a garnishing sauce for meat, game, vegetables, or even poured over corn husk bread.

Add all ingredients to a pot and bring to a boil, then reduce the heat and simmer for 15 minutes. Using an immersion blender, purée until smooth, being very careful of the hot liquid splashing out. Continue to simmer the sauce until it coats the back of spoon. Cool and serve.

Makes approximately 1 quart.

Prickly Pear

NOPAL **(NAHUATL),** ***NAAVO*** **(YAQUI),** ***IRAKÁ*** **(RARÁMURI), BARBARY FIG, CACTUS APPLE, DEVIL'S TONGUE**
OPUNTIA ENGELMANNII, O. FICUS-INDICA, O. HUMIFUSA, O. COCHENILLIFERA

PLANT FAMILY: *Cactaceae*
PARTS USED: *Pods, leaves, wood*
SEASON: *Summer, fall*

The Aztecs were one of the largest Indigenous empires of the Western Hemisphere. They subjugated nearby native communities while creating sophisticated mathematics, architecture, and agricultural practices that outmatched what was happening in Europe contemporaneously. However, none of it would have come to pass if not for the prickly pear cactus. The Aztecs were not originally from what today is Mexico City, where they eventually made their capital. According to legend, they originated far to the north in a land known as Aztlán, believed to be the region we know today as the American Southwest. The legend suggests that for centuries the Aztecs were in a state of constant migration, being pushed around and forced away from places that they were trying to settle by other tribes. This continued until an Aztec leader had a vision that prophesied that they should migrate south to a place near a lake, where he would see an eagle holding a snake in its beak while perched on a prickly pear cactus. Wherever they beheld this sight, they should settle. This place eventually became the Aztec capital of Tenochtitlan, today's Mexico City.

A prickly pear with abundant fruits growing in Saguaro National Park, Arizona.

The national flag of Mexico, with a central emblem reflecting the Aztec founding legend.

The legend is a central feature on the emblem of the flag of Mexico.

It is not only the Aztecs or today's modern Mexican who hold the prickly pear in high esteem, however. It is considered a gift from the land by many American Indians and is used widely for both food and medicine.

IDENTIFICATION

Prickly pears are evergreen perennials. Some species, such as *O. polyacantha*, grow only six inches tall while others such as *O. ficus-indica* grow up to sixteen feet. They are hardy plants and not frost tender. The plants tend to spread in all directions and flower between June and September. The pads are green, sometimes blue-green, generally obovate to roundish. Most prickly pear flowers are yellow, though sometimes occasionally reddish. The flowers will grow up to three inches in diameter and nearly as high. The blooms will open in midmorning and last an entire day. Later in the year, the plants will produce purple-reddish fleshy fruits that grow up to about three inches long.

Although prickly pears are often associated with the Southwest, native varieties grow across the continent. Opuntia cochenillifera *(left) is native to Florida, and* O. humifusa *(right) is native to New York.*

CULINARY USE

Prickly pear is a very nutritional food. I recall watching my grandfather sup on one of his favorite soups of chopped cactus fruits, pinto beans, broth, and rice. My grandmother made this dish for him all the time—perhaps it's part of why he reached the age of 106. I also enjoy carefully collecting young prickly pear pads, chopping them up, and adding them to soups, stews, or sautéing them with scrambled eggs. A Yaqui Deer Singer friend of mine enjoys bean burritos with chopped prickly pear.

Prickly pear can also be harvested and dried for later use. Prickly pear fruits, called *tunas* in Spanish, are a delicacy all around the Southwest. They can be eaten raw, but the sweet juicy flesh is studded with many seeds. More often, the fruit is sieved to remove the seeds and then made into syrup or jam. They can also be baked. The Apache save the seeds, dry them, and eat them as a snack or grind them into flour.

For medicinal use, prickly pear pads are scorched and then split to expose the interior and used to treat infections, cuts, burns, and to stop bleeding. The liquid from the boiled roots is taken to treat diarrhea and, conversely, as a laxative. The warm fruit juice is often rubbed onto joints to treat rheumatism. An infusion of the smashed pads is taken to ease childbirth. In a pinch, the thick pads can even be scraped of their spines and used as a temporary splint for a broken limb.

Prickly pear species such as *O. ficus-indica* and *O. engelmannii* are significant sources of soluble fibers, mucilages, amino acids, minerals, carotenoids, antioxidants, polyphenols, flavonoids, quercitin, gallic acid, rutin, and several are bioactive compounds. The therapeutic activities of these compounds makes *Opuntia* sp. valuable as an antiinflammatory, for preventing blood clots, as an antioxidant, as a diuretic, and to help lower blood pressure.

WHEN, WHERE, AND HOW TO COLLECT IN KINCENTRIC ECOLOGY

Although prickly pears are icons of the Southwest and Mexico, the species is widespread across North America. When the Lewis and Clark expedition began their journey to explore the western regions of North America in 1803, they expected to encounter wild animals, Indians, and perhaps difficult weather as they passed through what today are the Dakotas and Montana. What they did not expect to be major difficulties were mosquitoes, clouds of gnats, and stands of prickly pear. The short spines of plains prickly pear, *Opuntia polyacantha*, made their trek difficult as they could easily puncture the moccasins worn by many on the Corps of Discovery. On September 8, 1805 William Lewis wrote in his journal,

> *On this part of the river on the head of the Clark's River [the name they gave the Bitterroot] I observe great quantities of a peculiar sort of prickly pear growing in clusters, oval and about the size of a pigeon's egg, with strong thorns which are so bearded as to draw the pear from the cluster after penetrating our feet.*

Prickly pear species such as *Opuntia cochenillifera* can be found in Florida while *O. humifusa* is native to New York. Hundreds of species and varieties are spread throughout the continent.

Opuntia polyacantha, *which grows low to the ground and caused so much trouble for Lewis and Clark as they made their way West.*

Generally prickly pear grows well in light, sandy soils in full sun. The larger varieties of prickly pear often create habitat for certain species of birds, provide shelter from predators for small mammals, and offer a food source for insects, pollinators, birds, and some mammals.

When harvesting prickly pear for food, it is best to collect the young pads during the spring. Older pads over seven inches long begin to fill with bitter gallic acids and grow thicker fibers, making consumption unpleasant. After collecting, the glochids—the small nodules holding the spines—can be scraped off with a sharp knife. The fruits are harvested during the late summer and into the fall. Be careful, as the fruits are also covered with many glochids that have tiny spines.

If you have spent much time in areas where prickly pear grows, you may have observed how, if left to itself, a prickly pear can grow into an impassable wall of spiny globular green. In some places, locals even plant prickly pear as a security or privacy hedge. However, if intentionally planted it is important to periodically cut the plants back, as it will outcompete any other plants nearby.

Indigenous communities will sometimes burn patches of prickly pear in order to control its spread. In addition, careful mechanical pruning will not only control the growth of prickly pear but will also encourage the growth of the fruits as well as the desired young pads.

Sopa de Nopalitos

INGREDIENTS:

- 2 cloves chopped garlic
- 1 small yellow onion, diced
- 1 c. young prickly pear pad (chopped into ¼-inch squares)
- 1 tsp. dried Mexican oregano (*Lippia graveolens*)
- 2 tbsp. fresh cilantro, chopped
- 4 c. chicken or vegetable broth
- ¼ c. white rice
- 3 tbsp. tomato paste
- 1 or 2 crushed dried chiltepin peppers (optional)
- 1 c. cooked pinto beans
- Salt and pepper, to taste

Sopa de nopalitos (prickly pear soup) is a something that returns me to my grandmother's kitchen. I can easily recall the pungency of the onions and garlic sautéing in a pot while my grandmother chopped cilantro and the nopalitos. Prickly pear, or nopal, can be added to any recipe or dish as one might add chopped spinach to scrambled eggs or peas and carrots to a pot of soup. The key to incorporating prickly pear into a dish is the preparation. After removing the glochids, as noted previously, rinse the pads in fresh water to remove any dirt or any remaining tiny pieces of the spines. This dish makes for a perfect lunch or a side dish for dinner. I like to dip tortillas into the soup while eating.

Sauté the garlic and onion for about a minute over medium heat. Do this in the same pot that you plan to cook the soup in. Next, add the chopped nopalitos, oregano, and cilantro. Cook until the little squares of cactus just begin to change color. Add the broth, rice, and tomato paste. Also add the chiltepins for some heat and added flavor, if you like spice. Lower the heat and simmer for 15 minutes. Add the beans and cook for another 5 minutes. Salt and pepper to taste.

Serves 2.

Saguaro

HA:SAÑ **(TOHONO O'ODHAM),** ***HOSHCHOH*** **(APACHE),** ***SAUWO*** **(YAQUI)**
CARNEGIEA GIGANTEA

PLANT FAMILY: *Cactaceae*
PARTS USED: *Fruits, seeds, ribs*
SEASON: *Summer, fall*
REGION: *Southwest*

Cacti with fruits atop their tall "arms" in Saguaro National Park, Arizona.

The flowers of a saguaro, which only appear after the cactus is at least thirty-five years old.

Every summer, normally sometime in July, Tohono O'odham and Pima people venture into the hot Sonoran Desert armed with very long sticks that have a shorter stick attached perpendicularly near the end, making them resemble a ten- to fifteen-foot-long crucifix. This time of year is known in the Tohono O'odham language as *Hashañi Mashad*—the Saguaro harvest moon. They will gather the sweet, ripe fruits that sprout from the tops of the tall cacti in preparation for the *vikita*, a harvest ceremony. This ceremony is crucial for the Tohono O'odham and Pima, as traditionally it was celebrated to ensure that the summer monsoon rains would come and nourish their crops, as well as all the sensitive flora and fauna of the desert.

IDENTIFICATION

The saguaro cactus's only natural range is within the borders of the Sonoran Desert. Look for the tallest columnar cactus growing there, and you have found saguaro. It is characterized by an erect central stem. During its younger years the central stem grows to about ten feet tall and about twenty-five inches in diameter. Later, after about a hundred years, the cactus can reach heights of up to forty feet with a trunk diameter of around thirty inches—this is also when the cactus begins to sprout "arms." Saguaro is also characterized by its prominent radial ribs that number from twelve to thirty. The stem and arms are covered with dense spines. Throughout its lifetime, saguaros sprout funnel-shaped flowers from the tops of the central stems and arms. The flowers are green at the outer sides and borders. The inner petals are white and yellow. After flowering, dark-red, scaly fruits that grow to about two inches long appear.

Tribes that call the Sonoran Desert home believe that the saguaro was once human. One legend suggests that a little boy fell into a hole in the ground and when he came out, he emerged as a saguaro. Another legend describes how a mischievous little boy and his brother were arguing and accidentally knocked over a clay jar full of precious water. To avoid getting into trouble from their grandmother, they escaped into the desert. At that point, the two boys decided to transform into desert plants. One boy changed into a palo verde tree while the other became a saguaro so he would live forever and bear edible fruit for the people. Finally, the Tohono O'odham believe that every saguaro in the desert represents the place where a bead of sweat fell onto the ground from the brow of their trickster creator, I'itoi. Saguaro is not only a keystone Sonoran Desert plant, it is also central to O'odham and Pima culture.

CULINARY USE

Saguaro mostly provides American Indians a source of sweet food, but is aso an important ceremonial plant and provides materials for tools and construction. The sweet fruits that grow atop of the columnar cacti are collected and eaten directly. The insides of the fruit are scooped out and made into syrups and preserves. The juice is mixed with other foods as a sweetener. The juices are allowed to ferment into an alcoholic drink that is consumed during ceremonies; they can also be filtered and taken as a refreshing beverage.

The fruits may also be dried for later use, in which case the seeds of the fruit are separated from the pulp, allowed to dry or are parched, and later ground into flour that is used for making cakes, breads, and porridge.

Saguaro cacti are very long-lived plants. Many live for more than four hundred years. When a saguaro does finally die, its inner ribs are exposed The medium-hard ribs are a source for the fruit-picking sticks mentioned above. The ribs are also used as warp material for basketmaking, for roofing houses, fencing material, and for making cooking implements. The ribs can be split and made into small traps, cages, and rough baskets, and many other tools and construction materials.

We:sic 'em ki: (Everybody's Home) *by late Tohono O'odham artist Terrol Dew Johnson. It draws from that nation's house-building traditions to reinterpret mesquite support poles and roof slats made from saguaro ribs in a contemporary structure.*

An interesting symbiotic relationship the occurs among the saguaro, gila lizards, woodpeckers, elf owls, and several desert birds. The woodpecker drills holes into the sides of the cactus to get to the moisture inside, then creates a nest in the resulting cavity. In the meantime, the cactus lines the cavity with scar tissue from the injury. Later, once the nest has been abandoned, desert birds such as screech and elf owls, flickers, and many others will move in and occupy it. Finally, after the cactus has died, desert dwellers such as the Tohono O'odham, Apache, or Pima collect the hard skinned burls, or "boots," to be used as containers for water and other items.

Finally, although saguaro is not really thought of as a highly medicinal plant, Apache, O'odham, and other desert peoples feel strongly that eating saguaro fruits helps to prevent arthritis and rheumatism.

A Tohono O'odham canteen made of a saguaro woodpecker cavity, with agave carrying ropes, circa 1915.

WHEN, WHERE, AND HOW TO COLLECT IN KINCENTRIC ECOLOGY

Saguaros are endemic to the Sonoran Desert. Their northernmost range is about twenty-eight miles north of Phoenix, Arizona. They grow most thickly in the Tucson, Arizona, area and grow south into the northern half of Sonora, Mexico. They begin to dissipate above 2,500 feet in elevation. They are sometimes found near the California-Arizona border, but are only sparsely dispersed east of Phoenix or Tucson. The cactus prefers gravelly slopes and rocky ridges.

Harvesting saguaro fruit is difficult. Like the people indigenous to the Sonoran Desert, some kind of 20-to-30-foot-long pole, tall enough to reach the tops of the central stem and arms, is required. The pole should have some kind of hook or perpendicular arms for pulling or knocking off the fruit.

Generally, the fruit pulp is scraped from the inside of the pod and into a vessel. The seeds should then be strained from the flesh. It takes about twenty-five pints of the fruit to make a gallon of syrup. Seeds are not wasted, but dried after being separated from the flesh of the fruits.

The O'odham and other Piman-speaking peoples of the Sonoran Desert do not really engage in much mechanical management of the habitats near the giant saguaro. Until the invasion of buffelgrass (*Cenchrus ciliaris*), which competes with young saguaro for moisture and nutrients, there was little need for physical land management. However, kincentric ecological relationships are founded in the Indigenous recognition that plants are related to us, therefore, require our care.

The Tohono O'odham maintain a deep relationship with saguaro. The saguaro plays a crucial role as a keystone species in the Sonoran Desert ecosystem. It provides food and shelter for a variety of animals, including birds that nest in cavities they excavate within the cactus. This translates into management practices that are interwoven with their ceremony. The saguaro is a central figure in O'odham cosmology, as exemplified by the stories noted above. The stories suggest that the O'odham recognize saguaro as having once been human. This respect is reflected in their kincentric ecological practices.

Tohono O'odham management practices of saguaro are twofold; they include harvesting and ceremony. The annual saguaro fruit results in more than the production of a simple syrup. The fruit is collected to be eaten raw, processed into syrup, jam, or ceremonial wine. Seeds are dried and turned into flour or chicken feed. In addition, they use other parts of the saguaro, demonstrating a comprehensive and sustainable approach to resource management. Ribs from dead saguaros are used for building materials and for crafting other tools. The saguaro will create a hardened callus tissue, called a saguaro boot, around wounds created by desert woodpeckers. This boot is often extracted and utilized by the O'odham as storage vessels or containers. Finally, O'odham interaction with and especially consumption of the fruits plays an essential role in in the propagation of the cacti.

Every summer, the *Nawait I'i*, the rain ceremony, is aimed at encouraging monsoon rains. A fermented saguaro syrup is used to make ceremonial wine as part of these rituals. Participants drink the wine, *nawait*, to the point when they must vomit. The vomiting is seen as a sacred act;

Tohono O'odham people, circa 1950, engage in their traditional harvest of saguaro fruit which they call bahidaj. *Harvesters knock or pull the fruits off the tops of the saguaros using a tall pole made of saguaro ribs, called a* kukuipad.

it is a cultural reminder of a legend about when Raven drank too much *nawait*, too—his vomit turned into the clouds that brought precious rain.

The Tohono O'odham treat the saguaro with respect, and imbue it with a sacred status. This respect inherently promotes conservation, as the cactus is never intentionally harmed. The annual harvest of fruits is also traditionally seen as a communal activity and sacred practice. O'odham management of saguaro is based on a deep understanding of the Sonoran Desert ecology and a reverence for the plant that promotes sustainable harvesting and kincentric ecological balance.

5

Nuts *and* Seeds

So often, when modern people consider the foods that pre-Columbian peoples of North America ate, the foods that are most often spoken of include corn or some kind of wild game. However, it turns out that of all the foods that American Indians ate before the arrival of Europeans, nuts comprised more of the typical American Indian diets than any other foods. The exception would be populations of people up near the Arctic Circle where there are not any nut-bearing trees or bushes. Although, according to a study published by the Geological Survey of Canada in 2024, up until about 37 million years ago three species of Juglans (walnut trees) existed in a rich forest on Axel Heiburg Island. The canopy of the forest included ginkgo, redwoods, birches, cedars, and hickories. This was during the Earth's Eocene period, when conditions were much warmer in both the Arctic and Antarctica.

An oak tree branch with acorns, growing in California.

Millions of years later, the reason for the popularity of nuts and also seeds is due to several factors: nuts and seeds are readily available, they are relatively easy to gather, they can be stored for long periods, and they are an excellent source of nutrients and calories. Nuts and seeds can also be prepared in so many different ways. They can be eaten directly, roasted, and toasted. They can also be dried and ground into a flour and then used to make cakes and added to soups and stews. Finally, nuts and seeds are sometimes central figures in narratives meant to teach values and lessons and also played a role in the Creation.

Every summer on the reservations where Apache people still live and practice their ceremonies, the Sunrise Ceremony is performed. The ceremony, also known as *Na'ii'ees*, occurs over four days. It is a spiritual event meant to honor a young girl's passage into maturity.

During the Apache Sunrise Ceremony, which marks the transition of a young lady into womanhood, participants are prayed over and sprinkled with pollen.

During the four days the girl temporarily becomes White Shell Woman, also known as Girl-Without-Parents. To the Apache, White Shell Woman is a figure that appears during the Creation. She survives a flood by floating on a large ball of sticky gum taken from a piñon tree and becomes the caretaker of the Apache and essentially the First Mother and protector of the Apache and the Earth.

Acorns

XUNTÁPAN **(KARUK),** ***MITIGOMIN*** **(OJIBWE),** ***CHI CH'IL*** **(WESTERN APACHE)**
QUERCUS **SP. &** ***LITHOCARPUS DENSIFLORUS***

PLANT FAMILY: *Fagaceae*
PARTS USED: *Inner nut*
SEASON: *Late summer to fall*

According to the Karuk people from the middle Klamath River region of what today is northern California, acorns were one of several kinds of spirit people who lived among the rivers, mountains, and redwoods of their current homeland in a previous time period, prior to when the Karuk arrived. The Karuk refer to these people as Ikzareyavs. As is the case today, there were different kind of acorn Ikzareyavs. There was the black oak acorn (*Quercus kelloggii*), the post oak acorn (*Q. stellata*), maul oak acorn (*Q. chrysolepis*), and the tan oak acorn (*Lithocarpus densiflorus*). Before the acorn Ikzareyavs traveled from their previous dimension to today's Earth, they were instructed to weave their own hats in order to be presentable. They each began to weave, but

A California live oak (Quercus agrifolia), *growing near Santa Barbara.*

black oak did not finish hers; instead, she just picked up a woven bowl and put it on her head. Tan oak did not properly clean her hat, so the unfinished wefts were visible sticking out from the edge of the hat. Post and maul oak did properly finish their hats, however. And thus, this was how the acorn people arrived to the land. Recalling this story helps one tell the visual difference between different kinds of acorns.

California Indians are not the only Indigenous peoples to have a connection to oak trees and acorns. According to the Western Apache during the time of emergence, when the world was still empty and dark the tree people were among the first people to climb up from the lower world and into the current one. The first tree people include juniper, willow, chokecherry, mesquite, and oak.

If asked to name the most important pre-contact plant foods for American Indians, I would guess that most people would suggest foods such as corn, beans, and squashes. Perhaps some would include specific berries or perhaps regionalized nuts and other plants. However, I imagine that most would not consider the importance of acorns to the Indigenous diets.

Prior to the arrival of Europeans, acorns were the most widely gathered and eaten food in North America. In California alone it has been speculated that supply far outreached the consumption of acorns. This is largely due to the inherent availability, abundance, storability, and nutritional content of these bitter nuts.

IDENTIFICATION

There are ninety different species of oaks native to North America. About sixty of those are native to the United States. In California there are about twenty species that are found throughout the state. In Arizona about twelve, in Georgia thirty-four, and in New York sixteen. Oaks can be found in every region in North America and in every ecosystem, from scrub oak that endures the aridity and heat of the Sonoran Desert to the valley oaks in California that thrive near riparian zones. In addition, oaks can grow up to sixty feet tall or, like the Sonoran scrub oak, survive as medium-sized shrubs and bushes.

Due to the diversity of oak species throughout the continent, there are only a couple of identifiers that can be used to determine oak-ness. The most important identifier would be the presence of acorns, but acorns appear in different shapes and sizes depending on the species. The only commonality is the presence of a cap at one end of the nut. The leaves of oaks tend to be leathery, but this is not always the case. Oak leaves do tend to grow alternately and are most often lobed or serrated. Finally, young oak trees have smooth bark that becomes deeply furrowed.

Oak acorns vary by species, and, along with leaf shape, can aid in identification. Clockwise from top left: Quercus kelloggii; Quercus stellata; Quercus emoryi; Quercus chrysolepis.

CULINARY USE

During one summer ethnobotanical field school, I and my students spent a couple of weeks among the Western Apache in the White Mountains of eastern Arizona. A handful of the students that summer where from the Western Apache community and had invited us to a puberty ceremony. Different kinds of traditional dishes were being served at the ceremony including oak and venison stew. It was a hearty dish. The acorn served as the base of the stock, which was more of a thin mush. Between the mush and the venison there was a bit of the sliminess to the stew that many of my students were not accustomed to. Fortunately I had lectured them about the protocols of conducting ethnographic fieldwork beforehand, which included maintaining politeness and not making weird faces if consuming something that you might not enjoy.

Apache chefs prefer to cook with acorns gathered from Emory oak (*Quercus emoryi*). Among some California Indians the acorns of tanoak are preferred and prepared as soup, but is often prepared as a thick mush, and in biscuits and bread.

Nutritional Values

Acorns, along with the seeds of native grasses and forbs, provided carbohydrate-rich food sources that could be stored throughout the year. Some health benefits of the tanoak are that the acorns are low in protein but are high in caloric value due to the high amount of nutritious fats they contain. Protein and fat content varied a lot throughout different kinds of acorns. However, the protein content is low, while fat and carbohydrate content are typically high in tanoak acorns. Tanoak acorns are also soft enough to chew without the need of processing, but the tannic acid found in them needs to be removed in order to make them useful as human food. Also compared to most acorns, tanoak acorns are much larger than those of other oak trees, making them much easier to eat.

WHEN, WHERE, AND HOW TO GATHER IN KINCENTRIC ECOLOGY

On October 8, 1542, Spanish explorer Juan Rodriguez Cabrillo noted in his journals the presence of smoke rising from hillsides behind San Pedro Bay which is today Los Angeles, California. For centuries fire had been a tool employed by Native Californians to maintain the oak groves, hunting areas, and other locations where they gathered foods, medicines, and basketmaking materials. It is not an accident that approximately one-third of the Indigenous population that was present in what today is the United States in 1491 occupied the coastal areas reaching from Baja up to what today is British Columbia. As a result of sustainable fire management, coppicing, pruning, and selective harvesting, the West Coast of North America presented a cornucopia to Indigenous communities. Not surprisingly the western region of North America was also one of the most culturally and linguistically diverse areas in the world. To this day there are around a hundred different tribes, bands, and subgroups that are recognized by the state government of California. Many of these Indigenous California communities have

A 1622 engraving of Abanaki/Wabanaki people hunting on Mount Desert Island, Maine, showing the use of controlled fire to drive deer into the water.

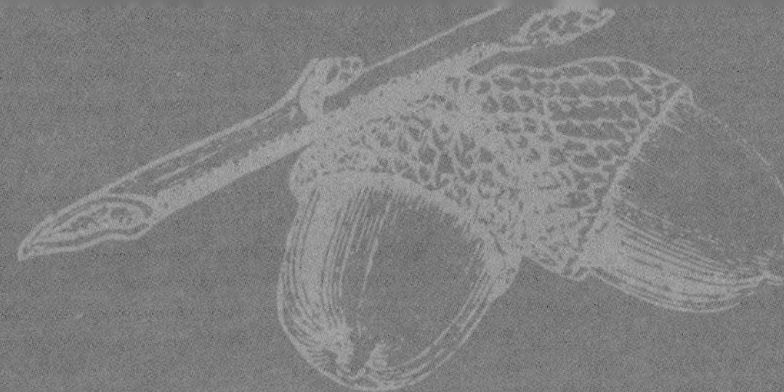

Acorn Stew

INGREDIENTS:S

- 4-5 quarts (or more) of fresh water
- 1 lb. bite-size chunks of wild game meat (optional)
- ¼ c. wild onions, chopped
- 4 summer squash, chopped into 1-inch pieces
- 8 whole ears of corn (de-husked shaved from the cob into kernels)
- ½ to 1 c. of finely ground acorn meal
- Salt and pepper, to taste

Cooking with acorns is a bit of a process. After the acorns are carefully harvested in the fall, the nuts are laid out to dry for a few weeks. The inner nut meat is then removed from the shell. Next, the meat is ground into a flour, placed through a fine sieve, and leached in water of the bitter tannins. Depending on the variety of oak tree that the acorns have been harvested from, the leaching process might require up to six changes of water to remove the tannins. Today's Indigenous chefs insist that the leaching process be done using only fresh spring or river water—apparently chlorinated water ruins the flavor of the acorns, making them seem to still retain tannins. The leached flour is then allowed to dry before it is used for making acorn mush, cakes and cookies, or as a base for acorn stew.

In a large pot, sear the meat if meat is being used. Add the water and simmer with the onions until the meat is tender, for about an hour. Add the corn and squash and simmer for another 20 minutes. Slowly add acorn flour until the desired thickness is reached.

Serves 6.

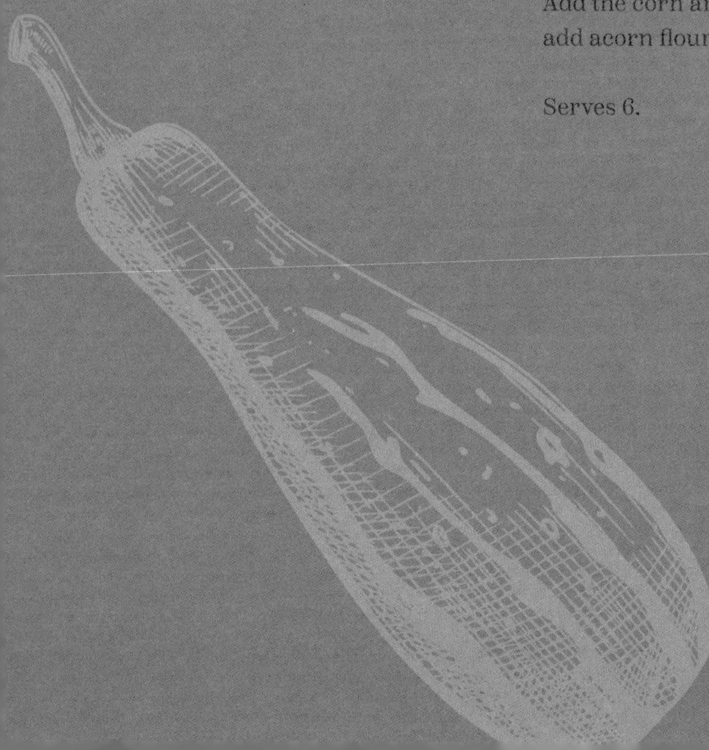

managed to maintain their languages as well as their cuisines. This includes gathering and cooking with acorns.

Bay Laurel

CALIFORNIA BAY, CALIFORNIA LAUREL, MYRTLEWOOD
UMBELLULARIA CALIFORNICA

PLANT FAMILY: *Lauraceae*
PARTS USED: *Nuts, seeds*
SEASON: *Year-round*
REGION: *West Coast*

Ask people what they feel is California's most important tree; most likely the response will be sequoia or redwood. Perhaps someone might suggest almonds, as they are a lucrative agricultural export for the state. However, ask a California Indian the same question, especially one who is steeped in their culture's traditions, and the answer would likely be different. They might suggest that oaks are very important. Other native Californians, especially those from the Bay Area, might put forward bay laurel.

Bay laurel, Umbellularia californica.

I used to live with a large, multi-trunked bay laurel. It was an old tree, rooted on a slope near the back of the property that I occupied. It shared its space with a large redwood, some oak trees and other native and introduced plants. This laurel was at least one hundred years old. Its trunks curled up and away from the slope. One trunk had wrapped its way around a wooden structure. The tree created habitat for the many songbirds in the area and shade for the few herbaceous plants that sprung up in the area beneath it. I enjoyed the pungent scent that drifted from the tree as well as waiting for the small yellowish flowers and fruits to appear every year. Bay laurels are incredible trees. California Native peoples thought so as well, since they have been usesd as essential elements in ceremonies across the region.

IDENTIFICATION

Bay laurel is a hardy evergreen tree that can grow up to eighty feet tall. The dome-shaped canopy that is formed by several slender, erect branches can reach about thirty feet across at maturity. In good conditions, bay laurel can live to be several hundred years old. The dark-green to yellow-green leathery leaves are narrow, alternate, oblong to lance-shaped. The leaves are between two and half to four inches long, smooth-edged and pointed at the end. Throughout the year, some leaves on the tree will become light brown before they drop to the ground. When broken or crushed, the leaves give off a pungent peppery, menthol-like scent. The small yellow-green flowers are arranged in umbel-shaped clusters of six to ten flowers that all

Clockwise from lower left: *Ripe bay fruits, shelled hulls of bay fruits (unroasted), shelled bay nuts, roasted bay nuts, bay nut powder, bay leaves, and a drink made by steeping bay nut powder in water.*

spread from a common point. The fruits are olive green and olive shaped, about one inch long and about five-eigths inches in diameter. The flowers will emerge during the late winter and into the spring. The fruits that emerge around April turn to a brown-purple color as they mature. Inside the fruit is a single, large, light-brown seed surrounded by a light-brown shell that sort of resembles a small avocado.

Before a bay laurel reaches maturity, the bark is thin, whitish-grey, and only slightly creased. As the tree ages the bark thickens, becomes reddish-brown, and will peel away on different parts of the trunk.

CULINARY USE

Laurel leaves offer many medicinal and ceremonial uses for California Indians, including the relief of headaches, a treatment for rheumatism, stomachaches, colds, sore throats—and even a way to help get rid of head lice and fleas. People from my tribe, the Rarámuri, often drink a tea of a close cousin of bay laurel, *Litsea glaucenscens*, after meals in order to assure good digestion and to calm the nerves.

However, laurel trees also produce an edible fruit referred to as a bay nut. It is not a true nut, but California Native peoples eat both the flesh as well as the large inner seed of the olive-sized fruits (nuts). The outer flesh is often acrid tasting due to the concentrations of volatile oils. This is why only the inner parts of the flesh are eaten. The flesh can be boiled to rid it of these oils. Most often, the fruits are dried until they split, revealing and loosening the large seed. The dried flesh can be eaten at this point. The inner seeds are then roasted until they are brown, at which point they are eaten whole or ground or pounded into a meal. The meal is pressed into cakes, mush, and added to stews. Roasting removes much of the pungency of the seeds, leaving a spicy, roasted chicory-like flavor. California natives also make the meal into a chocolate-like drink. The leaves of bay laurel are similar to bay leaf, *Laurus nobilis*, which is the kind of culinary bay leaf common in the the spice sections of grocery stores. However, the leaves of bay laurel but are more pungent; they can similarly be added to soups and stews, but produce a stronger flavoring. It helps to first dry the leaves before adding them to any recipes. Drying removes some of the strong pungency. It is recommended that only about a quarter of a bay laurel leaf be used in place of a full bay leaf.

WHEN, WHERE, AND HOW TO GATHER IN KINCENTRIC ECOLOGY

Look for bay laurel along the West Coast from Southern California north into southwestern Oregon. It grows also along the coastal ranges of these regions and in the Sierra Nevada. Bay laurel does well in both full sunny areas and shady conditions. It prefers well-drained moist soils. It will often be found growing in shady hillsides among oaks, mixed evergreens, redwood forests, and even chaparral up to five thousand feet in elevation.

Bay laurel is one of many plant species impacted by incipient California Indian land management practices. Periodic burning across what today is California was employed to maintain a mosaic if chaparral and other habitats in different differing stages of succession. The result was an abundance of different food sources and and materials for basketmaking and other utilitarian needs. This kind of management ensured that trees such as bay laurel acted as part of a planned forest and chaparral architecture that afforded space and nutrients to the trees and their plant and animal neighbors.

Because it is an evergreen, the leaves can be collected any time of the year. For sensitive people it might be prudent to wear a mask and gloves as bay laurel is known to produce headaches as well as skin rashes due to the heavy volatile oils present in the leaves, twigs, and bark of the tree.

Black Walnut

BLACK WALNUT, ARIZONA WALNUT, *NOGAL*
JUGLANS* SP., *J. NIGRA*, *J. MAJOR

PLANT FAMILY: *Juglandaceae*
PARTS USED: *Nuts, wood, leaves, bark*
SEASON: *Spring to fall*

Whenever I think of walnut trees, my mind immediately makes a temporal-dimensional journey to when I was a little boy. My family was having a gathering in a sunlit corner of a wide canyon area. At one edge of the area ran a stream that I and my brother and cousins were drawn to. At the other side of the area, next to a canyon wall, stood a huge black walnut tree. Many of my family members escaped the sun under the tree and we set up our tables and food there. I recall one of

*Black walnuts (*Juglans nigra*) are coated in a yellow-green husk.*

my aunts pointing out the large ripe walnuts and encouraging us boys to climb the thick limbs of the tree in order to collect some of the nuts. Later, we enjoyed each other's company while cracking open and eating the sweet nut meats. It is not only my family who think so highly of walnut trees; American Indians across the continent value walnut trees for the durable and beautiful wood they offer as well as for medicinal and utilitarian uses. We also just like having picnics in their shade.

The Apache of the American Southwest valued the black walnut tree so much that they named a clan after it. The White Mountain Apache, whose territory includes the region of east-central Arizona and into western New Mexico, have a clan named *Chilimeyadnaye*, walnut. The Pinal Coyotero Apaches also named a clan, *Chisnedinadinave*, after the tree. Black walnut trees also play a role in Apache cultural narrative. They have a story about how Coyote used a walnut tree to trick a group of soldiers. One day, Coyote was resting in the shade of a black walnut tree. He had just stolen a horse from a man. The saddlebags on the horse were filled with money. Coyote heard the soldiers chasing after him and devised an idea. He placed a few coins in the branches of the tree. When the soldiers arrived to arrest him, Coyote convinced the soldiers to wait and hear him out. He told them that if they let him go that he would tell them how to make a lot of money. The soldiers did not believe Coyote until he told them to shake the branches of the walnut tree. When they did this, the coins that Coyote had hidden in the tree fell down. Coyote then suggested that if the soldiers were to give him their pack mules as well as the packs on the mules that he would trade them the "money-growing" tree. The soldiers agreed, and Coyote made off with the pack mules while the soldiers were stuck with a plain old walnut tree.

IDENTIFICATION

Black walnut, *Juglans nigra*, is a medium-sized deciduous tree that can grow up to ninety feet tall. The central trunks of black walnut can be as wide as three feet in diameter. In some cases, black walnut can grow up to one hundred and fifty feet with eight-foot-diameter trunks. The branches are normally widely spread, forming a large crown. The thick brown and gray-black bark is deeply furrowed often in a diamond pattern. Black walnut leaves grow between two and three feet long. They are pinnate with up to twenty leaflets. The leaflets are normally rounded at the base, with pointed tips. The leaves are dark green in color and hairy below. Between May and

June the elongated panicle-like flowers appear. The flowers contain between seventeen and fifty stamens. The fruits are spherical, and often appear in groups of two or three. Most parts of black walnut trees emit a pungent and spicy odor.

Arizona walnut, *J. major*, is similar to black walnut. The main difference is that the Arizona walnut tree grows up to fifty feet tall with a trunk diameter of about two feet and sometimes up to four feet. The branches are also more widely spaced than black walnut. In additon, Arizona walnut sometimes grows as a shrub. The bark is also furrowed, but is not as thick as black walnut. The new growth of Arizona walnut is reddish-brown. The pinnate leaves of Arizona walnut grow up to about one foot. The are serrated at the edges and overt to lanceolate in shape.

*The Arizona walnut (*Juglans major*) has slightly smaller nuts than the black walnut; it occurs in Texas, Oklahoma, Utah, New Mexico, Arizona, and Mexico as far south as Guerrero.*

CULINARY AND MEDICINAL USE

Walnut trees are used for more than tricking soldiers. In the Southwest the Apache, Yavapai, and other tribes collect and store the nuts of Arizona walnut, *Juglans major*, for winter food. The nut meats are often mixed with mesquite flour and made into a sauce that other foods are cooked in. The Yavapai also mix the pounded nut meats with the sweet syrup of mezcal agave and use it as a nutritious beverage. The bark of Arizona walnut can be made into an infusion and taken to treat rheumatism and arthritis as well as a wash for aches and pains. The nuts of black walnut, *J. nigra*, is eaten by many eastern tribes. The Iroquois, for example, boil the nut meats and use the resulting brew as a refreshing beverage. The nut meats of black walnut are also an important ingredient in corn soups and several other traditional native dishes. In order to bring the complex flavors of a black walnut to the surface of a dish, the meats are often roasted before being added to recipes.

The flavonoid content of black walnut affords anti-inflammatory, anticarcinogenic, antitumorigenic, antioxidant, and antimutagenic pharmacological properties. The naphthoquinoe, juglone,

Walnut and Watercress Pesto

INGREDIENTS:

- 1 ½ tsp. apple cider vinegar
- ¼ c. olive oil
- 2 cloves of garlic, minced
- 1 tsp. fresh lemon juice
- ½ c. of watercress (or substitute parsley or cilantro)
- ½ c. cooked pinto or similar beans
- ½ c. roasted black walnuts
- ½ tsp. salt
- ¼ tsp. black pepper
- 2 tbsp. water

I look forward to experimenting with long-established recipes with substitutions of some of the ingredients. Pesto is essentially a ground mixture of herbal greens, olive oil, some hard cheese, and nuts. Here is an Indigenous version of this recipe that uses black walnuts, beans, and watercress. The vinegar can be omitted if desired, but it does add a tanginess to the recipe. Be sure to toast the walnuts before incorporating into the mix in order to bring out more of the unique flavors. Also, if you wildcraft the watercress, be sure to thoroughly rinse the spicy greens in order to eliminate possible giardia contamination that may have been present in the water where the plant was growing.

Blend all the ingredients exept the water in a food processor until smooth. Add water in small amounts until the desired consitency for the pesto is achieved. Serve over pasta, wild rice, or as a dip.

Makes approximately 1 cup.

demonstrates effective antifungal and antimicrobial activity. Several studies have demonstrated that walnuts reduce blood glucose and lipids, protect the liver, are antidiabetic, and helpful for reducing blood pressure.

WHEN, WHERE, AND HOW TO COLLECT IN KINCENTRIC ECOLOGY

Black walnut is an eastern tree that is found mostly in riparian areas. It often grows alongside poplar, ash, cherry, beech, oak, and hickory trees. Toward the edge of its eastern range, it will be found in floodplains growing with elms, hackberry, ash, red oak, and boxelder. The range of black walnut is from South Dakota to New York, south to Georgia and Florida, and west to Texas. Arizona walnut, *J. major*, grows at elevations between 1,000 to 7,000 feet from West Texas and Oklahoma and to New Mexico and Arizona. It will very occasionally be found in Utah. It can be found in riparian zones and along streams. It often is found in deep canyons and ravines growing alongside cottonwoods, sycamores, and ponderosa pines.

The nuts normally fall and are ready for harvesting beginning in midsummer and into the fall. Be careful to wear gloves when collecting black walnuts in order to avoid staining your hands with the shells, which turn black after they fall. It might be a good idea to also wear old clothes. Walnuts can be eaten fresh, or stored in a cool, dry area away from direct sunlight for several months. If the sap is collected for medicinal use, it should be used immediately or it will dry out, crack, and transform into fine dust. The bark and shells can be stored away from the sun for up to a month, but will begin to lose their potency quickly after that.

Butternut

WHITE WALNUT, OILNUT, LONG WALNUT
JUGLANS CINEREA

PLANT FAMILY: *Juglandaceae*
PARTS USED: *Bark, nut fruits, fruit shells*
SEASON: *Year-round*
REGION: *Eastern North America*

The nuts of Juglans cinerea *are oblong, and usually mature to about 1.5 to 2.2 inches long.*

Cherokee writer Thomas King writes in *The Truth About Stories* that our tales are "all we are." For Native peoples, stories are the source of our values, morals, and identity. Stories are also the dominant path along which we transfer and reproduce plant knowledge. A person can *read* about plant knowledge, they can *listen* to an herbalist's lecture, but unless that knowledge resonates with them personally, chances are that the knowledge will not be retained. However, if knowledge of plants is transferred through a *story*, the information becomes connected to mental images and related to commonly understood ideas. Therefore, it become easier to retain and retrieve that critical plant information.

There is an Indigenous story in the Southeast about the "walnut cracker." Apparently, there was a man who enjoyed walnuts so much that people from his village would often find him sitting under his favorite walnut tree, cracking and eating walnuts. He even devised a simple tool to helped him crack walnuts more easily. Unfortunately, the man died. Not too long afterward, however, another man who was passing through the area stopped at the same walnut tree. The new man noticed all the walnuts piled up there and began to crack and eat walnuts too. He did this only in the night. The people from the nearby village heard the sound of walnuts being cracked and assumed that the ghost of the walnut cracker had returned. Some of the villagers decided to investigate the sound, even though some of them were sick and one man even needed to be carried due to an injured leg. The visitor, thinking that he was being attacked when he saw them approaching, suddenly ran off. The people of the village were in turn scared by *that* sound, and fled. But they realized that the people who had been sick suddenly felt better, and that even the man with the injured leg could suddenly walk on his own—their fear had scared the illness right out of them. Ever since, it is said that walnuts have the power to remove sickness through their very proximity; walnuts have since been known as a medicine.

The seeds of butternut are often described as being sweet and oily; the fruit husks can be used to make an orange-yellow dye.

IDENTIFICATION

Butternut is a medium-size, deciduous tree that grows between sixty and eighty-five feet tall. The pinnately compound leaves are large, reaching about fifteen to twenty inches long with eleven to nineteen leaflets. The edges of the leaves have small teeth. The short trunk is normally ashy gray bark with broad, flat plates and deep furrows. Butternuts are not particularly long-lived trees, usually surviving sixty to eighty years. The unisexual flowers form into narrow catkins that get about six to ten inches long. The tree flowers from May to June, and the fruits ripen from October to November. The greenish oblong fruit (nuts) usually form singularly but sometimes in clusters of two to five. The fruits are hard, with a thick, deeply furrowed shell enclosed by a thick husk. The husk has a sticky, glandular surface. The fruits will typically stay on the tree until after the last leaves fall.

CULINARY USE

Before strangers came to North America's shores, the foods available to American Indians were a vast and varied cornucopia. Nuts made up a good portion of those Native foods. Every region of the continent provided at least one, if not several, varieties of nuts for its Native inhabitants. In places such as what today is California, nuts such as acorns were a staple part of the diet. In the east especially, walnuts were an important food supplement. Butternuts are eaten similarly to other nuts, and are prepared most like black walnuts. The nut meat of butternut has a smoother and milder taste compared to black walnuts. The meat can be crushed and added to corn stews. It is also added to cornbread dough. It can be crushed, mixed with berries, and formed into small cakes for travel food. The nut meat is also boiled and pureed into a drink.

WHEN, WHERE, AND HOW TO COLLECT IN KINCENTRIC ECOLOGY

Look for butternut in the northeastern and north-central United States and southern Canada. It will sometimes be found in Missouri and eastward through Tennessee, North Carolina and Virginia, and rarely in Arkansas, Mississippi, Alabama, South Carolina, and Georgia. Butternut does not form dense stands and is often difficult to find in its range. In fact, butternut trees have been in decline across North America due to a canker disease that has been decimating the population. In some places it is actually illegal to attempt to propagate butternut as a way to control the disease. However, butternuts are still available across the northern U.S., often in plain sight.

Butternuts prefer moist, sandy, well-drained soils with some clay. They grow well in sunlit areas near river banks, among mixed woodlands. Due to presence of juglone and plumbagin in this species, there will not be much understory at the base of butternut trees. If you are able to locate a butternut tree and plan to collect the football-shaped nuts, be careful to wear gloves when processing them, as they have strong dye. Also, do not allow the nuts to sit around for very long after collection; the juices from the outer husks will leach into the nut, causing them to become bitter. In order to get to the nut, the thick green husks have to be cut away. The clear juices from the husks will seem harmless at first; however, after even brief contact, the juices can create a black stain that is very difficult to clean away. The nuts must be dried for a about a month before consumption. The easiest way to do this is to spread the nuts out on a flat surface away from direct sunlight. The nuts should be rotated and turned every few days, to ensure air contacts all surfaces. After this, the nuts are ready for cracking open and eating.

If it has not been expressed directly enough before, butternut is indeed a type of walnut, so preparation and gathering is similar. There are at least six varieties of walnuts native to North America—all of which were valued by Native peoples. In the east, the two native species are butternut, *Juglans cinerea*, and black walnut, *Juglans nigra*. In the western states of Arizona, New Mexico, Oklahoma, Texas, and Utah grows the Arizona black walnut (*Juglans major*). A species of walnut found in Texas, Kansas, New Mexico, and Oklahoma is the Texas black walnut or Mexican walnut (*Juglans microcarpa*). A little further west, in California, there exists another black walnut (*Juglans californica*), as well as the Northern California black walnut (*Juglans hindsii*).

Top left: Juglans microcarpa, *the little walnut, aptly named as its nuts are the smallest in the genus and the tree grows only to a relatively modest twenty feet tall.* Top right: Juglans californica, *the Southern California black walnut, is recognizable for having multiple trunks.* Bottom: Juglans hindsii, *the Northern California black walnut, features one straight trunk.*

Mesquite

***PROSOPIS* SP.**

PLANT FAMILY: *Fabaceae*
PARTS USED: *Pods, leaves, wood*
SEASON: *Spring to fall*
REGION: *Southwest North America*

*The pods of honey mesquite (*Prosopis glandulosa*) are often regarded by modern cattle ranchers as weeds and eradicated; Indigenous peoples have valued them as food and medicine.*

The Paiute elder was looking directly at the Park Service employee, shaking her forefinger back and forth in the air while making her point. We were inside an air-conditioned government building, sitting around several tables; outside the Mojave Desert heat caused distant objects to shimmer in blurry waves. The meeting had been arranged in order to discuss how to manage local groves of mesquite. The elder continued to scold the Park Service ranger about how the Service had allowed the groves to "become a mess." For years, the Park Service assumed leaving the mesquite groves alone would encourage the trees to return to their "natural" ecological state. Therefore, humans, including local native peoples who had relied on the mesquite trees for food, wood, and medicine, had not been permitted access to the mesquite. The result was that the groves had become overgrown with invasive and competitive plants. Their numbers were dropping—along with other native species.

Local Paiute, Mojave, Chemehuevai, and other Native peoples have argued for decades that mesquite groves must be managed by pruning, small-scale controlled burns, and harvesting. In other words, humans play a part in the ecological dynamics of certain plants. When people properly harvest the mesquite, their gathering and pruning encourages more edible pods to grow. Small-scale fire reduces competition of other plants, encouraging the healthier trees and more pods. Open mesquite groves in turn encourage native flora and fauna to remain in the area. Natural diversity returns. Everyone wins.

IDENTIFICATION

Mesquites are generally medium-size deciduous trees or tall shrubs. *Prosopis velutina* can reach up to forty-five feet tall. *P. pubescens* can grow up to thirty feet, while *P. glandulosa* grows between twelve and eighteen feet tall. Mesquites tend to create spreading, rounded crowns. All parts of the trees contain short, dense hairs. The branches tend to grow crookedly and sprout half-inch or longer spines that appear at the nodes. The leaves are fernlike, compound, and are divided into many tiny leaflets. The trunk of *P. velutina* has shaggy bark. The inflorescence of mesquite grows into a spikelike yellowish raceme. The flat bean podlike fruits of *P. velutina* grow to between

Dried pods of mesquite; the contemporary English name may be an adaptation of the Aztec word mizquitl.

six to ten inches and are tan-colored, sometimes streaked with red. The pods of *P. pubescens* appear in clusters of two to ten pods that are tightly coiled and grow to between two and four inches long. The pods of *P. glandulosa* are the largest of the mesquite species; they grow between four and twelve inches long. They are thick, reddish-brown in color, and contain half-inch-long seeds.

CULINARY AND MEDICINAL USE

From West Texas to California, desert mesquites have long been a source of food and medicine for several Native communities. The phytochemical components of *Prosopis* sp. include flavonoids, terpenes, tannins, the alkaloid juliflorine, and quinones that demonstrate different pharmacological activity including analgesic, anthelmintic, antibiotic, and antiemetic properties, and act as a microbial antioxidant, antimalarial, anticancer drug, antidiabetic, anti-inflammatory, and antiulcer.

The juice from the leaves of honey mesquite, *P. glandulosa*, is applied to the eyelids to treat irritation. The Comanche chew the leaves of mesquite and swallow the juice as an antacid. The Pima boil the bark of the root of the screwbean mesquite, *P. pubescens*, and make it into a poultice for wounds. The root bark is also made into a tea to regulate a woman's menstrual cycles. The gum from mesquite trees is gathered, soaked in water, and used as a cleansing eyewash for pink eye and to treat sores and skin infections. A poultice of the chewed leaves is used to treat red ant bites and sores. A cold decoction of the leaves is also applied to the head to relieve headaches and stomachaches. A decoction of the beans is used to treat sunburn. An infusion of the roots is taken to treat diarrhea. The black gum from the mesquite is an important medicine to the Pima. It is boiled with a little water and applied to sore lips and gums, chapped fingers, and taken internally to cleanse the system. Mesquite leaves are pounded and boiled and placed on the eyes of Pima individuals as a treatment for pink eye. Terpenes are used as insecticides and are also antibacterial, antifungal, antihelminthic, and antimalarial. The Pima even use black gum in a concoction to dye gray hair black.

In addition to the numerous medicinal applications of mesquite, it is a wonderful food source. The pods of mesquite are an important ancestral food to the Maricopa, Pima, Apache, Haulapais, Cahuilla, Luiseno, Mohave, Panamint, Shoshone, Chemehuevi, Ute, Gosiute, Comanche, Navajo, Pueblo, and Southern Paiute peoples. The pods, along with the large inner seeds, are ground into meal in a mortar. The result is a sweet, hearty flour that is made into breads, cakes, mush, and thick, nourishing drinks. My favorite chocolate chip cookie recipe includes mesquite flour. The seeds are also sometimes parched and ground into a meal for an extra-tasty flour. The pods can also be collected directly from the tree and chewed on for an immediate sweet snack.

WHEN, WHERE, AND HOW TO COLLECT IN KINCENTRIC ECOLOGY

Look for mesquites in the desert regions of the Southwest, from Southern California to West Texas. They tend to grow in or near washes, ravines, and arroyos. The leaves, bark, and roots of mesquite can be collected at any time of year. The pods can be harvested in the spring while they are still green. They can also be collected during the later summer after they have ripened—when they're the sweetest. Most Native peoples collect mesquite pods during the late summer; this is when the pods are traditionally pounded by stone or hardwood mortars into flour. Be careful of the spines when collecting mesquite pods. Since the natural habitats of mesquites are in the Mojave, Chihuahuan, and Sonoran Deserts, be mindful of spiny plants such as cholla, ocotillo, prickly pear, and barrel cacti that also tend to grow nearby.

Groves of mesquites have been carefully managed by Indigenous peoples in the arid West for centuries. This is accomplished by small controlled burning and careful pruning. Their value

An old mesquite tree growing in the Santa Rita Mountains, with Josephine Peak at left, in the Coronado National Forest, Arizona.

Mesquite Flour Chocolate Chip Cookies

INGREDIENTS:

- 1 ¼ c. mesquite flour
- ¾ c. whole wheat flour
- ½ tsp. baking soda
- 1 tsp. salt
- ⅔ c. unsalted butter, room temperature.
- ¾ c. white sugar
- ½ c. brown sugar
- 2 eggs
- ¼ tsp. vanilla extract
- 1 ½ c. chocolate chips

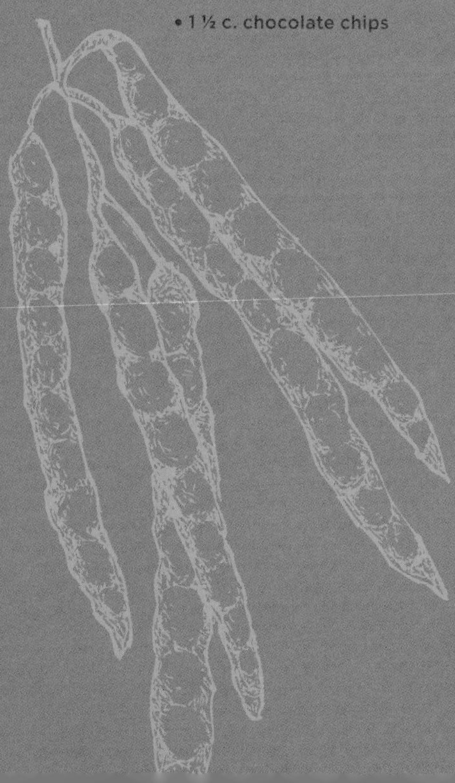

When I hear the word "cookie," my default mental image is of a chocolate chip variety. I have tried several recipes for this treat. They mostly satisfy in different ways, but there is one that I continue to revisit: chocolate chip cookies made with mesquite flour. Mesquite flour is naturally sweet and adds a nutty and slightly floral flavor to any cookie recipe. Mesquite flour can be substituted for any recipe that uses whole wheat, oat, or other non-gluten flours. Due to the nonbinding nature of mesquite flour, whole wheat flour is normally included in a baking recipe with mesquite. Mesquite flour is available for sale through different specialty outlets; I recommend that you avoid buying flour milled outside of the United States, as the quality and flavors are not the same.

Warm an oven to 375° F. In a small bowl, mix together the flours, baking soda, and salt. In large bowl, cream the butter and sugars. Add the eggs and vanilla and mix until everything is well combined. Add the flour mixture and stir until everything is consistently moist. Fold in the chocolate chips. Be careful to not overmix the dough. Place the dough in a refrigerator for about 20 minutes in order to stiffen it up.

Scoop out ¼-cup balls of dough. Place them onto a baking sheet lined with parchment paper. Bake the cookies for about 15 minutes, or until the cookies are beginning to turn dark golden at the edges. They will still be a little soft in the center. Enjoy.

Makes approximately 2 dozen.

is also shown by the fact that the Creation stories of many Indigenous nations in the West include mesquite; a common thread is that pods of mesquite or the trees themselves were placed upon the land as a gift for the people and that they should be carefully managed.

Piñon

PINYON, *KAWI-CHU-RI* (RARÁMURI), *CHA'O* (HOPI), *NEESCH-IL* (NAVAJO), *NUKÛMA* (PAIUTE), *WA'A"PIN* (SHOSHONE), *TSHI* (APACHE), *KO* (HAVASUPAI), *ŤÁGIM* (WASHO)
***PINUS EDULIS* (TWO-NEEDLE PIÑON), *P. MONOPHYLLA* (SINGLE-LEAF PIÑON)**

PLANT FAMILY: *Pinaceae*
PARTS USED: *nuts (seeds), needles, wood, resin*
SEASON: *Late summer to early fall*
REGION: *Southwest and intermountain west*

Top and above: *The nuts of the piñon pine have long been consumed by peoples of the Southwest.*

Piñon nuts are typically pretty small; about ⅞ inches long. The ones handed to me by some Washo Indians one day, though, were about an inch long and nearly five-eighths of an inch thick. These were not the pine nuts I was used to—the ones that Indigenous peoples and Hispanos from around the American Southwest savored and anxiously waited to collect during the early fall. These were strangely, unusually huge.

I was attending the annual California Indian Conference in the Bay Area. Native Californians from across the state travel to the conference to share their experiences with each other, to trade, to listen to academic presentations, and to celebrate their traditions. I had been speaking with some Washo people who were sharing their experiences of reviving their language. During the conversation, I was handed the unusually large piñon nuts. I have not come across such large nuts ever since. I suspect that these people from the Lake Tahoe/Reno region were hoping

Top: *Aracauria nuts, from the monkey puzzle trees of South America, are often 1.5 inches long;* Above: *Piñon pine nuts of North America are often only 0.5 inches in length.*

to demonstrate some of the traditional foods available from the historical landscape of their ancestors, but did not have any available. So they somehow got a hold of some Paraná pine nuts (*Araucaria angustifolia*) from South America and were substituting them for local nuts.

IDENTIFICATION

Every fall in the American Southwest, the Great Basin region, and into the eastern Sierras of California, Indigenous peoples laden with baskets, tarps, and buckets will migrate to the foothills toward their favorite groves of piñon trees. Piñons are one of two dominant trees in the piñon/juniper woodland plant community. This is an ecosystem that can be found in the mid-elevations of the Greater Southwest between 3,900 and 7,000 feet. The region extends from southern Idaho to Baja California. Piñon trees are medium height, reaching up to about 65 feet. The trunks of the trees are marked with irregular furrows and often laden with very sticky resin. The leaves (needles) of *Pinus edulis*, the two-needle piñon, appear in pairs; *Pinus monophylla*, as the name suggests, is the only pine species with single leaves. Both produce globular-shaped cones that grow up to two inches long. Before maturity, the cones are green and scaled; toward late summer, the cones turn brown and begin to open. Each cone will hold several reddish-brown to dark brown seeds. Although the seeds are referred to by those who enjoy these flavorful foods as "nuts" they are actually an edible seed.

CULINARY USE

Piñon nuts are not a staple for any single Indigenous nation, but they have played a role in the overall nutrition and seasonal caloric intake of several Native peoples. They are considered a delicacy across the Great Basin region and the Greater Southwest. During the fall especially, the tasty little nuts are consumed much like sunflower seeds or chips. It is not unusual to come across locals passing time by cracking open toasted piñon nuts, the nearby tabletop or ground scattered with the dark brown shells. Piñon nuts are eaten both raw and toasted; I prefer the latter. The inner meat is also separated from the outer shell, ground into a meal, dried, and used in several dishes including soups, stews, sauces, and small grilled cakes.

Piñon nuts are an incredible source of valuable nutrients, healthy fats, and minerals. One of the fats, pinolenic acid, is a a heart-benefitting polyunsaturated fat. It has been shown to help lower LDL cholesterol while increasing HDL cholesterol, the good cholesterol. Other fats include oleic acid, which is also a heart-healthy fat. Piñon nuts also contain the antioxidant vitamin E, as well as protein, fiber, zinc, phosphorus, calcium, thiamin, niacin, and manganese—all important for bone strength, metabolism, and antioxidant protection.

WHEN, WHERE, AND HOW TO COLLECT IN KINCENTRIC ECOLOGY

Late summer to early fall is piñon nut harvesting time. The beginning and end of the harvest period depend on the location. Other factors include elevation, the cardinal direction that a particular grove of piñon trees is facing, the latitude, and when the last time was when a particular grove produced nuts. It turns out that after a group of trees has produced, it will be between two and seven years before the trees will once again produce cones with nuts. The duration between nut production is influenced by the degree of sunlight that the trees receive, the elevation, the kind of soil underneath the trees, and water availability.

Local nut harvesters will secretly surveil their favorite piñon groves throughout the year. If the trees are on public lands, they will reveal the location only to close family and trusted friends. If the trees are on private land, a deal must be made with the landowner, who will indicate how much of the harvest they will receive as payment. During the growing season, harvesters will pay attention to the number and size of green cones, the local rain patterns, the color of the leaves, and many other signs that the trees are ready to produce. I recall attending to trees where I lived in southern Colorado, observing the cones throughout the summer and picking a cone or two in September to determine if there were any nuts inside yet. By the end of the summer, gatherers will have decideded where they will go to collect nuts.

Assuming that squirrels and piñon jays have not already taken all of the nuts, collecting piñon nuts involves big tarps or blankets and long sticks. The tarps and blankets are spread around the base of the trees. Next, at the risk of getting your hands and clothing sticky from the very gummy sap, you can climb the trees and begin shaking the branches in order to loosen the cones and nuts. Many people prefer to knock the cones and nuts from the trees with poles and sticks. Either method results in the cones and nuts falling onto the tarps and blankets below. The next step

A photo from circa 1930 depicting mealtime under a piñon tree for Navajo girls.

Bean and Piñon Nut Dip

INGREDIENTS:

- 2 c. cooked pinto beans
- 1 c. fresh, shelled piñon nuts
- ¼ c. pinto bean liquid
- Salt and pepper, to taste

I often eat piñon nuts toasted—easy and simple. After rinsing the nuts, just add them to a hot, dry skillet and shake them continuously. Since they have just been rinsed, the nuts will steam at first, but will soon dry out. Continue to move the nuts around until they begin to sweat a little bit. This will normally take about 10 to 15 minutes. Every now and then, remove one in order to double-check that they are not burning. Once they're golden brown, spread them on a flat surface to cool down. Some people soak the nuts in salted water before toasting, but I prefer the simple, unadulterated taste of the pure toasted nuts.

The earthy flavor of toasted piñon nuts will add an incredible layer of deliciousness to many dishes, including soups, stews, sauces, and dips. This bean and piñon nut dip is an easy and tasty way to try these traditional nuts.

Add the pinto beans, piñon nuts, and bean liquid to a blender or food processor. Blend until smooth. Add more bean liquid from the cooking water or can to achieve the desired thickness. In order to bring out the flavors a bit more, add some salt and pepper. To add herbal favors, try including some chopped cilantro and perhaps a chiltepin pepper or two into the mix.

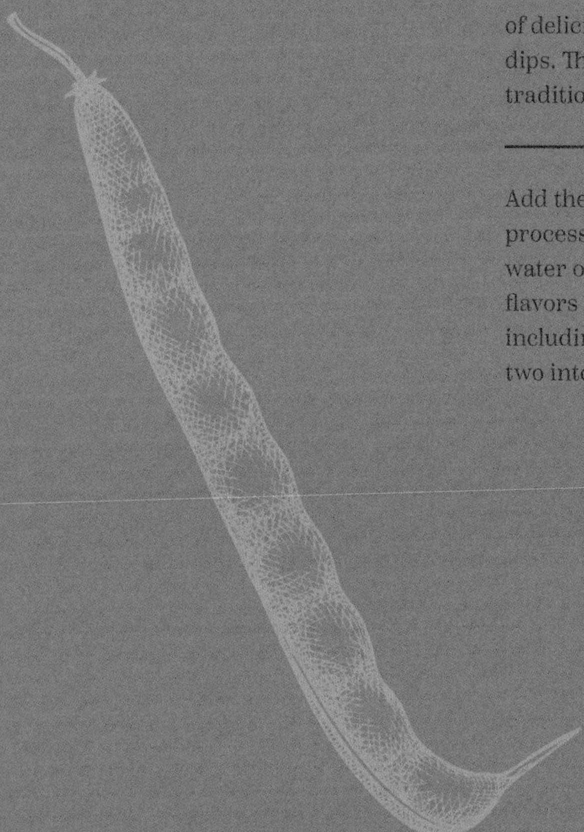

involves the painstaking job of separating the nuts from the cones. Once this is accomplished, they're toasted and then shared with friends and family. In the Southwest, fall is also the time to look for vendors selling small plastic bags of these nuts. They can often be found at farmers markers, local grocery stores, and sometimes even sitting at small tables in front yards, where they're often sold alongside local honey and dried local chiles.

It is not an accident that some of the longest and most productive piñon collecting areas are near places where local Indigenous and Hispano communities have been managing the lands. As has been noted in other sections of this book, Indigenous peoples feel that it is their responsibility to carefully manage the sources of foods that have been afforded to them by the Creator, the spirits, or other land-based entities. Not only is it essential that humans do what is asked as caregivers of the land and plants, it is felt by many Indigenous peoples that the plants themselves rely on interactions between people and plants for survival. If the interaction ends, the plants might feel lonely and eventually stop producing; in the case of piñon trees, this could be seen as a reason that the nuts produce some years only.

A Moapa Paiute elder once told a researcher: "We're doing the tree a service. They're there for us to eat. Creator gave it to us as a food. So when you pick them . . . the tree's thankful. The mountain's thankful, because they're seeing Indian people up there doing what they used to do. They're probably crying out for us."

The elder's sentiment results in kincentric ecological management such as selective harvesting, periodic pruning, and low-level burning. These practices serve to reduce competition for soil nutrients and moisture. Fire returns nutrients to the soil, while pruning the branches increases cone production.

Wild Rice

MANOOMIN

ZIZANIA AQUATICA, Z. PALUSTRIS, Z. TEXANA

PLANT FAMILY: *Poaceae*
PARTS USED: *Grain, stems*
SEASON: *August to September*
REGION: *Northern Great Plains*

Many American Indians understand that they owe their very existence to the natural world around them. So many of our origin stories remind us of how specific animals, plants, and sometimes stars in the night sky played a direct role in our emergence. In some cases, even if a food did not play a role in the emergence of a people per se, it might have been recognized as essential for their ongoing existence and identity. A part of Anishinaabe (Ojibwe) history, for example, includes a time when the people were forced to migrate west from their original homeland on the northeast coast of Turtle Island (North America). They were informed by a prophet that they should travel and not stop until they came to a land where food grew on water. The people followed these instructions until they reached the area around the Great Lakes. One day, a hunter was returning to his camp without any game. When he reached his camp he found a duck near his cooking pot. The duck flew away when the hunter came near, but left some unknown grains in the pot. The

Northern wild rice, Zizania palustris, *features pistillate spikelets that turn tan at maturity. Minnesota has more acreage of natural wild rice than any other state.*

hunter made some soup in it, and did not remove the grains left by the duck. It was the best-tasting soup he had ever had. The next day, the hunter traveled in the direction the duck had flown. He reached a lake, and found ducks and many other water birds feasting on the grains of some tall grasses that grew on the water. The hunter brought this new food to his people. After that the people understood that they would never go hungry so long as they took care of the waters and lands where this gift, wild rice (*manoomin*), grew.

IDENTIFICATION

Wild rice is not a true rice such as the rice (*Oryza* sp.) that originates in Asia. Wild rice, *Zizania* sp., is a tall, annual water grass that grows between three and six feet tall. The plant sprouts a single plume that contains several slender, rodlike seeds. The seeds are tan to dark brown and are about half an inch long. The seeds are surrounded by a hull that terminates with a short beard. The elongated green ribbonlike leaves are about three-quarters to an inch-and-a-half wide, with rough edges. The plant will sprout a broom-like flower cluster that grows up to two feet long.

CULINARY USE

Simply put, wild rice is wonderful food. It is cooked and eaten like any other kind of rice. It can be a main dish or part of soups, stews, stuffings, casseroles, and wildcrafted salads. Unlike white or brown rice, wild rice is not starchy. The inner grain is chewy, and the overall flavor is sweet and nutty. It cooks in about thirty minutes and does not absorb as much water as white or brown rice. Wild rice is a high-protein grain; tests have demonstrated that a serving of wild rice provides between 12 and 15 percent of a person's daily protein requirement. Wild rice is also an excellent source of minerals such as iron, zinc, potassium, and phosphorus, as well as vitamins like thiamine, riboflavin, and niacin. The lipid content of wild rice is lower than other typical grains. In addition, antioxidant carotenoids can be found in wild rice,

Wild rice may still be harvested by permit in some areas, but only in a canoe, as depicted in this drawing, or nonmotorized boat and by knocking the stems with a wooden flail.

as well as cholesterol-lowering phytosterols, phenolics, and ferric acids. Finally, wild rice is high in both soluble and insoluble fibers.

Mature grains of wild rice are naturally dark brown and can be up to 1.1 inches in length.

WHEN, WHERE, AND HOW TO COLLECT IN KINCENTRIC ECOLOGY

In lakes and slower-moving streams around the Great Lakes region and northern Minnesota, the grains of wild rice begin to sprout underwater around May. The leaves of the plant will break the surface of the water beginning around June or July. The seed heads will appear toward the end of July, and will begin to be ready to drop in August. This is the short period when traditional American Indians will paddle their canoes into the wild rice areas to commence the harvest. *Z. palustris* is native to the upper Great Lakes region: Wisconsin, Michigan, and up into Ontario. Most wild rice grows in the north, but a rare species, *Z. texana*, is native to the upper San Marcos River region of Texas.

Wild Rice and Berry Salad

INGREDIENTS:

- 1 ½ c. cooked wild rice
- 2 tbsp. maple syrup
- 3 to 4 c. mixed berries
- Mint, optional

Sometimes the best dishes are the ones that require little preparation, allowing the ingredients' freshness to speak for themselves. This is one of those dishes, best eaten in late summer.

This is an easy recipe. After cooking the wild rice according to the package's directions, chill it in a refrigerator. Just before serving, simply mix together the rice, berries, and maple syrup in a large serving bowl. Garnish with mint if you like.

Serves 4.

6

Tubers, Roots, *and* Corms

Edible tubers, a crop native to the Americas, have been cultivated here by certain Indigenous peoples for more than 11,000 years. They are a delicious and nutritious source of seasonal foods for American Indians across the continent. They are often baked to increase the complexity of their flavors, and they nourish us with a variety of proteins, complex carbohydrates, and minerals—often during times of the year when other foods are not available. As with most other plants, tubers are perceived by Indigenous peoples to be living members of other nations. Some legends even tell of them playing a role in the Creation. Because their roots thrive deep down in the earth, they remind us also of our relationship to the entities that occupy the underworld; most American Indian worldviews do not associate the underworld with being a place of dread.

*A field of blue nahavita (*Dichelostemma capitatum*) growing on an oak savannah in Pacheco State Park, California.*

The immediately recognizable beautiful and unique flower of the groundnut, Apios americana.

Seasonal kincentric management of tubers is often related to how the plants are collected. In some cases it is important to collect tubers of only a certain size—not so small they're not worth cooking, and not so big that they've become old and tough. This is so that the population can continue to produce the following season. Sometimes, while collecting, we will also bury the aboveground growth (stems and flowers) of the plants back in the earth. This forces the plant's seeds to dry out and "plant" themselves to ensure future populations.

Most important, tubers are recognized by most Indigenous nations as seasonal relatives who come to visit only once a year. Just as we welcome our human relatives with joy on the rare occasions that they might visit, we celebrate the emergence of tubers and corms as well. This is why the arrival of camas and bitterroot in the Pacific Northwest and timpsila and groundnut farther to the east are associated with ceremony and communal gatherings.

Groundnut

HOPNISS, INDIAN POTATO, POTATO BEAN
APIOS AMERICANA

PLANT FAMILY: *Fabaceae*
PARTS USED: *Tubers, seed pods*
SEASON: *Year-round*
REGION: *Eastern North America*

Look into the worldview of virtually all American Indian belief systems and there will be a domain of knowledge, or several knowledge domains, connected to the idea that humans are intimately related to the natural world. In some cultures, such as mine, the Rarámuri, this idea is expressed via language itself. For us, the same adjectives that describe human relatives are also used for certain plants. Other cultures that maintain a clan system have created plant clans or have named their own clans after particular plants. Clans are culturally sanctioned extensions of human kinship systems.

The eastern Creek tell a story about a time when a new group of people arrived in their territory. These people were friendly and so were permitted to live in peace with the Creek. Soon, marriages began taking place between the Creek and the new people. Mixed-blood children were born, but the Creek could not figure out how to include the people and their children in their existing clan system. There was some turmoil and confusion, so some of the mothers of the classless people left the area looking for a sign. In the interim, the Creek decided to create a new clan to accommodate them, called the white potato (aka the groundnut) clan, as a way to create kinship with the new people.

Groundnuts present more as tubers than tree nuts, despite the name.

IDENTIFICATION

The groundnut is a climbing perennial that forms low thickets. The stems are half an inch to one and a half inches thick. The stems become vines that can grow to ten feet. The pinnate leaves are alternate, ovate, about three to four inches long, and about one half to two and a half inches wide. They are often hairy. Between summer and fall, flowers form into rounded clusters among the leaves and bloom from July to October. They are white to reddish-brown, with two brown-purple side "wings" that curve down. The flower also has two brownish-red lower petals that surround a brown-red sickle-shaped protrusion. The slightly curved seed pods are between two and five inches long and about half an inch wide. They start out green but dry to brown in the fall, then split open to release the edible seeds. The seeds are oblong and dark brown.

CULINARY USE

Groundnuts are a tasty food source for many Native peoples east of the Mississippi River. Although they are a different genus and species than potatoes, which originated in South America, they are collected, processed, and eaten in much the same manner.

Groundnuts should not be eaten raw. This is because the tubers contain protease inhibitors and glycosides that can cause severe stomach upset and even allergic reactions. When boiled or baked, however, these compounds leach out. Groundnut tubers are a good source of complex carbohydrates and contain 13 to 17 percent protein. Groundnuts are also high in soluble fibers. The seeds, which are also edible, contain as much protein and fiber as other legumes, such as pintos and other domesticated beans. They are also a good source of a type of amino acid called proline.

If not eaten fresh, groundnuts can be dried and stored for later use or dried and ground into a flour to use in soups, stews, bread, and cakes. Because the groundnut is technically a legume, the plant produces pods full of pealike seeds that can be cooked like beans. Some tribes with access to maple or birch syrup bake groundnuts in it to produce a dish similar to candied yams. The taste of groundnut resembles roasted sweet potato mixed with a bit of peanut butter.

Although groundnuts are primarily a food source, some New England tribes also use the tuber for a severe skin condition known as "proud flesh." This is a condition when granulated skin grows back into a healing wound, creating a cauliflower-like growth. To treat it, the groundnut tuber is boiled, made into a poultice, and then applied to the growth.

WHEN, WHERE, AND HOW TO COLLECT IN KINCENTRIC ECOLOGY

Groundnut plants form low twining or climbing thickets that often grow over other plants and nearby trees. They are mostly found east of the Mississippi River, but appear occasionally in some of the central prairie states from Texas to North Dakota. Look for groundnut in wet meadows, near stream banks, streams, ponds, and sloughs. It can also be found in the moist soils of prairie ravines and woodlands.

The tubers of groundnut can be harvested any time of year, but are best when collected during the fall. The tubers grow several inches below the surface of the soil and are distributed about every ten to twelve inches along the plant's rhizomes. Care must be taken not to damage nearby roots and rhizomes, in order to ensure future growth of the plant and tubers. The tubers should be cleaned of any dirt and the small nitrogen-fixing nodules before consumption. The seeds can be collected in the fall, when the pods have dried and sprung open.

Candied Hopniss with Maple Syrup

INGREDIENTS:

- 2 lbs. hopniss (groundnuts), peeled and scrubbed
- 1 tbsp. butter or butter substitute
- ¼ c. maple syrup
- 1 tbsp. apple cider vinegar

The first thing to know about cooking with groundnut is that the skin contains a bit of a sticky mucilage. After you peel a tuber, rinse it off and scrub it under running water to remove any of this remaining substance. Groundnut tubers can be substituted in most recipes calling for potatoes, yams, sweet potatoes, or carrots. For your next fall family celebration, perhaps try this candied hopniss recipe in place of candied yams or glazed carrots.

Preheat the oven to 350° F. Slice the peeled and scrubbed hopniss into quarters. Place them in a pan and add water just to cover them. Cook them over low heat until they are tender, about 30 minutes. Drain the hopniss and place it into a buttered 9-inch baking dish. Pour the maple syrup evenly over the potatoes. Top the mixture with dots of the butter. Sprinkle the apple cider vinegar over the mixture. Bake for about 45 minutes, uncovered. Serves 6.

Wapato

WAPATO, KATNISS, DUCK POTATO
SAGITTARIA CUNEATA, S. LATIFOLIA

PLANT FAMILY: *Alismataceae*
PARTS USED: *Roots, leaves*
SEASON: *Late summer and fall*

Wapato's arrow-shaped leaves make it easy to identify in riparian locations.

I often wonder what went through the minds of Meriwether Lewis and William Clark back in October of 1805. They and their Corps of Discovery, composed of thirty-two military recruits, had barely survived the westward crossing of the Continental Divide following their guide, Sacagawea. They were unfamiliar with the challenging environment of the high Bitterroot Mountains and the ridge-top Lolo Trail and therefore not equipped to forage the land for edibles. They survived the crossing by eating candles, their horses, and something they referred to as "portable soup." The were rescued by the Nez Perce on the Clearwater River. The Nez Perce fed them one of their staple foods, wapato, in order to return the band to health.

Wapato is a tuber that Lewis and Clark described as reminiscent of small potatoes. Half starved, they and their men ate heartily of this new food—only to find that the next day the entire Corps of Discovery was laid up with dysentery. The culprit was the glycosides present in wapato, which their digestive systems were unaccustomed to. It does not bother the Nez Perce and other tribal peoples of the area, who have co-evolved with the tubers for many generations; they no longer have a negative reaction to the slightly toxic glycosides, which are also mostly removed during the traditional preparation and cooking processes. The feast stalled the Corps on their journey west for several days. They must have been so dismayed to have finally had a decent meal, only to find out so quickly that it wreaked havoc on their systems.

IDENTIFICATION

There are leaf variations between *Sagittaria cuneata* and *S. latifolia*, but on both the arrow-shaped foliage growing alternately from a rhizome is its immediate and best means of

Wapato is an aquatic plant that often grows in colonies.

identification. Each leaf, which ranges between two and six inches long, grows on one stem. The leaves of *S. latifolia* can grow up to twelve inches long. The leaves are erect, though sometimes they rest on the water. The whole plant can grow up to three feet tall. Between July and September, the flowers of this perennial bloom in sets of three on a central stem. Each flower has three white, three-quarter-inch-long petals and yellow stamens.

The walnut-sized tubers grow on rhizomes about three feet beneth the bottom of the pond or stream that forms wapato's aquatic habit. The tubers have a white-to-bluish color on the outer layers and contain a milky juice inside.

CULINARY USE

The small tubers of wapato are eaten by Indigenous peoples across North America, and are also particularly beloved by ducks, giving them another common name, "duck potato." *Sagittaria latifolia* is found in most of the lower forty-eight states, while *S. cuneata* is found primarily in the Pacific Northwest. The tubers are traditionally cleaned, then boiled or roasted before being eaten. They are also dried and then reconstituted for consumption later. The dried tubers are often pounded into a flour and then added to soups and stews or baked into cakes.

Wapato also has a long history as a medicine. An infusion of the leaves is rubbed onto a person suffering from a fever, and the same is taken to treat rheumatism and headaches. An infusion of the roots can act as a laxative and is also taken for indigestion. The Potawatomi apply a poultice of the tubers to wounds and sores.

Wapato is such a valuable plant, in fact, that it once acted as a trading currency among Pacific Northwest peoples, and the tubers have been used similarly to contemporary poker chips in gambling.

Wapato tubers share a distinct shape but can come in colors ranging from beige to bluish to purple.

WHEN, WHERE, AND HOW TO COLLECT IN KINCENTRIC ECOLOGY

Wapato grows in shallow pond edges, swamps, marshes, and slow-flowing creeks throughout most of North America and into Mexico. It is best to gather wapato tubers in early spring or during the fall. When gathering wapato tubers, reach below the surface of the water and down into the mud or sandy bottom of the pond or stream. Beginning from the central stems of the plants, reach down to the root zone and follow the rhizomes outward with your hands. The tubers grow at the end of each rhizome.

After collecting the tubers, peel them and clean them carefully before roasting, boiling, or drying them. To remove the potentially irritating glycosides, boil the tubers in salted water for about fifteen minutes. The tubers can also be sliced into disks and strung on a line for faster drying.

Roasted Wapato

INGREDIENTS:

- 2 lbs. wapato, cleaned and cut in halves
- 2 tsp. vegetable oil
- 3 cloves garlic, minced
- 1 ½ tsp. chopped herbs, such as chives, wild marjoram, sorrel, bittercress, or even a bit of juniper
- Salt and pepper, to taste

I think that the best way to enjoy wapato at home is to simply roast it and serve it as a side dish with other Indigenous foods, as you could most other tubers, roots, and corms. Be sure to carefully scrub and peel wapato prior to preparing the dish, to remove the sticky layer of mucilage just under the peel.

Preheat the oven to 450°F. Mix the sliced wapato in a bowl with the oil, salt, and pepper. Place the mixture onto a baking sheet and spread it out evenly. Roast the wapato for about 40 minutes, stirring after about 20 minutes. Meanwhile, mix the garlic and herbs in a small bowl. Sprinkle the garlic-and-herb mixture onto the wapato for its last 5 minutes of roasting time.

Serves 6.

Throughout the Pacific Northwest in spring, fields and hillsides used to be absolutely covered in the purple blooms of nahavita, timpsila, and, as here on the Centennial Marsh Wildlife Management Area in south-central Idaho, camas.

Nahavita

BLUE DICKS, BRODIAEA, WILD HYACINTH, CONGESTED SNAKE LILY
DICHELOSTEMMA CAPITATUM

PLANT FAMILY: *Asparagaceae*
PARTS USED: *Tubers, flowers*
SEASON: *Spring to Summer*
REGION: *West Coast and Southwest*

Every Native culture in North America was reliant on what their local habitats provided in the way of natural resources, and every landscape affords unique and endemic food staples, if you know where to look. On the eastern lee of California and Oregon's coastal ranges, Paiute, Shoshone, and other Native peoples relied heavily on nahavita tubers, harvesting them in such great quantity they were given the nickname "diggers" by white intruders. It was meant as a derogatory moniker, but nevertheless reflects how important this food staple truly was.

By the middle of spring, many rangelands and hillsides in California and Oregon used to be blanketed in purple due to the emergence of blooming nahavita plants. Armed with digging sticks, Paiute, Cahuilla, Karuk, Miwok, Pomo, and other western peoples scoured the hillsides and ranges for the tasty little tubers growing underneath the plants. Today, due to the introduction of non-native and invasive species—and changes in how the landscape has been managed by first the Spaniards, the Mexicans, and now the United States—nahavita has since become difficult to find. Whenever I am out on a hike in the hills near my Bay Area home, I keep my eyes peeled for the little purple flowers peeking their heads up among the grasses next to the trail. Occasionally, I spot a nahavita and stop to reflect on how grateful I am to see it persisting.

The delicate blue-purple flowers of Dichelostemma capitatum *grow in clusters.*

IDENTIFICATION

Nahavita is an herbaceous perennial. The main visible characteristic is a fleshy central stem ending with a dense cluster of purple-blue flowers that grow on stems between one and three feet high. Each flower has six stamens. The central stem will sometimes twist around nearby plants for support. The plant has a set of several narrow basal leaves. Underneath the plant are several yellowish-white cormlets covered with a light brown husk.

The clustered, edible corms of nahavita.

CULINARY USE

Although nahavita is primarily harvested for its edible corms, some tribes such as the Apache also eat the young purple flowers as a snack. Nahavita is a good source for complex carbohydrates, soluble fibers, nutrient, minerals, and protein. The corms can be eaten raw, roasted, baked, or boiled. They are also commonly dried and ground into a flour to be added to stews, soups, or made into cakes and breads. In the past, the corms were most commonly stored for use after the harvest, to bridge the gap between when fresh foods were readily available and when people had to rely on food stores. The Kawaiisu have a particularly interesting use of nahavita corms: they rub them on a stone, forming a sort of glue that could then be spread onto seed-gathering baskets in order to seal the small openings between the fibers.

WHEN, WHERE, AND HOW TO COLLECT IN KINCENTRIC ECOLOGY

Nahavita grows well in open, grassy habitats, on open hillsides, around vernal pools, and in mixed evergreen and deciduous forests, oak woodlands, and chaparral. It often emerges in open areas with recently disturbed soils and in post-woodland fire environments. It is native to California, Oregon, and parts of Arizona and New Mexico.

Tubers are best harvested between the middle of spring and into the summer, via a digging trowel to help lift the corms. Better yet, fashion a digging stick from a hardwood branch at least one inch in diameter and about thirty inches long. To make it easier to push the stick into the ground, grind or whittle one end into a sort of flattened taper. Remember to always leave the smallest corms and a couple of the largest bulbs so that the population can repropagate—harvest only the mid-sized bulbs. Rub the largest clumps of dirt off the tubers at the harvest site to leave it in place; rinse the tubers with water thoroughly before eating.

There is no one specific, traditional recipe for nahavita. Generally, Indigenous peoples prepare these small corms by steaming them in an earth oven, roasting them in cooking ashes or large earth ovens, drying and then storing them for later use, or grinding them into a powder either before or after they have been roasted. The ground corms can then be used for thickening or as a flour.

Timpsila

***TIMPSULA*, *TIPSINA*, PRAIRIE TURNIP, INDIAN BREADROOT**

***PEDIOMELUM ESCULENTUM*, (SYN. *PSORALEA ESCULENTUM*)**

PLANT FAMILY: *Fabaceae*

PARTS USED: *Root*

SEASON: *Late spring to early summer*

REGION: *Great Plains*

What happens when a young woman falls in love with and marries a star? According to a Lakota story, a young woman had been spending a lot of time outside in the evening. She became enamored with the night sky, and especially with one particularly bright and handsome star. She decided that she wanted to marry this star. One night, the bright start that the woman had fallen in love with descended to the earth to introduce himself to the young woman. They did indeed fall in love and marry. The star took his young bride back up to the star world to love with his family, in the Lakota way. They believe that the star world is much like earth—it's a series of vast plains where women can move about and gather plants.

The star people taught the young bride about a special plant with bluish-purple flowers that likes to grow on moist, sandy soils. This plant was called *timpsila*. It is a plant that grows rounded tubers underneath the ground, with long tap roots. The star people taught the bride how to carefully dig up the tuber, how to peel off the thick woody skin, and then how to braid the tubers and upper part of the plant for storage and for later use. They also reminded the young bride to leave the largest *timpsila* plants so that the colony would continue to grow and feed the people.

One day, out of curiosity, the young bride decided to dig up one of the biggest plants. When she did this, she found that she had created a significant hole in the ground—one so big she could see back down to the land where her family still lived. She became homesick. By that time, she had become pregnant, and she yearned to raise her child back among her own people. She kept returning to where she had dug the hole, and this made her ever more homesick. While braiding the *timpsila* plants that she had collected, she had the idea to create a braid so long she could use it as a rope that would allow her to attempt to climb all the way back to Earth through the hole. Unfortunately for the young bride, the rope broke and she fell. She died, but not before giving birth to a child who was raised by meadowlarks. The meadowlarks kept him until they realized they could teach him only so much, and then returned him to his people.

This story, like other Indigenous stories, is not only entertaining, but serves also to transmit ecological knowledge. In this instance, it teaches us that digging up mature timpsila can only lead to problems. It reminds the people of their responsibilities to the land, and simultaneously of their relationship to the star realm.

IDENTIFICATION

The part of *timpsila* most sought after is the underground tuber. However, collectors must be able to find the aboveground part of the plant somewhere on the vast prairies in order to harvest the tubers, of course. From Manitoba in the north, down into Texas, and from eastern

The densely packed light-blue flowers of timpsila *turn to a cluster of ripe seeds that detach and blow across the prairie in fall, almost like a tumbleweed.*

Timpsila *corms.*

Colorado to the Mississippi River, *timpsila* can be found on sunny sandy low angled hillsides—hence its common name, "prairie turnip."

During the early spring, young, densely hairy shoots emerge from the soil. The sprouts, growing up to about a foot in height, produce several palmate leaves. In early summer, purple-blue clusters of flowers emerge. These are followed later in the season by flattened seed pods. The plant will produce one to four tuberous roots each, located about four to five inches below the surface, each with a long tap root.

CULINARY USE

Timpsila corms can be eaten immediately after harvesting, either raw or boiled, but not until the tough skin is peeled away. They can also be sliced and sun-dried, braided and hung to dry, or pounded into flour—a common traditional preparation to preserve food into the winter season. The fresh roots can be added to soups and stews or roasted in order to bring out more of the flavor. *Timpsila*, notably, does not have a particularly distinct taste. At first bite, the mouth is met with a very mild radish or chayote sensation, followed by a slightly sweet taste reminiscent of potato. The mild flavor, in fact, is what makes *timpsila* a great addition to other dishes—it adds nutrition without adding a strong flavor.

WHEN, WHERE, AND HOW TO COLLECT IN KINCENTRIC ECOLOGY

Historically, in late spring and early summer, the women of the various Great Plains nations would venture onto the prairie to collect *timpsila*. Using a tapered, fire-hardened digging stick, they would collect hundreds of the roots and bring them back to camp for processing. Today, entire families attempting to regain and revitalize ancestral foodways travel to their favorite collecting sites to gather these prized tuberous roots. Instead of digging sticks, the people now generally use small shovels, carefully pushing them into the earth with their feet so as not to accidentally damage the precious roots. *Timpsila* roots, however, still have to be processed one way or another after harvesting. The roots have a hard, dark skin that must be peeled before eating. Processing is time-consuming work that goes by much more pleasantly if there is company around to share gossip and stories with.

The story about the young woman who married a star is one such example of a tale that might be told during the harvest, and emphasizes the importance of respecting the land when harvesting *timpsila*. It's crucial to return the disturbed soil and the plant's base to the earth after harvesting to ensure future growth and regeneration. And as was expressed in the story, collectors are reminded to leave the largest *timpsila* plants (and some of the small ones) in the ground so that they can continue to grow and regenerate amply to feed the entire populace in following years. For Indigenous people, foraging is practice rooted in mindfulness. The very act reminds people of traditional ecological knowledge that sustains the land, communities, and future generations.

Timpsila Stew with Fresh Greens and Wild Rice

INGREDIENTS:

- 2 tbsp. vegetable oil
- 2 cloves garlic, finely chopped
- 1 medium yellow onion, diced
- 2 c. greens, such as pigweed, purslane, amaranth, or collard
- 4 c. vegetable broth
- 1 ½ c. fresh or dried sliced timpsila root
- 1 ½ cups cooked wild rice

The mild flavor of *timpsila* makes it an easy addition to recipes where it will not overpower the flavors of other ingredients, but will add thickness or nutrition.

Sauté the onions and garlic in the oil until soft but not brown. Add the greens and cook until they begin to wilt. Next, add the broth and *timpsila*. Cover and simmer for at least 1 hour and up to 2 hours. Add the cooked wild rice and simmer for another five minutes. If desired, add venison, elk, or bison meat and/or some fresh herbs such as sage or wild mint. Serves 2 to 4.

7

Edible Greens

My friend and ethnobotanical colleague Karen Adams once told a group of my students "a weed is just a useful plant with a lousy press agent." Many edible and useful greens are today often overlooked as weeds. Even the use of the word "greens" is a nod to the western culinary tradition, which somehow feels a need to create a separate category of foods for plant-based ingredients that are not meat, dairy, grains, starches, or legumes. American Indians typically gather greens along watercourses, in the understory of forests and woodlands, or at the edges of open meadows. They are often seasonal and sometimes have a short collection window where the optimal times for harvesting rely on observational awareness in order to pick vegetables before they become too tough or bitter to eat.

Kincentric harvesting often involves knowing where to look for prime ingredients even in challenging landscapes, like these stands of lush cattails that quickly transition to high desert in Malheur County, Oregon.

Amaranthus spinosus, *spiny amaranth plant, a nutritional powerhouse that is often overlooked.*

Edible greens benefit particularly from the type of seasonal fire management some tribes practice. Cultural burns return essential nutrients to the soils and loosen soils for the easier propagation of small seeds. Controlled burning also decreases competition among plant species and often removes diseased plants from specific habitats and ecosystems. The thinning of woodlands and forested areas allows sunlight into locations where seasonal or ephemeral greens in particular can thrive. In some instances, and especially among agriculturalist tribes, edible greens are sometimes intentionally planted at the edges of the fields or, such as the epazote and wild red amaranth that somehow keep popping up in different parts of my garden every year, and are permitted to propagate as volunteer plants.

These types of volunteer plants in particular are often species that today non-Indigenous farmers and gardeners consider weeds. But Indigenous land management has resulted in a long list of plants known as semi-domesticates—plants whose characteristics have been influenced by human interaction. For example, away from direct human influences chenopods (saltbush, goosefoot, and pigweed), for example, tend to be smaller and produce less foliage.

Many greens can also be encouraged to repropagate every year with selective collection practices. It is important to collect the leaves of edible greens during their early growth stages, so that mature leaves stay on the plant and continue to photosynthesize, feeding the mother plant and keeping it healthy and strong. Indigenous gatherers look for leaves that are not too small to be worthwhile and also not too big. Some of the plant must be permitted to continue to grow so that leaves from the same plant can be collected again during the season, but also so that eventually, the plant will go to seed and replace itself the following year—pulling up an entire plant while gathering would substantially blunt the entire population. While collecting plants late in the season, gatherers often dig fully formed seed heads back into the earth nearby or scatter them by hand to aid propagation.

Indigenous nations are grateful for their edible green relatives, and often talk about their growth periods as "visits" from any other family member. Some greens only visit once a year, on rare occasions akin to holidays. Some, like chicory nettles and watercress, are homebodies who can be found in the same place year after year. Chenopods and purslane might be like the slightly crazy uncles who surprise us by showing up in unexpected places virtually without warning.

Finally, it's worth noting that some of the plants in this chapter have questionable ancestry. Taxonomists are still debating whether or not plants such as watercress and purslane are native to the New World, or if some goosefoots and epazote were brought to North America by migrating animals and humans. Generally, however, Indigenous botanists are not unduly concerned about the origin of a plant; if we know it's been here for five hundred or a thousand years and has been used for just as long, it qualifies as native. An Indigenous botanist thinks only about how the plant is related to our local community of people and plants; we mediate the definition of kincentricity for plants that have been with us for many years.

Cattail

BULRUSH
TYPHA LATIFOLIA **(BROADLEAF CATTAIL),**
T. ANGUSTIFOLIA**, (NARROWLEAF CATTAIL)**
T. DOMINGENSIS **(SOUTHERN CATTAIL)**

PLANT FAMILY: *Typhaceae*
PARTS USED: *Fresh flowerheads, leaves, roots*
SEASON: *Year-round*

Several parts of the broad-leaved cattail, Typha latifolia, *can be used for various practical household purposes.*

An Apache girl being dusted with pollen during her Sunrise Dance on the San Carlos Indian Reservation in Arizona.

The Nuts and Seeds chapter introduced the wonderful and tasty piñon nuts, and discussed how piñon trees played a central role in the creation of the Apache universe and especially in the survival of White Shell Woman, who survived a flood by floating on a large ball of sticky gum taken from a piñon tree and became the First Mother and protector of the Apache. Every summer, thirteen-to-fifteen-year-old girls enter large ceremonial circles around large bonfires of piñon wood that light up the cool nights on different Apache reservations across the Southwest. During the four-day ceremony, the young women become living embodiments of White Shell Woman. For those four days, the initiate assumes the healing and other powers of White Shell Woman. Elderly and ailing Apache will approach individual girls, asking them for a healing touch or a blessing.

Gaan dancers (Mountain Spirits) appear in the circle during this ceremony. They are accompanied by the rhythm of singers and drummers. At the edge of the circle the young initiates, attired in buckskin clothing, have their hair caked with a mixture of yellow cornmeal and cattail pollen. The young girls who endure this ritual represent the finest example of Apache womanhood and are spiritually invested with the pollen of a plant that many wildcrafters consider primarily a food plant.

IDENTIFICATION

The easiest modern way to identify cattails is to look for corn dogs on a stick. The "hot dog" is actually the female part of the seed and flowerhead, which rises above tall cattail plants. In optimal conditions, cattails can reach up to ten feet tall. They colonize an area via rhizomes, and are perennial plants. If you look at a colony a few years in a row, so long as the environment is favorable, you'll notice it spreading gradually. Most of an individual plant is composed of long, slender, green stalks topped with a brownish, fluffy, flowering head. The dark brown male spike that holds staminate flowers and rises directly up and out of the flower head. Surrounding the central stem are several thin, basal leaves with parallel veins running their long, narrow length. The leaves are about a half inch to an inch and half wide in narrowleaf cattail species, and a bit wider for southern and broad-leaved cattails.

A basket by an Akimel O'Odham (Pima) artisan, circa 1923, woven with cattail, willow, and devil's claw.

CULINARY USE

Cattails truly provide a multitude of uses, because practically every part of the cattail is edible. The plant has been important to American Indians for millennia. Material culture excavated at the ruins in and around Chaco Canyon in northwest New Mexico have included the remnants of cattail pollen, shoots, and roots. Parts of cattail have also been identified in the bundles of ancestral Puebloan healers. The Hopi of northern Arizona mix the fluffy flowerheads with tallow to create a substance they use as chewing gum. In southern Arizona, the Pima bake the pollen into biscuits or mix it into a gruel. They also eat the young stalks. At the bottom of the Grand Canyon, the Havasupai eat the flowerheads like they would corn. Over at San Felipe Pueblo, cattail shoots are ground and mixed with cornmeal. The Paiute take the seed heads and strike them with a firebrand to separate the seeds from the down, which makes the tasty seeds easier to eat. The Paiute dry the rhizomes and grind them into a flour to be used in mush or made into cakes. The rhizomes can also be chewed fresh—but be ready to engage in lots of spitting out the stringy pulp. Cattails contain more calcium, iron, potassium, and carotenoids than other starchy foods including rice and potatoes.

WHEN, WHERE, AND HOW TO COLLECT IN KINCENTRIC ECOLOGY

Throughout North America, cattails can be found in or near slow-moving and still waters. They occupy marshes, ponds, lakes and wet depressions. The leaves, seeds, fluff, pollen, stems, and leaves must be collected between spring and fall. The flower head pops open during early fall. The edible stems should be collected early in the season, before they become too fibrous. The roots can be collected year-round. Late spring to early summer is the best time to collect the edible male parts of the plant.

The edible part of the plant head is actually the more narrow male staminate that pops up above the corn dog–looking cluster of flowers. The upper and narrow male stamina is where the pollen is held, and it's the pollen that is generally collected and eaten. When collecting any kind of pollen, it is best to choose a day that is not windy. It is also advisable to wear shoes that you will not mind getting wet and muddy as you wade into shallow water. Bring a paper or plastic bag to collect the pollen in; I prefer a good paper bag. Pollen tends to stick to the sides of plastic bags, which will waste a lot of the pollen that you collect. Place the bag over the top of the flower head, bend it over, and gently shake to encourage the pollen to drop into the bag. The next step is to filter the pollen from the plant fibers that will also fall into the bag. This is best done with a fine-mesh strainer. Once filtered, pollen can be stored in the refrigerator for several weeks.

Native gatherers of cattail are mindful of the time of year when they collect the different parts of the plants, generally collecting in late spring and early summer. Improper collecting can damage the stand's fertility, diminishing future generations. It is important to not overharvest the plants. The overall health of cattails is directly connected to the health of the wetland or riparian area that the cattails occupy. When appropriate, Indigenous peoples do sometimes work to keep stands of cattails in check, as if they spread too far, they might happily create a monoculture and outcompete other worthy species nearby, limiting the overall diversity of nearby plants as well as potentially insects and other aquatic life.

The staminate at the top of the whole flower spike is the part most frequently used in cuisine, though the stems and roots are also edible.

Cattail Pancakes

INGREDIENTS:

- ½ c. cattail pollen
- ½ c. wheat flour, preferably einkorn or emmer
- ½ c. fine cornmeal or masa
- 1 tsp. salt
- 2 tsp. baking powder
- ½ tsp. baking soda
- 1 tbsp. brown sugar or coconut sugar
- 1 c. plain kefir or buttermilk
- ½ c. milk or milk substitute
- 2 large eggs
- 2 tbsp. melted unsalted butter or butter substitute

Much of Indigenous cuisine calls for ingredients such as seeds, nuts, and other plant parts to first be dried and then ground into a flour that can then be included in recipes for cakes and other foods. This recipe calls for cattail pollen—since it's fine by nature, this is one recipe where we can skip the the grinding part of the process. Cattail pollen does not bind readily with other ingredients, however, so it must be mixed with other flours. I like to mix cattail pollen with whole wheat and fine corn flour.

Mix all the dry ingredients (pollen, flours, salt, baking powder, baking soda) in a medium bowl. In another bowl, mix the sugar, kefir, milk, eggs, and melted butter. Add the dry ingredients and gently mix just until the batter is smooth and all dry ingredients are incorporated. For the best results, allow the mixture to rest, covered, for about five minutes. Heat a skillet or griddle to medium. Pour about ¼ to ⅓ of a cup of the batter into the skillet and cook for about 2 minutes, or until the bubbles that form on the surface begin to pop. Flip the pancake and cook it for about one and a half minutes on the other side. I like to serve these pancakes with real maple syrup. Makes approximately one dozen pancakes.

Goosefoot

GOOSEFOOT, LAMB'S QUARTERS, PIGWEED, *QUELITE* (SPANISH), *CHUAKA* (RARÁMURI), *WAH-PE TO-TO* (LAKOTA)
***CHENOPODIUM ALBUM*, *CHENOPODIUM* SP.**

PLANT FAMILY: *Chenopodiaceae*
PARTS USED: *Leaves, seeds*
SEASON: *Spring to fall*

The origin of one common name for Chenopodium album, *goosefoot, is based on its easily identifiable leaves.*

Once, after having given a talk at a small college in Indiana, I borrowed a car so that I could try to get in a little fishing and maybe do some vintage shopping at one of the large antique malls in the area. I wrote about this in a previous article a few year ago:

> *I had the impulse to stop and take in the maizery. Maize (corn) was everywhere, interrupted only by old farmhouses with faded paint and large harvesters. I stepped out of my car into the oppressive heat that felt like a steamy weight on my shoulders. The horizon ran green for miles and resembled corduroys. The air was silent except for the rustle of large leaves of corn as they brushed against each other in the light wind. Except for small willows, dock, and a handful of grasses that struggled in the ditches that separated the road from the field there was nothing else growing. There weren't even any crows around to scold me at my invasion of their space.*

In stark comparison to this type of modern monoculture cropping, American Indian cornfields fairly invite you to stroll among their wide, uneven rows and to enjoy the process of identifying and perhaps collecting some of the edible and medicinal herbaceous plants such as goosefoots, or lamb's quarters that grow in, around, and through crop areas. We recognize the benefit of allowing this nutritious wild edible to pop up wherever it volunteers. It can be gathered and prepared in many of the same ways as spinach.

In a modern monoculture planting, goosefoot is often labeled a noxious weed. Indigenous foragers see it as a beneficial volunteer; the intended scale of production and intended technique for harvesting of the main crop makes the difference in how it's labeled.

IDENTIFICATION

Goosefoot is a common name applied to a very large family of plants of the genus collectively referred to as chenopods. There are currently known to be 170 species of chenopods. Some taxonomists still consider chenopods to be a subfamily of Amaranthaceae. The common name, goosefoot, was applied to this genus due to the shape of the leaves of many species that resembled the feet of geese. They can be both annuals and perennials herbaceous plants, depending on the type.

The edible chenopods, such as goosefoot/lamb's quarters tend to be annuals; they develop tall terminal inflorescences that drop hundreds of seeds during the late summer and early fall. The leaves are often thin and best harvested young, before they turn bitter. The lobed leaves can be rhombic, triangular, and/or have dentate margins. Some species' leaves can be as small as one inch long while others, such as *Chenopodium giganteum*, can grow up to eight inches long. The most commonly known goosefoot, *Chenopodium album*, can grow up to five feet tall as a plant, with leaves on the bottom part of the plant

North American chenopods are relatives of their South American counterpart, Chenopodium quinoa, *though it's interesting the southern hemisphere variety is valued mainly for its protein-rich seeds, while the northern hemisphere plant is harvested primarily for its nutrient-dense leaves.*

In late summer, the top inflorescences of lamb's quarters turn into spikes of seeds.

reaching up to three inches in length. The leaves toward the top of the plant tend to be shorter and not as clearly lobed.

It should be noted here that the Spanish term *quelite* can be applied to some chenopods, but also includes other species of edible greens such as purslane, squash blossoms, epazote, nettles, and the leaves of amaranth.

CULINARY USE

Goosefoots are edible wild greens. They can technically be eaten raw, but the tiny hairs that grow underneath the leaves often make them feel a bit unpleasant on the tongue; cooking removes these. Wildcrafted goosefoot greens can be cooked in any of the ways people generally prepare spinach, collards greens, or chard. They can be sautéed in a skillet with mushrooms or nuts, or simply boiled with a few spices, salt and pepper as a tasty side dish. They are often added as greens in soups and stews.

WHEN, WHERE, AND HOW TO COLLECT IN KINCENTRIC ECOLOGY

Goosefoot and other edible chenopods begin to appear during the late spring and continue to grow into the fall, when they go to seed. They can be found in sunny areas at the edges of meadows and particularly in recently disturbed areas. They do best at lower elevations, but can be found in foothill areas, up to around 3,000 feet in elevation.

The edible greens are best harvested early in the plant's growth cycle. They become bitter and less pliable later in the season. When collecting, be careful not to pull the entire plant from the ground; leave the upper part of the plant where

Chenopodium giganteum *can be differentiated from* C. album *by its pink inflorescence, though its common name of "tree spinach" alludes to it being equally as edible.*

the seeds are located so it can continue to grow and propagate the following year.

I mentioned earlier that many Indigenous farmers encourage and sometimes intentionally propagate useful plants at the edges of their fields. One reason for this is convenience—it saves the time of having to go search for edible greens such as goosefoots. In addition, many semi-domesticates contribute to the functioning ecosystem created in the microhabitat of an Indigenous field, milpa, or terrace system. Goosefoot attracts pollinators, and its root system encourages soil health. Goosefoot and other chenopods also help to control pests that would otherwise eat the main crops in a field—leaf miners, for example, are highly attracted to chenopods, and will often eat them preferentially, sparing the nearby crops.

Tepary Bean Soup with Fresh Greens

INGREDIENTS:

- 3 c. water
- 1 c. dried tepary beans (or precooked beans, optional)
- 2 tbsp. olive or vegetable oil
- 2 cloves garlic, minced
- 1 yellow onion, finely chopped
- 1 tsp. Mexican oregano *(Lippia graveolens)*
- 1 tsp. cilantro
- 3 c. freshly collected chenopod leaves
- 2-3 c. chicken or vegetable broth
- Salt and pepper, to taste
- Chile peppers, optional

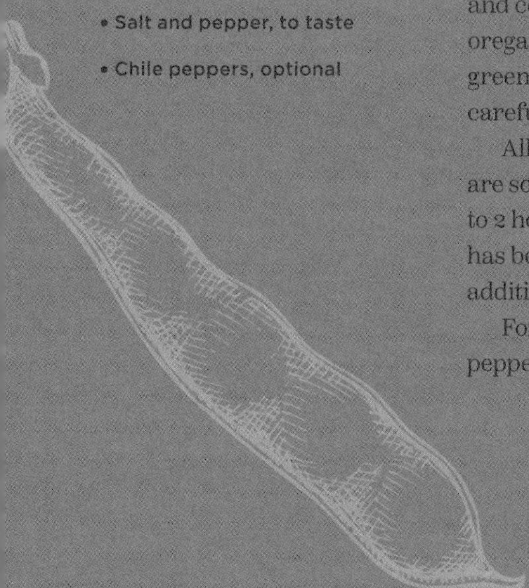

I enjoy preparing soups using whatever ingredients happen to be fresh in my garden. This recipe includes the little tepary beans mentioned in Chapter 3. The beans can be cooked or soaked ahead of time and added to the soup after everything else has been prepared. However, I prefer to cook the beans along with everything else so the complex flavors can dance around with each other while the soup is simmering. If goosefoot plants are not available, substitute chard, collard greens, or young amaranth leaves.

In a deep pot, bring the water to a boil. In the meantime, spread out the beans on a flat surface and pick over them to remove any little stones, dirt clods, or cracked beans. Rinse the beans in a wire sieve. Once the water is boiling, add the beans. Boil the beans for about 10 minutes (skip this step if using precooked beans). Remove the pot from the heat and allow the contents to cool for about 5 minutes. Drain the water and place the partially boiled beans in a large bowl.

Rinse out the same pot, dry it, then place it over medium-low heat. Add the oil and heat it until it begins to shimmer. Add the garlic and onion and cook while stirring until the onion just turns translucent. Add the oregano and cilantro and sauté it for 1 minute, until fragrant. Add the greens and stir until they have wilted and are thoroughly cooked—be careful not to burn them. Add the broth, and then add the beans back in.

Allow the soup to simmer for a minimum of 1 hour, or until the beans are soft. Depending on the age of the beans, the soup may need to boil for up to 2 hours. If you decide to use precooked beans, add them after the soup has been simmering for 20 minutes, then simmer the soup for about 10 additional minutes. Taste, and adjust seasoning with salt and pepper.

For a little heat, drop a jalapeño, a serrano, or even a couple of chiltepin peppers into the pot while the beans are cooking. Serves 6.

Epazote

MEXICAN TEA, WORMSEED, YERBA ZORILLO, *BASOTA* (RARÂMURI)
DYSPHANIA AMBROSIOIDES, D. GRAVEOLENS

PLANT FAMILY: *Amaranthaceae*
PARTS USED: *Leaves, seeds*
SEASON: *Spring to fall*

The long, jagged leaves of epazote make it recognizable as a member of the amaranth family.

There was a period during my mother's life when she decided to move into an apartment complex in Southern California that served older members of the community. Many of the residents were Latino, and from other countries. It was a great complex for someone like her—the residents looked out for each other, visited each other regularly, and shared meals. Many of the balconies and front stoops were cluttered with pots and planting boxes growing flowers, herbs, edible greens, and vegetables. At one point, my mother and a couple of her neighbors decided to engage in a little guerrilla gardening and planted some herbs in and among some of the landlord-maintained landscaping that separated the apartment blocks. They planted yerba buena, ruda, and epazote. All are important culinary and medicinal herbs to that community.

Unfortunately, the gardener hired by the apartment complex viewed my mother's herbs as weeds and threatened to eradicate them. A fierce plant-based battle ensued, and—much to the satisfaction of my mother and her friends—the epazote and other herbs were allowed to stay and become permanent members of the landscaping.

Since I was a little kid, I have always been captivated by the word "epazote." To me the name feels exotic, somehow a bit dangerous—this is fitting because those things are true and representative of this plant and how it is used as a food and as a medicine.

IDENTIFICATION

Until recently, epazote was classified as a member of the goosefoot family (Chenopodiaceae). This was due to the plant's morphological similarities. However, over the course of the twentieth century, taxonomists gradually accepted that *Dysphania* species belonged in a different family (Amaranthaceae).

The individual plants are erect, herbaceous annuals; but in tropical regions, the plants can be perennial. The plant grows to between two and five feet tall. The central, woody stems hold irregular branches, with leaves that become gradually smaller as they near the top of the plant. Large light-green and yellowish, ovate leaves occur at the base of the small branches. The leaves grow up to about five inches in length, wider at the base and tapered at the end. The edges of the leaves have several outward-facing, rounded teeth. Spikes of florescence emerge at the top of the plant and at the ends of the topmost small branches. From a distance, epazote resembles plants from the goosefoot or amaranth family—but once you rub up against it, you'll realize your skin or clothes will have taken on a strong, pungent odor that resembles a cross between creosote and turpentine. Even young plants give off this particular scent, which can be helpful for identification.

CULINARY USE

Despite its strong scent—or perhaps because of it—epazote is often used as a culinary herb in Mexican and Central American cuisine. There were not that many dishes from my family that did *not* include epazote. It is added to soups and sauces and is often seen as an essential ingredient for making a pot of beans. Epazote adds a unique flavor to the beans and is known to help reduce the flatulence beans can cause. This helpful quality is due to chemical compounds, including terpenoids and alkaloids, present in the leaves. You may have noticed that the bean recipe on page 65 calls for only a single leaf of epazote: more than one leaf in any recipe will overpower the other ingredients.

A bunch of fresh green epazote waiting to be added to a dish as a culinary herb.

Dried epazote can be added to dishes or brewed as a tea long after the growing season ends.

WHEN, WHERE, AND HOW TO COLLECT IN KINCENTRIC ECOLOGY

Epazote grows best in sunny, dry areas. The young sprouts begin to appear in groups during late spring. The plants grow very quickly, reaching maturity by midsummer. It is best to collect the leaves before the plant goes to seed; afterward they can turn tough. I often pick entire plants just before they go to seed and hang them in bunches to dry so I can enjoy adding the dried herb to dishes throughout the culinary year, or drinking it as a tea. Although it does not contain caffeine, it's often described as stimulating due to its intense flavor profile, akin to a strong, citrusy mint tea.

I do allow some of the epazote plants in my garden to go to seed, knowing it will disperse several feet away from the mother plant and reliably come back as volunteer epazote somewhere in my garden the following year. Due to the strong scent of the plants from its volatile oils, epazote is often planted around crops known to attract damaging insects, as a natural pesticide.

Fiddleheads

***PTERIDIUM AQUILINUM* (BRACKEN), *MATTEUCCIA STRUTHIOPTERIS* (OSTRICH FERN), AND *OSMUNDASTRUM CINNAMOMEUM* (CINNAMON FERN)**

PLANT FAMILY: *Polypodiopsida, with several subclasses*
PARTS USED: *Young sprouts*
SEASON: *Spring to summer*
REGION: *Northeast*

I still vividly recall the pleasant textural surprise in my mouth and flavor surprise on my tastebuds the first time I ate fiddleheads. The soft, curling heads were slightly chewy, but so fresh and tender it only took a couple of bites to break them down. A gentle bitterness mixed with complex earthy tones settled onto the edges of my tongue. The closest experience of forest-floor umami I can compare it to would be morel mushrooms.

*Tightly furled ostrich fern (*Matteuccia struthiopteris*) heads appear in spring throughout the Northeast.*

There was a hint of asparagus as well—and now I realize this shouldn't have been surprising, since fiddleheads are also young sprouts. And that it reminded me of mushrooms may have had to do with the fact that they use spores for reproduction. Although they're from different families of the natural world entirely, my palate could discern deep-rooted, primal similarities.

Fiddleheads are more than a wonderful addition to the dinner table: they also provide essential nutrients and have a medicinal value too.

IDENTIFICATION

In the woods, search for the little three-to-four-inch tall, bright-green curled fronds pushing their way up above the dark soils, twigs, and leaves. They prefer to grow near springs, along creeks, and in damp, forested areas that do not receive too much sun. Imagine the tops of small bright green colored violins, or fiddles, sticking up from the ground. Remember, fiddleheads are just the young sprouts of new ferns; many ferns die back to the ground in autumn in areas with

Clockwise from top left: *bracken fern, cinnamon fern, and ostrich fern.*

Ostrich ferns often grow in colonies on damp, shady forest floors.

severe winters, so also look on the forest floor for brown leaves from the previous year, indicating a nearby colony. One way to identify fiddleheads is to look for the thin, light-brown papery material that covers that outside of the furled head. This will come off the plant on its own, or can be brushed off. There should also be a slight groove along the stem.

CULINARY USE

Fiddleheads are primarily considered an early spring food source. Before modern grocery stores, they came as a welcome and tasty green addition to meals after long winters spent eating dried meats and stored nuts and grains or reconstituted flours.

After collection, rinse the fiddleheads of the small debris that can get caught up in the furls. Next, boil the plants for between seven and ten minutes. This step is important, to leach the bitters and toxins such as ptaquiloside, or PTA, that are often found in bracken ferns and older fern species. Certain varieties of fiddleheads such as ostrich fern, *Matteuccia struthiopteris*, and bracken fern, *Pteridium aquilinum*, have been shown to be toxic and possibly carcinogenic if not fully cooked. Next, simply sauté the fiddleheads in butter or olive oil. I like to cook them with a little white wine and some shallots. In the past, Native peoples simply boiled fiddleheads and added them to spring meals.

Contemporary scientific research on the nutritive value of fiddleheads upholds what Native peoples already knew about many pre-Columbian foods from North America: they are exceedingly good for you. They are source of antioxidants. The furled heads are also chock full of omega-3 and omega-6 fatty acids. In addition, fiddleheads are high in iron and insoluble fiber. They also contain iron, magnesium, potassium, selenium, and phosphorus.

WHEN, WHERE, AND HOW TO COLLECT IN KINCENTRIC ECOLOGY

After the harshness of a Northeast or New England winter has subsided but the land is warming and the ground is still moist, fiddlehead fern gatherers trek to their favorite collecting sites in search of the new sprouts as they push up through the wet leaf clutter and natural mulch leftover from the previous fall. The ideal time in New England for fiddleheads is normally around mid-April. Be ready to collect on short notice. As an Abenaki elder told me, "You have to be ready to harvest as soon as you see the first of them, because they unfurl quickly and become bitter." Fiddleheads tend to grow in small clumps of about six plants. They like damp places away from roads and other disturbed areas. In some locations across the country, it's possible to find adventurous vendors offering fiddleheads at farmers markets. I have tried these, and although they are passable, they are not quite as tender as fresh, personally harvested fiddleheads.

Once you locate a group, be careful to harvest only the part of the plant that has emerged above the soil. Leave the roots and rhizome below ground so that it can return next season. Also, be careful not to harvest all the plants in one clump—leave the majority of the group to grow on and ensure future harvests. Avoid fiddleheads that are already starting to unfurl, as they are unfortunately likely to be taking on a bitter note already.

Sautéed Fiddleheads with Mushrooms

INGREDIENTS:

- 2 tbsp. butter
- 1 garlic clove, finely chopped
- 2 chives
- 1 c. fresh fiddleheads
- ¾ c. morel mushrooms
- 2 tbsp. white wine
- Salt and pepper, to taste

Fiddleheads can be added to any dish that calls for a mix of sliced or chopped vegetables—they can replace green beans, asparagus, or prickly pear with delicious results. Just substitute the equal amount of fiddleheads. My favorite way to enjoy fiddleheads is to simply sauté them with butter and other simple ingredients.

Carefully wipe or rinse away any dirt from the fiddleheads and mushrooms. In a saucepan, melt the butter over medium-low heat. Add the garlic to the butter and sauté until the garlic softens. Chop the chives into ¼-inch pieces and add them to the pan. Add the fiddleheads to the pan. Chop the mushrooms into quarters, and add them to the pan. Lower the heat and cook until the fiddleheads and mushroom begin to soften. Add more butter if the pan begins to seem dry. Add the wine and cook for a few more minutes. Add the salt and pepper, to taste. This sauté works well as a side dish or simply served over a bed of wild rice.

Serves 2.

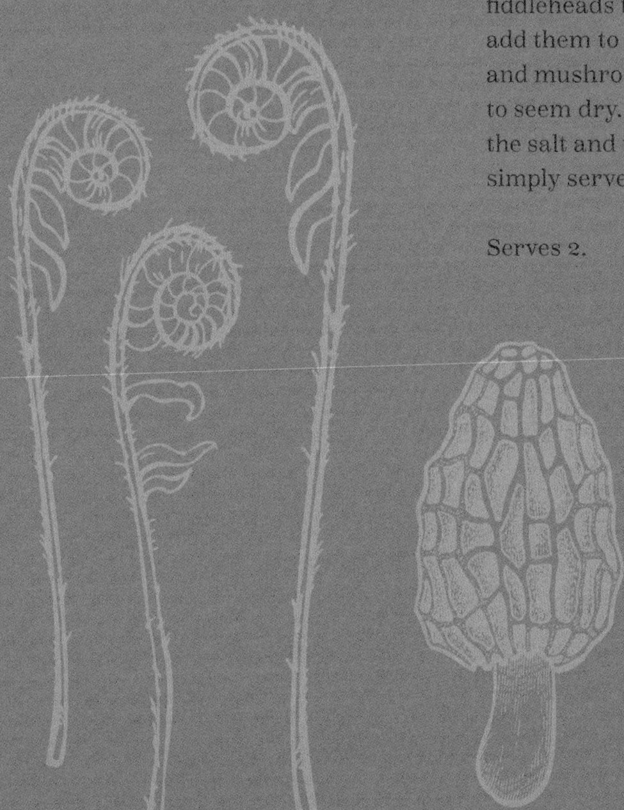

Purslane

PORTULACA OLERACEA, P. RETUSA

VERDOLAGAS, PIGWEED, LITTLE HOGWEED, MEXICAN PARSLEY, MOSS ROSE

PLANT FAMILY: *Portulacaceae*

PARTS USED: *Leaves*

SEASON: *Year-round*

REGION: *Western United States*

Although wild and semi-domesticated greens have always been a part of American Indian cuisine, western botanical taxonomists are unable to determine whether some of these plants are truly endemic to the ancestral homelands of people who are native to North America.

It has been suggested that purslane (*Portulaca* sp.) is actually native to Europe and Asia, and that it was introduced to North America via Norsemen and/or during European explorations. However, other studies suggest that purslane could be native to South America. At the same time, an archeological site located south of Toronto, Canada, revealed purslane pollen and seeds that date back to the mid-fourteenth century. Purslane seeds and pollen of the species *Portulaca retusa* have also been identified at ancestral Puebloan sites including Salmon Ruins, Chaco Canyon, and Mesa Verde. It seems that many pre-Columbian peoples across North America shared a taste for these tiny little greens.

IDENTIFICATION

It should be noted here that the name purslane is not to be confused with *Claytonia* sp., often referred to as pink purslane or winter purslane.

Purslane's reddish stems, yellow flowers, and oblong leaves make it easy to identify.

Nevertheless, it is likely that you have already seen purslane somewhere in your garden and have even dug it up, assuming that it is a weed. Purslane does resemble a low-growing succulent with small yellow flowers that open in the mornings. The plant appears in the summer months growing in large, sunlit patches in rocky and sandy soils. The small ovate leaves that grow in clusters at the end of reddish stems are no bigger than half an inch long. The little yellow flowers hold five heart-shaped petals and grow up to about a quarter of an inch across. Later in the season, the flowers are replaced by a seed capsule that eventually releases several very dark brown nearly black kidney-shaped seeds.

CULINARY USE

Many Indigenous communities native to North America use purslane for several medicinal purposes including for tuberculosis, as an antiseptic wash, and to treat digestive problems. However,

Try adding purslane to any salad, even those with origins outside North America, such as Greek salad.

purslane is mainly enjoyed as a tangy addition to meals. The leaves are picked and added to salads, soups, and stews. The leaves can also be sautéed, fried, and boiled. I like to add the little leaves to a dish of scrambled eggs along with Southwestern spices, jalapeños, and a bit of cheese. The seeds of purslane are also edible; if enough are collected, they can be ground into meal and added to cakes and cereal mixes. It is recommended for those with kidney ailments to use caution when ingesting purslane, due to the presence of organic crystalline oxalates.

WHEN, WHERE, AND HOW TO COLLECT IN KINCENTRIC ECOLOGY

As noted above, purslane is largely present as a summer plant. In parts of the Southwest and along the southern half of the West Coast, the plants appear in the spring and remain until later in the fall. Look for purslane in sunny, flat, disturbed areas such as in your garden where you've recently planted other things, and in open fields. It's tenacious and will often grow at the edges along sidewalk edges or in hellstrips. Since purslane is so widely distributed, overharvesting is not usually a concern, but it's always recommended to cut stems instead of uprooting an entire plant if you value your collection site. As with other plants, however, carefully consider your intended area: if it's on or near a residential lawn or city street, there's a fair chance that the plants could be polluted with herbicides, pesticides, or by a passing canine.

The leaves of purslane are the tasty part. They tend to cluster at the end of the short stems. If harvesting on the go, snip whole stems and separate the leaves back at home. Purslane is a low-growing plant and therefore collects a lot of dirt. Be sure to carefully rinse the leaves before preparing them for a meal.

Purslane can be substituted wherever a dish calls for greens such as arugula, kale, chard, or other bitter or peppery greens. Whenever I am cooking outside in the open and there is some purslane available, I like to chop up the green leaves and add them to a wild salad—they pair well with watercress and wild-harvested berries.

Stinging Nettle

RAHEWAKA **(RARÁMURI)**
URTICA DIOICA

PLANT FAMILY: *Urticaceae*
PARTS USED: *Leaves, roots, stems*
SEASON: *Year-round*

I had carefully moved down toward the small, narrow stream. The water flowed over rounded stones and around mosses, watercress, and other aquatic plants. As I dropped into the small ravine, I was engulfed in shade created by the towering redwoods and coastal spruces that provide so much of the habitat of the Lost Coast Wilderness in Northern California. I was loaded with a sixty-pound backpack. I carefully planned a route across several large, dry rocks that I could use as stepping stones to traverse the water. I managed to hop across the first two without getting my boots wet, then headed toward a thick wall of green shrubs and vines on the opposite bank. I paused midstream after hearing an unusual high-pitched sound emanating from the tangle of green before me. I moved another foot or two closer and came face-to-face with the large, snorting face of a Roosevelt elk. It stared back at me, nonplussed by my presence. It was casually chewing on a bunch of stinging nettles. The sound had nothing to do with pain—Roosevelt elk aren't bothered by raw stinging nettles, they simply have a bugle that can sound like a cross between a whistle and a screech. But if I had crashed into the nettles during a hasty jump from stream to bank, I would likely have made a similar noise—for different reasons.

The jagged form of stinging nettle almost seems to warn that the sharp, silica-tipped hairs painful to bare skin lurk just below, concealed on stems and on the underside of the leaves.

Plants play a role in many American Indian stories, often as a sort of tool or prop used by the main character. Among the Salish-speaking Klallam of Puget Sound, there is a story where stinging nettles are in fact the main character, and it again alludes to deep ecological knowledge about which plants are healthy long before they were ever tested for specific minerals by modern science; nettles contain high levels of calcium, iron, potassium, magnesium, zinc, manganese, copper, and chromium, making it remarkable for immune function and bone health.

This story begins at the time when The People (the Klallam) were living in deep fear from constant incursions and attacks by foes from the north. The persistent fear was so intense, in fact, that it was destroying their culture. One day, one of the Klallam men was wondering if there might be something that could be done to help his people.

That night, as he slept, the man was visited in a dream by a stinging nettle plant. The nettle told the man to tell his people to begin to pick its springtime leaves, then dry them. He advised that they should cook the dried leaves in boiling water and then drink the tea. The nettle told the man that if his people drank enough of this tea, they would begin to feel strong and brave. The man shared his dream with the people the next day, and they began to pick the stinging nettle leaves and make the tea as instructed.

Soon afterward, the man had another dream in which the nettle plant told the man that the strongest warriors in his tribe should pick the woody central stalks of stinging nettle plants and begin to flog their backs with them. The people again did as they were instructed by the man's dream. As they were flogging themselves, invaders from the north began to appear on the waters in canoes. But as the invaders got closer, they could see the Klallam warriors standing in a line on the shore, voluntarily flogging themselves while singing songs about bravery. The invaders were frightened by this display of obvious strength and turned their war canoes away.

IDENTIFICATION

Nettles are herbaceous perennials that can grow up to six feet tall. The one-to-seven-inch-long bright green leaves are narrow-lanceolate and sometime wide and ovate and arranged opposite on the central stem. The base of the leaves taper to cordate. The individual plants are topped with a spikelike inflorescence containing several panicle-like pistillate flowers. The

The stinging nettle makes flowers in long panicles in late summer.

small fruits are ovate. The whitish-tan roots are rhizomatous, and generally measure about half an inch wide at the top nearest the aboveground part of the plant, and can be several inches long under the soil.

CULINARY USE

Stinging nettle plants are known for being an edible green (once boiled or cooked). It is a potent medicine and provides materials for making utilitarian objects as well. Many native peoples do collect the leaves and simply cook them as an edible green—the tiny "stingers" disappear when cooked or dried. The whole (cooked) plant may be rubbed on the skin as a poultice to treat aches and pains, skin infections, rheumatism, and arthritis. The central stems of stinging nettles are pounded or twisted in order to make string cordage for bows, fishing nets, basketry, ropes, and twine. Some native fishermen rub the leaves onto their fishing gear in order to mask their scent and to turn the lines green so they're less visible in the water.

WHEN, WHERE, AND HOW TO COLLECT IN KINCENTRIC ECOLOGY

Look for growing and mature nettles from March through November. The plant will likely be in flower from May to October. It grows near stream banks that are in partial sunlight. Stinging nettle can also be found in disturbed areas along trails and roadsides throughout the western parts of North America.

Wear gloves and protective clothing when gathering the plants. The stinging sensation comes from contact with the silica-tipped hairs, technically called trichomes, on the underside of the leaves and stems. The stinging hairs almost function like teeny hypodermic needles, and inject skin with irritants like histamine and formic acid. If you are stung, wash the area with soap and water, ensure all the needles are removed, apply a mixture of baking soda and water, and then apply a cold pack or heat pack. If the rash persists, try a corticosteroid cream.

Gloves (and long sleeves, depending on the collection site's accessibility) are essential for collecting stinging nettle.

When collecting, be mindful to not overharvest the young leaves and stems and to leave some of the plants so they will go to seed and regenerate next year's nettles. It is also important to not disturb the root systems unnecessarily.

Stinging Nettle and Ginger Infusion

INGREDIENTS:

- 1-inch length of peeled ginger root
- ¼ c. of fresh stinging nettle leaves
- 1 qt. fresh water
- 2-3 spearmint leaves
- Honey or other sweetener (optional)

Many people like to consume nettles as a tasty green, often by making a pesto or adding it to soups and stews. However, nettles coupled with fresh ginger also make a tasty and healthy tea. Be sure to bring the leaves to a simmer to remove the stinging hairs on their underside before ingesting the tea.

In a saucepan, simmer the peeled and chopped ginger in the water for about 20 minutes. Add the nettle and spearmint leaves, stir well, simmer for a few minutes, then remove the pan from the heat, cover it, and let the mixture infuse for at least 45 minutes. For a stronger tea, leave the infusion in the pot for longer. If you decide to sweeten the tea with honey, add it to the mix while it is still warm. Strain the infusion into a small pitcher or other container. Enjoyed hot or iced.

Watercress

YELLOWCRESS, *BERRO* (SPANISH), *POHOHPAHTOOR* (PAIUTE), *ASILA AMAYA UDUHL* (CHEROKEE)
NASTURTIUM OFFICINALE

PLANT FAMILY: *Brassicaceae*
PARTS USED: *Leaves and stems*
SEASON: *Spring to late summer*

Watercress is an aquatic or semi-aquatic, trailing plant most commonly found next to sources of fresh, shallow, slow-moving water such as small streams, springs, and ditches.

When does a non-native plant become native to a place? Many plants migrated to North America along with the first Europeans who made their way to the continent. Phytogeographers (people who study the geographic distribution of plants) have determined that watercress migrated to the North American continent from Europe and Asia, however. They theorize that this migration somehow happened thousands of years before those first European explorers began to wonder if there was anything worth exploring on the other side of the Atlantic Ocean. The most likely solution is that migrating birds introduced watercress. And then moving water, insects, and animals contributed to the spread of watercress all across North America.

Watercress has been consumed by American Indians as a potherb since anyone can remember. The native language names for the plant all make some kind of reference to water. I do not recall the first time that I ate watercress, but I do recall being surprised by the slightly peppery, pleasant taste that is a little reminiscent of wasabi. This is not surprising, as watercress is in the mustard family of plants, which includes radishes, turnips, and collard greens. Now I enjoy every opportunity I get to add watercress to a campfire-side meal.

IDENTIFICATION

Watercress is normally a low-growing perennial, but it can grow up to three feet during the later part of its growth stage. The short stems are hollow. Watercress plants spread out as they grow, forming dense clumps. By early summer, little white four-petaled blooms with yellowish inflorescences will appear all over the plants. The small leaves grow pinnately along single stems.

CULINARY USE

The tender leaves and stems of watercress can be eaten raw, but it is mostly used as an ingredient in soups and stews, or as one of several varieties of mixed greens in a salad or on a sandwich. If enough of the greens can be collected, watercress

Watercress in flower shows how well it can colonize the banks of water sources if the conditions are favorable.

is well suited to being transformed into a nutritious soup base. It is rich in vitamins K, A, C, B6, and manganese, calcium, and folate.

WHEN, WHERE, AND HOW TO COLLECT IN KINCENTRIC ECOLOGY

Watercress is most tender early in its growth stage, although it is still edible later, especially if cooked or puréed. In regions where there is freezing winter weather, the leaves and stems can usually begin to be harvested around late May. In temperate places such as parts of California, there are locations where watercress can be found year-round. Watercress tends to thrive in chalk and limestone, near streams and around springs. I like to look for the little distinctively shaped leaves around shady, seeping springs in mountainous areas. Be sure to thoroughly wash watercress if collected in the wild, to remove potential giardia and liver flukes.

Watercress is so tenacious it is classified as an invasive species in some locations. Long before state agricultural offices began to worry about protecting local crops and irrigation courses, however, watercress populations were subject to oversight by Indigenous land managers. They were careful not to overharvest the plants to ensure a steady population, but at the same time ensure that the watercourses where it grew best remained clean and free from debris, so that it would be healthy to eat.

Watercress and potato soup.

Watercress and Potato Soup

INGREDIENTS:

- 2 medium potatoes
- 2 tbsp. olive oil
- 2 leeks, chopped
- ½ white onion, chopped
- 2 c. fresh watercress leaves and stems
- 2 c. chicken or vegetable broth
- Salt and pepper, to taste

I once shared a lunch with the late Dakota actor Floyd Red Crow Westerman. I was eating a sandwich while he was enjoying a smoothie sort of drink made of different blended greens. He told me he believed eating a diet high in greens is what helped him to continue acting and playing music into his later years. This healthy watercress soup recipe reminds me of that wonderful meal.

Peel the potatoes and chop them into quarters. Fill a pot with water and bring it to a boil. Add the potatoes and cook them until they are soft enough that a fork or knife pierces them easily, usually for between 15 and 25 minutes. Drain the potatoes and set them aside.

In a saucepan, heat the olive oil and then add the leeks and onion. Sauté them until the onions and leeks soften and begin to turn translucent. Add the potatoes, leeks, onions, half of the watercress, and the broth to a blender (or use an immersion blender) and blend until the ingredients are liquified and smooth.

Add the rest of the watercress and blend for a few seconds until the leaves and stems are just chopped but still visible. (You can add all the watercress earlier if you want a very smooth purée.) Return the blended soup to the pot and warm it up over low heat. If you prefer a more soupy dish than a thick, stewlike dish, simply add more or less broth. Adjust the seasoning with salt and pepper to taste. Serves 2.

Allium bisceptrum, aspen onion, grows in high-elevation meadows across the western United States.

Wild Onions

TAFVMPUCE **(PAIUTE),** ***SV-GI*** **(CHEROKEE),** ***SIBOWE*** **(RARÁMURI),** ***PŠÍŅ ŠIČÁMNA*** **(LAKOTA)**

ALLIUM **SP.**

PLANT FAMILY: *Amaryllidaceae*

PARTS USED: *Leaves, ramps, and bulb*

SEASON: *Late spring to fall*

Onions are a tasty and tangy addition to so many dishes. Indigenous peoples across North America have taken advantage of the abundance of wild onion species for millennia. There are roughly 130 different species of wild allium on the continent, and recently chefs everywhere have started to hunt for one specific type, *Allium tricoccum*, the ramp. They begin to send up leaves in spring, like any spring bulb (think tulips, daffodils), and are identifiable as an onion

Onions are responsible for reminding some of us about the kincentric role that humans occupy as mediators between the Earth and Sky realms.

According to a Mono Nation story, when the Earth was still being formed, six women traveled out into the fields near their village to collect edible plants. One of the women had brought her baby along for this gathering trip. The women were digging in the earth for bulbs when they discovered a little white one that they had not seen before. They tasted the new bulb and were immediately taken with the sweet-tangy taste. They collected and ate the new bulbs for much of the day and finally brought some back to the village to share with their husbands once they returned from a hunting trip. The husbands were immediately repelled by the stench—not only did this new food stink, they thought their wives smelled, too.

They told their wives that they had to go sleep that night out in the open air, away from them. They left again in the morning to hunt, and the wives once again collected these fascinating new onion bulbs and brought more back to the village. When the husbands returned from the hunt that night, they were as repelled by the smell of the onions and their wives as before. Even after the wives tried to convince their husbands how much the onions would improve the flavors of their foods, the husbands once again ordered the wives to sleep out in the open, away from their homes. The hunters told their wives that they also should not get anywhere near the animals that they were trying to hunt, because the onion smell that surrounded them would give away their position. This pattern continued for several days.

Finally, the wives announced they would leave their husbands and the village and would find a way to live on their own. So the six wives, including the one who had brought her baby along, left the village for good. They brought ropes twisted from eagle down and hemp. They traveled to a place where there was a huge rock and climbed it. Using their magic, they began to sing; the ropes that they made began ascending into the sky. The wives held on to the ropes and traveled into the Sky realm too.

When the husbands realized that their wives had truly left them, they became lonely and tried to follow their wives into the sky world using magic ropes of their own. But their ropes could only fly partway to the sky—once the wives realized that they were being followed, they used their magic and caused the husbands' ropes to stop wending their way upward when they had only reached partway into the sky.

To this day, the six wives and the one baby can still be seen floating in the night sky as stars—in modern times this constellation is called the Pleiades. The faintest star in the constellation is, of course, the baby. The husbands who followed their wives can be seen as the constellation Taurus.

by their onion smell, which only members of the onion family give off. Unlike grocery store cooking onions or even scallions, wild onions generally have very small bulbs; the lower leaves have plenty of onion flavor, so it's a question of whether to dig up the entire bulb or leave it to regenerate and just snip off the leaves.

IDENTIFICATION

It is not always easy to find wild onions. The long, narrow leaves often blend in with wild grasses. However, foragers often accidentally step on onion leaves without realizing it, smell the strong onion smell, and are able to identify a clump of onions nearby. Later in the growing season, it is easy to spot them by their quintessentially allium-shaped, the umbellate flower clusters. Depending on the species, there will be between ten and thirty separate flowers in an umbel. The flowers of some species, such as *Allium unifolium* are white. The flowers of *A. hyalinum* are whitish-pink while the pointy tipped flowers of

Allium unifolium, *left, and* Allium hyalinum, *right.*

A. bisceptrum can range in color from white to pink to rose.

The whitish bulbs of wild onions tend to be elongated or oval-shaped, and run between three-quarters of an inch to one and a half inches.

The flat, narrow, and linear leaves of wild onions grow between twelve and thirty inches high.

CULINARY USE

The leaves and scapes of wild onions are enjoyed by American Indians across North America. They are chopped and added to a wide variety of savory dishes to add an earthy note, very similar to how contemporary chefs use scallions and chives. Some Indigenous nations, including the Pomo and Miwok, eat the raw bulbs or bake them in pit ovens.

Wild onions can be substituted wherever a dish calls for ramps, scapes, chives, leeks, or even garlic. Whenever I am cooking outside in the open and there are wild onions available, I like to chop up the green leaves and scapes and sprinkle them onto whatever I am cooking. I also like to add them to bannock bread, cornbread, or Johnny cakes.

WHEN, WHERE, AND HOW TO COLLECT IN KINCENTRIC ECOLOGY

Wild onions will begin to spring from the moist earth not long after the last snows melt. The umbels will begin to appear by midsummer, sprouting pointed flowers in umbellate clusters within a few weeks. Look for wild onions in sunny and moist areas: near springs and creeks and at the moist edges of forest meadows. Wild onions can also be found near the lower elevations of hillsides, below 3,000 feet in elevation.

When collecting wild onions, be mindful to leave some of the bulbs in the ground in order to encourage future growth. It is also important to not collect all of the onions in one clump, so that some of the plants can go to seed and establish additional plants for the following year. If you come across a clump of a dozen or so onions, take the time to look for the largest and perhaps only harvest that one—since the bulbs of wild onions are not large, only the largest of them may be worth harvesting to cook with at all. Leave the smaller ones for the health of the overall population.

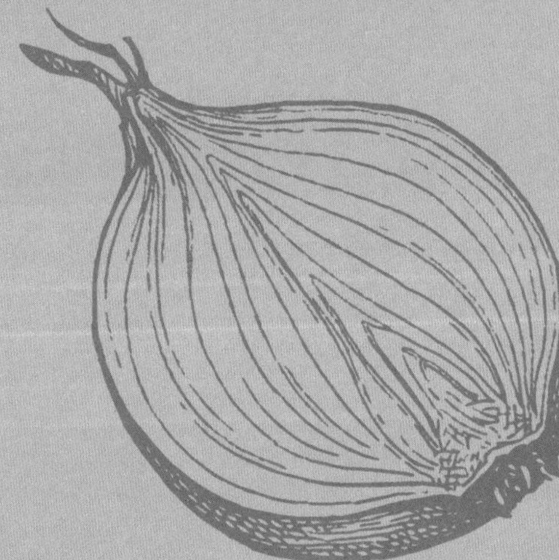

Glossary

GLOSSARY

ABORTIFACIENT	induces or brings on menstruation or a miscarriage
ALTERATIVE	restores the proper function and balance of the body
ANALGESIC	decreases the body's response to pain
ANDROGENIC	reduces the absorption of testosterone and dihydrotestosterone
ANTHELMINTIC	rids the body of parasites
ANTIANGIOGENIC	prevents tumors from growing their own blood cells
ANTIARTHRITIC	prevents and relieves symptoms of arthritis
ANTIBACTERIAL	seeks out and kills (or inhibits the growth of) bacteria
ANTIBIOTIC	inhibits the growth of microorganisms
ANTICANCER	demonstrates activity against malignant diseases
ANTICARCINOGENIC	counteracts carcinogenic effects and inhibits cancerous growths
ANTICOAGULANT	retards or inhibits the coagulation of blood
ANTICONVULSANT	inhibits convulsive seizures
ANTIDIABETIC	helps to regulate diabetes by lowering blood glucose levels
ANTIFUNGAL	prevents or inhibits the growth of fungal organisms
ANTIHYPERTENSIVE	reduces high blood pressure, peventing strokes and heart attacks
ANTIHYPERURICEMIC	prevents the overproduction of uric acid

ANTI-INFLAMMATORY	minimizes the body's response to injury by reducing pain and the release of neurochemicals to the injury site
ANTILITHIATIC	prevents the formation of kidney stones
ANTIMICROBIAL	kills or stops the growth of microorganisms
ANTIMUTAGENIC	reduces the rate of cell mutation
ANTIOXIDANT	protects cells against damage from harmful free radicals
ANTIPLEURITIC	decreases inflammation in the tissue surrounding the lungs
ANTIPROLIFERTIVE	restricts cancerous cell growth in tumors
ANTIPYRETIC	prevents and reduces fever
ANTIRHEUMATIC	slows the progression of rheumatoid arthritis
ANTISEPTIC	retards the growth of microorganisms
ANTISPASMODIC	reduces muscle spasms
ANTITUSSIVE	suppresses coughing
ANTIULCER	prevents the progression of ulcers
ANTIVIRAL	prevents and inhibits viruses
ANXIOLYTIC	relieves anxiety
ASTRINGENT	encourages the contraction of skin cells and body tissues

CARMINATIVE	prevents or relieves flatulence
CATHARTIC	a purgative herbal therapy
COMPOUND	the metabolic chemicals of plants (e.g. phytosterols, lipids, essential oils)
CONSTITUENT	the medicinal phytochemicals of plants
CYTOTOXIC	toxic to living cells
DEMULCENT	helps to relieve inflammation
DERMATOLOGICAL AID	helps skin heal from wounds, cuts, rashes, and dermatitis
DIAPHORETIC	helps to increase perspiration
DIURETIC	promotes the production of urine
EMMENAGOGUE	stimulates and increases menstrual flow
EXPECTORANT	promotes the secretion of mucus and saliva in the air passages
FEBRIFUGE	reduces fever
GASTROPROTECTIVE	protects the stomach lining from irritation
HEMOSTATIC	helps to prevent or stop bleeding
HEPATOPROTECTIVE	helps to prevent liver damage
HEPATOTOXIC	associated with liver damage

IMMUNOMODULATORY ACTIVITY	stimulates antibodies to strengthen the immune system
LARVICIDAL	targets the larval stage of an insect
LAXATIVE	helps to loosen stools and promote bowel movements
PHYTOCHEMICAL	biologically active plant chemicals
PHARMACOLOGICAL	effects and actions of plant chemicals on and in the body
PHARMACOLOGICALLY ACTIVE	plant constituents that are metabolized and demonstrate effects on and in the body
PHARMACOTHERAPEUTIC	beneficial effects of plant constituents
STOMACHIC	promotes appetite and helps with digestion
STYPTIC	stops bleeding
SUBTONIC	retards growth
URICOSURIC	increases the secretion of uric acid in the urine
VASODEPRESSOR	promotes the loss of consciousness
VASODILATOR	helps to widen blood vessels

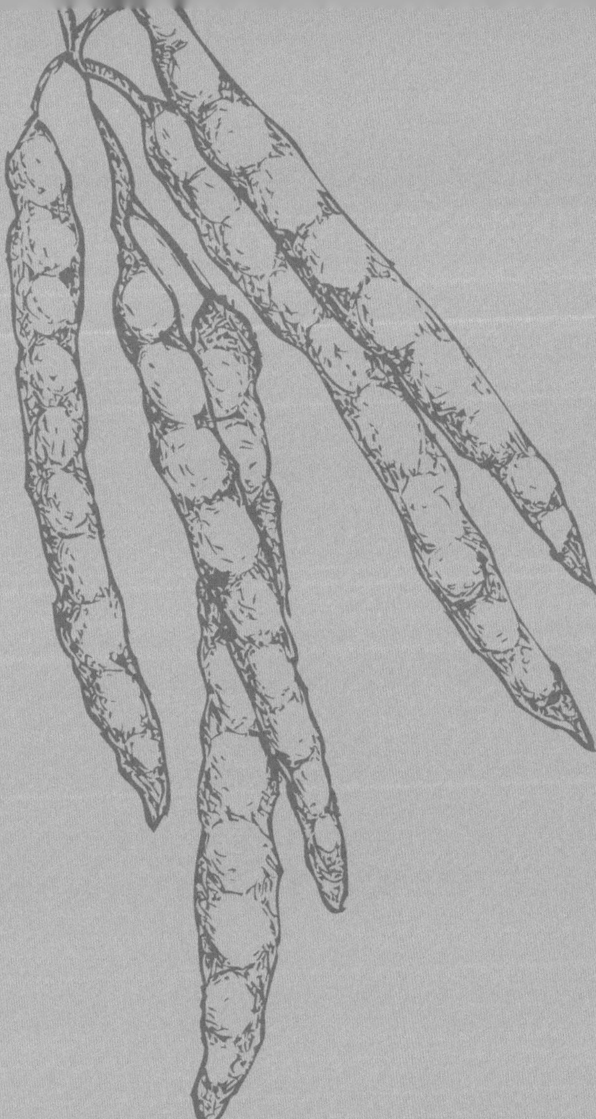

Further Reading and References

REFERENCES

Benz, B. F., & Staller, J. E. (2006). "The Antiquity, Biogeography, and Culture History of Maize in the Americas." In *Histories of Maize* (pp. 665–672). Academic Press.

Bowcutt, Frederica. "Tanoak Landscapes: Tending a Native American Nut Tree." *Madroño* 60, no. 2 (2013): 64–86.

Bruchac, Joseph, with Michael J. Caduto. *Native Plant Stories.* Fulcrum Publishing, 1995.

Buchmann, Stephen L., and Gary Paul Nabhan. *The Forgotten Pollinators.* Island Press, 1996.

Bye, R. *Ethnoecology of the Tarahumara of Chihuahua, Mexico.* Dissertation. Harvard University, 1976. Cambridge, Massachusetts.

Bye, R. "Quelites-Ethnoecology of Edible Greens—Past, Present, and Future." *Journal of Ethnobiology* no. 1 (1981): 109–123.

Caduto, M. J., and J. Bruchac. *Native Plant Stories.* Fulcrum Publishing, 1995.

Cajete, Gregory. *Look to the Mountain: An Ecology of Indigenous Education.* Kivaki Press, 1994.

Courlander, Harold. *The Fourth World of the Hopis.* Crown Publishers, 1971.

Evers, Larry, and Felipe S. Molina. *Yaqui Deer Songs/Maso Bwikam: A Native American Poetry.* University of Arizona Press, 1987. https://doi.org/10.2307/j.ctv348f929.

Felger, R., et al. *Northern Sierra Madre Occidental and Its Apachian Outliers: A Neglected Center of Biodiversity.* Drylands Institute. Tucson, 1994.

Hummer, Kim E. "Manna in Winter: Indigenous Americans, Huckleberries, and Blueberries." *HortScience* 48, no. 4 (2013): 413–417.

Hunn, E. S., with James Selam and Family. *Nch'iWána "The Big River": Mid-Columbia Indians and Their Land.* University of Washington Press, 1990.

Lefler, Lisa J. *Anthropology: Weaving Our Discipline with Community.* Newfound Press, University of Tennessee Libraries, 2014. https://doi.org/10.7290/akiz914.

Mackendrick, Norah, "Foodscape." In *Contexts* 13, no. 3 (2014): 16–18.

Martinez, Dennis. "Managing a precarious balance: wilderness versus sustainable forestry." *Winds of Change* 8, no. 3 (1993): 23–28.

Martinez, D. "Karuk Tribal Module for the Main Stem River Watershed Analysis: Karuk Ancestral Lands and People as Reference Ecosystem for Eco-cultural Restoration in Collaborative Ecosystem Management." Issue 41. Prepared by the Karuk Tribe of northern California under the Auspices of Cultural Solutions for the U.S. Klamath Nation Forest, 1994.

Martinez, D. "Traditional Environmental Knowledge Connects Land and Culture: American Indians Serve as the Link." *Winds of Change* 9, no. 4 (1994): 89–94.

Nabhan, Gary Paul. *Growing Food in a Hotter, Drier Land: Lessons from Desert Farmers on Adapting to Climate Uncertainty.* Chelsea Green Publishers, 2013.

Peacock, Sandra L. and Nancy J. Turner. "'Just Like A Garden': Traditional Plant Resource Management and Biodiversity Conservation on the British Columbia Plateau." In B*iodiversity and Native America.* University of Oklahoma Press, 1999. pp. 113–79.

Ramamoorthy, T. P., et al., eds. *Biological Diversity in Mexico: Origins and Distribution.* Oxford University Press, New York, 1993.

Silko, L. M. *Yellow Women and a Beauty of the Spirit.* Simon & Schuster, New York, 1996.

Salmón, E. 1995. "Cures of the Copper Canyon: Medicinal Plants of the Tarahumara with Potential Toxicity." *Herbalgram* 34:44–55.

Salmón, E. "Tarahumara Healing Practices." *Shaman's Drum* 24: 34–45.

Valle, Gabriel. *Gardening at the Margins: Convivial Labor, Community, and Resistance.* University of Arizona Press, 2025.

Wilson, Gilbert L. *Buffalo Bird Woman's Garden: The Classic Account of Hidatsa American Indian Gardening Techniques.* Minnesota Historical Society Press, 1987.

Zingg, R. *Report on Archaeology of Southern Chihuahua.* No. 1 of the University of Denver, Center of Latin American Studies, Denver, 1940.

FURTHER READING

Calvo, Luz, and Catriona Rueda Esquibel. 2015. *Decolonize Your Diet: Plant-Based Mexican-American Recipes for Health and Healing*. Vancouver, BC: Arsenal Pulp Press.

Curtin L.S.M. 1997. *Healing Herbs of the Upper Rio Grande*. Santa Fe: Western Edge Press.

Dunmire, William W., and Gail D. Tierney. 1995. *Wild Plants of the Pueblo Province*. Santa Fe, NM: Museum of New Mexico Press.

———.1997. *Wild Plants and Native Peoples of the Four Corners*. Santa Fe: Museum of New Mexico Press.

Frank, Lois Ellen. 2013. *Foods of the Southwest Indian Nations: Traditional and Contemporary Native American Recipes*. Berkeley, CA: Ten Speed Press.

Goodrich, J., C. Lawson, and V.P. Lawson. 1996. *Kashaya Pomo Plants*. Berkeley, California: Heyday Books.

King, Thomas. 2003. *The Truth About Stories*. Toronto: House of Anansi Press.

Moerman, Daniel E. 1998. *Native American Ethnobotany*. Portland, Oregon: Timber Press.

———. 2009. *Native American Medicinal Plants*. Portland, Oregon. Timber Press.

Sherman, Sean, and Beth Dooley. 2017. *The Sioux Chef's Indigenous Kitchen*. Minneapolis: University of Minnesota Press.

Timbrook, Jan. 2007. *Chumash Ethnobotany*. Santa Barbara Museum of Natural History Monographs. Berkeley, CA: Heyday Books.

Turner, Nancy J. 2014. *Ancient Pathways, Ancestral Knowledge*. Montreal: McGill-Queen's University Press.

Valle, Gabriel R. 2022. *Gardening at the Margins: Convivial Labor, Community, and Resistance*. Tucson: University of Arizona Press.

Willard, Terry. 1992. *Edible and Medicinal Plants of the Rocky Mountains and Neighbouring Territories*. Calgary: Wild Rose College of Natural Healing.

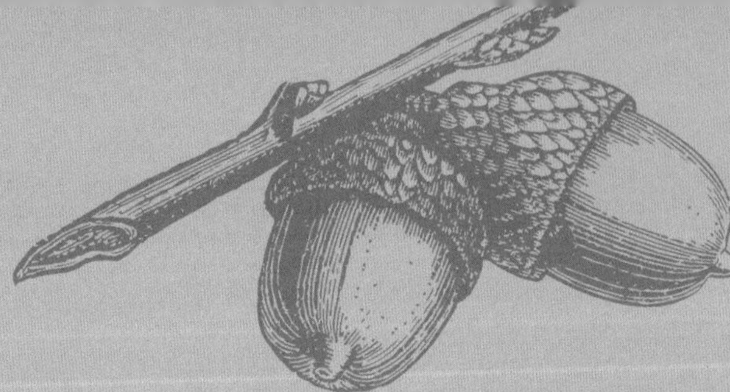

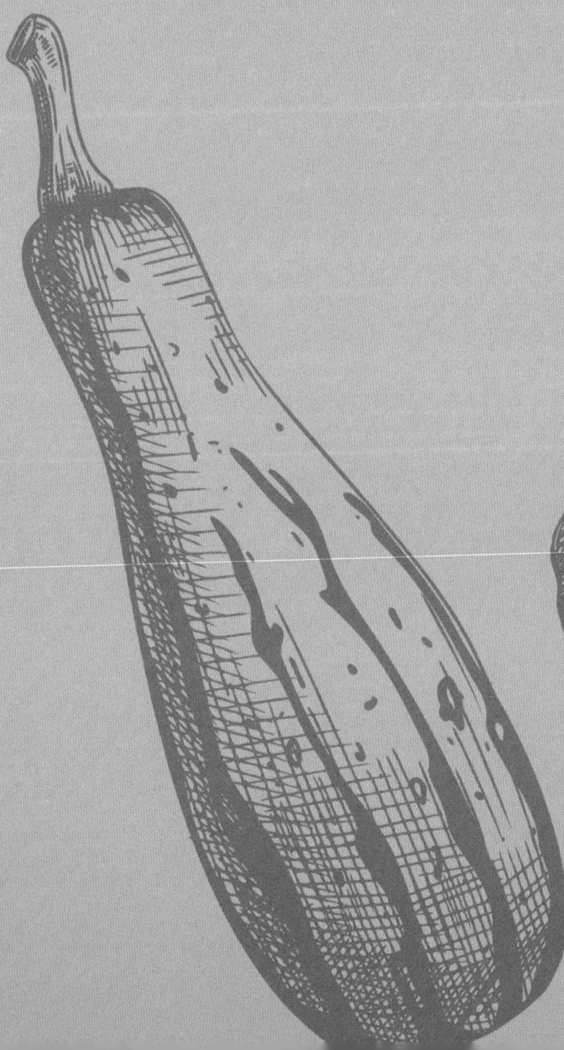

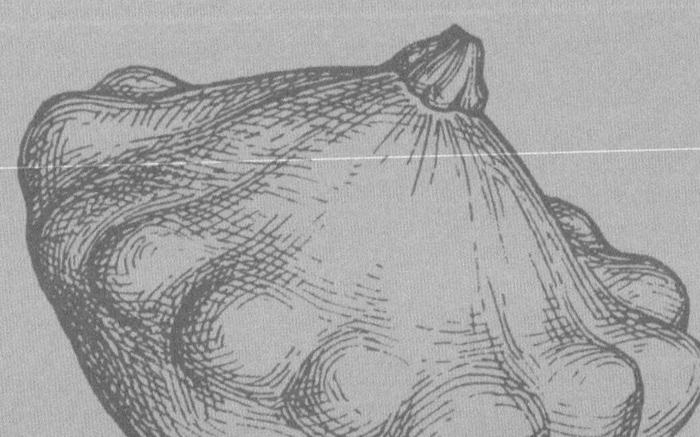

Acknowledgments

ACKNOWLEDGMENTS

This book is a result of a convivial confluence of events. It began with an email from Cydonia Editions founder Stacee Gravelle Lawrence, who was also the editor for my previous book, *Iwígara*. Stacee contacted me wondering if I "had another book in me." Turns out I did. Thank you, Stacee, for your confidence in my ability to get these writings onto the page, for your guidance and steady, unwavering support. These elements, for which I am grateful, have been essential for the completion of this work. Thank you Lauren Smith, the original graphic designer of the interior pages, and to Susan Evans of Design per se, who took over after Lauren left for maternity leave. My thanks as well to Rizzoli, for their willingness to bring this project to publication. Thanks also to Maria Pia Gramaglia, production manager, Lynn Scrabis, production director, and especially Charles Miers, Rizzoli's publisher.

Thanks should go also to the many students I have taught over the years. Their insights and questions continue to inspire my thinking and writing. I cannot forget to acknowledge my old friend Dennis Martinez for his contributions to the original concept of Indigenous kincentric relationships. I also appreciate and want to acknowledge the help from my network of ethnobotanical and ethnoecological friends. When I asked them if I should work on a book focused on kincentricity, their positive feedback and suggestions gave me the inspiration to carry this project to fruition. These people include John Hausdoerffer, Gavin Van Horn, Robin Wall Kimmerer, Luz Calvo, and Melissa Nelson. And my late, great amigo Phil Klasky—*Adios, hermano. Abrazos.*

Finally, I am grateful to my wife, Lisa Gaspari-Salmon, who provided editing, writing, and design ideas as well as loving support while working on this book. I couldn't have written it without you.

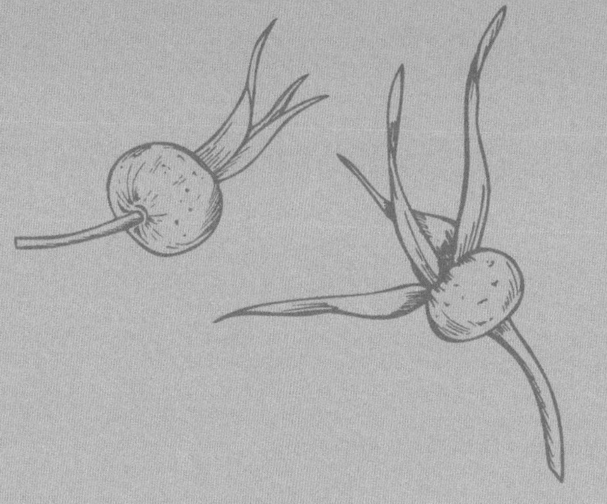

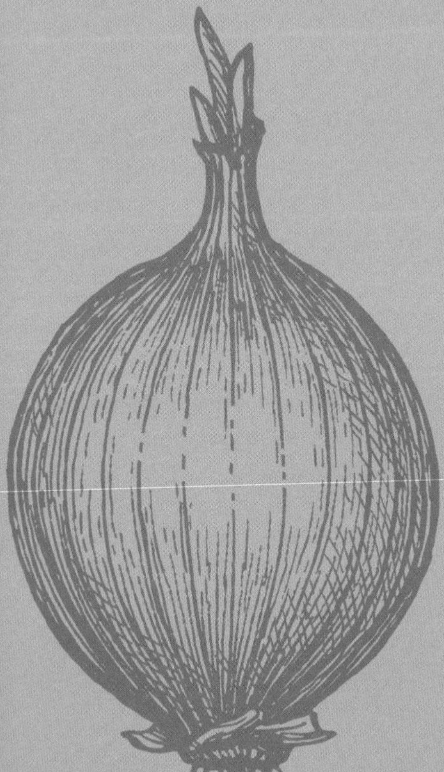

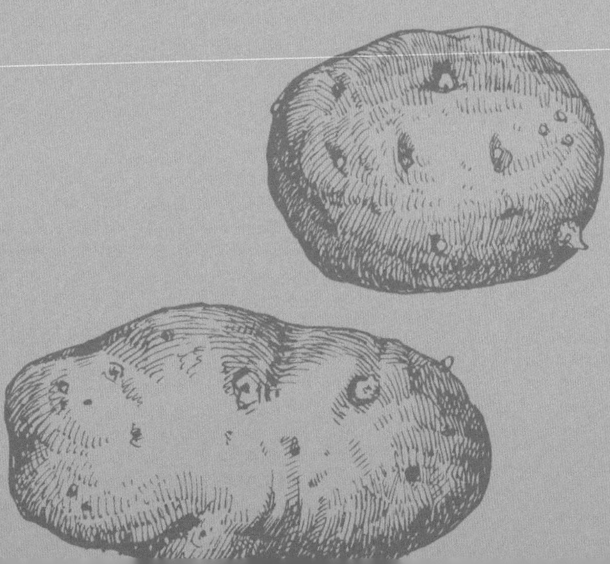

Photography Credits

PHOTOGRAPHY CREDITS

Every effort has been made to contact copyright holders of material reproduced in this volume. We would be pleased to rectify any omissions in subsequent editions should they be drawn to our attention.

Adobe Stock, 101
Adobe Stock/Foodlovers, 127
Alamy/AllCanadaPhotos, 28 top, 29 bottom left
Alamy/Anders Ryman, 148 bottom
Alamy/Andrew Profoto, 87 top
Alamy/Arina Habich, 66
Alamy/B Christopher, 114 top right
Alamy/blickwinkel, 114 top left
Alamy/Brent Hofacker, 44 bottom left
Alamy/Brian Reynolds, 102 top right
Alamy/CA Wadley, 116
Alamy/Charles Stirling, 91 right
Alamy/Chuck Place, 94 top
Alamy/Cliff LeSergent, 28 bottom left
Alamy/Cristina Lichti, 115
Alamy/Danita Delimont, 76
Alamy/David Pimborough, 125 bottom
Alamy/Esa Hiltula, 109
Alamy/Fabirano Sodi, 131
Alamy/factoraudiovisual@gma, 120 top
Alamy/Fay 2018, 42 bottom
Alamy/Florapix, 53 top left
Alamy/Garry Gay, 49
Alamy/George Ostertag, 128
Alamy/Grant Heilman Photography, 61
Alamy/Greg Vaughn, 94 bottom
Alamy/Heritage Image Partners, 17
Alamy/Historic Collection, 27
Alamy/Jared Quentin, 102 bottom left, 105
Alamy/Joseph Sorrentino, 31
Alamy/Karel Bock, 124
Alamy/Leon Werdinger, 144
Alamy/Matthijs Wetterauw, 153 top left
Alamy/mauritius images GmbH, 53 top right
Alamy/Maximilian Buzun, 135
Alamy/MBI, 44 bottom right
Alamy/MierCat Photography, 139 top
Alamy/Mindy Fawver, 108
Alamy/Nature Picture Library, 68
Alamy/North Wind Picture Archive, 119 bottom
Alamy/Oksana Golubeva, 112
Alamy/Panther Media Global, 63
Alamy/Pictorial Press Ltd, 74
Alamy/piemags/nature, 29 bottom right, 81, 114 bottom, 174 right
Alamy/Pulsar Imagens, 91 left
Alamy/RGB Ventures/SuperStock, 28 bottom center
Alamy/Rick & Nora Bowers, 102 bottom right, 109
Alamy/robertharding, 24
Alamy/Science History Images, 28 bottom right, 90 bottom

Alamy/Steffen Hauser/botanikfoto, 92
Alamy/Stone Nature Photography, 29 top left
Alamy/Sundry Photography, 98
Alamy/Suriel Ramzal, 54 left
Alamy/Svetlana Zhukova, 46 top
Alamy/Tetra Images, 44 top left
Alamy/Tim Ennis, 32 bottom right
Alamy/Tom Grundy, 44 top right, 120 bottom
Alamy/Trent Dietsche, 172
Alamy/William Mullins, 138
Alamy/William Tait, 29 top right
Alamy/Witold Skrypczak, 26, 117
Arizona Memory Project/MS1255F408_E.jpg, 97
Arthur Haines/Native Plant Trust, 51 bottom
Barbara Voorhees in Latin American Antiquity 24, 1 (2021), 10
Cass Gardiner, 141 bottom
Colorado State University/Are W, 47 left
Courtesy Andy Gonzales/@wildurbanist, 95
Courtesy Azusa Publishing/James Mooney 1893, 40 right
Courtesy Milwaukee Co. Historical Society Photographic Collection, 125 top
Courtesy NativeSeeds.org, 13
Courtesy Oregon Historical Society Research Library/48789, 21
Courtesy Wampanoag Tribe of Gay Head (Aquinnah), 88
Dean Hawn, courtesy Vesper Meadow, 32 bottom left
Dr. Michael Kotutwa Johnson, 36, 39
Dreamstime/© Khrystyna Herasymchuk, 69
Dreamstime/© Sandra Foyt, 53 bottom
Dreamstime/Picture Partners, 157 top
Eduwardo Verdugo/Associated Press, 11 bottom
Emily Moskal, 106
Flickr/Wild Edibles, 136, 139 bottom
Frasher's, Inc., 121
Getty Images/kojihirano, 38
Harvard University/Peabody Museum of Archaeology & Ethnology/Charles Fletcher Lummis, 1889-1899/63-22-10/99721.8, 19
Harvard University/Peabody Museum of Archaeology & Ethnology/Museum Purchase, Huntington Frothingham Wolcott Fund, 1900/00-30-10/62573, 18
Helmut Partsch/Science Photo Library, 150
iStock, 159 bottom
iStock/Adventure_Photo, 2
iStock/AleksandraKuzmina, 61
iStock/alexeys, 170 right
iStock/alffalff, 166
iStock/Alhontess, 4, 5 top, 48 bottom, 48 top, 49, 60 bottom, 60 top, 65 bottom right, 65 top, 71 bottom left, 71 top right, 93 top right, 104 bottom right, 133 top, 137 top, 143 bottom right, 176 top

left, 176 top right, 186 bottom right, 190 bottom left, 190 top, 206 top
iStock/Anastasiia Malini, 42 top
iStock/Andrii-Oliinyk, 5 bottom, 93 bottom
iStock/Antonio Jacome, 8
iStock/Arkadivna, 71 bottom right, 104 bottom left, 186 bottom left
iStock/Avalon Studio, 80
iStock/bonchan, 164
iStock/CarbonBrain, 159 top right
iStock/CliffWalker, 119 top
iStock/dabjola, 85
iStock/danikancil, 82 top
iStock/eAlisa, 153 top right
iStock/Eka Jaya Perman, 146, 163
iStock/Elena Chiplak, 89 bottom, 189 bottom
iStock/ErikAgar, 158
iStock/Hein Nouwens, 104 top, 186 top
iStock/Iamnee, 118, 133 bottom, 182 top, 182 bottom
iStock/Ievgeniia Lytvynovych, 122 left
iStock/Ievgeniia Lytvynovych, 155 bottom
iStock/ilbusca, 126 bottom, 127 bottom, 143 bottom left, 151, 155 top, 176 bottom left, 206 bottom
iStock/kellyvandellen, 83
iStock/Lakeview_Images, 170 left
iStock/Madeleine_Steint, 168
iStock/MarcQuebec, 160
iStock/Maria Tolkacheva, 89 top, 189 top
iStock/Marina Dekhnik, 122 right
iStock/MarinaVorontsova, 162 bottom right
iStock/Martina Cross, 165
iStock/Myatta, 168 right
iStock/Orest Lyzhechka, 152
iStock/rraya, 110 bottom, 162 bottom left, 171 bottom left
iStock/sara_winter, 90 top
iStock/seven75, 169
iStock/Sstajic, 167
iStock/Svetlana Striukova, 65 bottom left
iStock/Taste the Image, 153 bottom
iStock/TonyBaggett, 174 left
iStock/troyka, 159 top left
iStock/urbazon, 6
iStock/Veronika Yekimenko, 126 top, 189 middle, 196 middle, 196 bottom, 196 top
iStock/Victoria_Novak, 171 right, 190 bottom right
iStock/vicvaz, 148 top
iStock/weisschr, 154
iStock/yanjf, 78
iStock/Yulia Y, 102 top left
iStock/Yurii Sidelnykov, 110 top
Madeline McLeester, Dartmouth College, 14
Matt Witt, 32 top
Matthew Pendergast, 35
Minnesota Historical Society (7059.42), 46 bottom
National Museum of the American Indian, Smithsonian Institution (12/2412). Photo by NMAI Photo Services., 149
National Museum of the American Indian, Smithsonian Institution (15/4643). Photo by NMAI Photo Services., 41
National Museum of the American Indian, Smithsonian Institution (18/8656). Photo by NMAI Photo Services., 67 bottom
National Museum of the American Indian, Smithsonian Institution (23/7410). Photo by NMAI Photo Services., 40 left
National Museum of the American Indian, Smithsonian Institution (25/2652). Photo by NMAI Photo Services., 33
National Museum of the American Indian, Smithsonian Institution (25/6653). Photo by

NMAI Photo Services., 67 top
National Museum of the American Indian, Smithsonian Institution (25/9706). Photo by NMAI Photo Services., 55
National Museum of the American Indian, Smithsonian Institution (26/1749). Photo by NMAI Photo Services., 82 bottom
National Museum of the American Indian, Smithsonian Institution (26/6097). Photo by NMAI Photo Services., 34
National Museum of the American Indian, Smithsonian Institution (26/945). Photo by NMAI Photo Services., 57 top
National Museum of the American Indian, Smithsonian Institution (8/9757). Photo by NMAI Photo Services., 96
National Museum of the American Indian, Smithsonian Institution (9/5201). Photo by NMAI Photo Services., 57 bottom
Nelson DeBarros/Courtesy USDA, 79
Northern Arizona University/Colorado Plateau Digital Collections/Milton Snow, 50
Rebecca Hobert, 100
Shutterstock/Cacio Murilo, 156
Shutterstock/cctm, 141 top
Shutterstock/ChWeiss, 87 bottom
Shutterstock/Danny Hummel, 130
Shutterstock/Luis Echeverri Urrea, 157 bottom
Shutterstock/MTN2705, 51 top
Shutterstock/Sundry Photography, 72
Shutterstock/Victoria Tucholka, 134
Smithsonian Institution, Donald B. Cordry photographs from Mexico, 1937. NMAI-001.008_pht_007_P13392, 11 top
Smithsonian Institution, National Museum of Natural History (E424431-0), 54 right
Waltram Ravelombola, 47 right
Wikimedia Commons/Charles Horetzky, BC Archives, 30
Wikimedia Commons/Mattheüs Merian, 103

Index

INDEX

Note: Page numbers in *italics* indicate photographs and illustrations.

A

Abenaki people
  corn use, 18, *18*, 52
  creation beliefs, 23
  fiddlehead use, 161
acorns (*Quercus* spp. and *Lithocarpus densiflorus*), *98*, 100–105, *101–3*
Acorn Stew recipe, 104
Adams, Karen, 145
Adirondack blackberry (*Rubus lawrencei*), 77
agave fiber, 33, 96
Ageratina occidentalis (western snakeroot), 70
agroforestry practices, 20–22
ak-chin (mouth of the wash), 19, 47, 56
Akimel O'odham people, basket-making by, *149*
Algonquin-speaking peoples
  cranberry use, 87
  strawberry use, 85
Allium spp. *See* wild onions (*Allium* spp.)
ama'ca (Hidatsa word for beans), 42
amaranth family
  chenopods as member of, 153
  epazote as member of, 156, 156
Amaranthus spinosus (spiny amaranth plant), *146*
Amelanchier alnifolia (saskatoon), *29*
Andrew's blackberry (*Rubus andrewsianus*), 77
Anishinaabe people. *See* Ojibwe (Anishinaabe) people
Apache people
  acorn use, 100, 101, 102–3
  Arizona walnut use, 109
  black walnut use, 108
  mesquite use, 117
  nahavita use, 139
  piñon use, 119, 148
  prickly pear use, 91
  saguaro use, 94, 96
  Sunrise Ceremony, 100, *100*, 148
Arizona walnut (*Juglans major*), 107, 109, 111, 113
asila amaya uduhl (Cherokee term for watercress), 169
askutasquash (Narragansett word for squash), 66, 67
atole (corn beverage), *53*
Auguh, Pariscilla, 67
Aunt Vera's Salsa recipe, 65
Aztec people
  chili pepper use, 64
  prickly pear use, 90, *90*

B

bachi-ki (Rarámuri word for pumpkin), 66, 67
bachi-raka (Rarámuri word for pumpkin seeds), 67
bahidaj (saguaro fruit), 97
baking soda, for nixtamalization, 60
Balsamorhiza sagittata (balsamroot), *28*
balsamroot (*Balsamorhiza sagittata*), *28*
banana squash, 66
Basaseachi Waterfall, *8*
basket-making materials
  Akimel O'odham people use of, *149*
  blackberry canes, 77
  coppicing of, 20
  Hopi people use of, *82*
  Miwok people use of, 41
  purposeful harvesting of, 15
  saguaro ribs, 95
baskets, burden, *17*
bay laurel (*Umbellularia californica*), 105–7, *105*, *106*
bay nuts, 106–7
  Bean and Piñon Nut Dip recipe, 122
beans (*Phaseolus* spp.), 42–49
  in Bean and Piñon Nut Dip, 122
  corn interplanted with, 59
  living knowledge of, 41
  nutritional values of, 45
  profile of, 42–47, *42*, *44*, *46*, *47*
  in A Simple Pot of Beans, 48–49
  sprouted bean paste, 60–61
  in Tepary Bean Soup with Fresh Greens, 155
  in Walnut and Watercress Pesto, 110
berries, 73–89
  blackberry, 74–77, *74*, *76*
  blueberry, 78–79, *78*
  cranberry, 86–88, *87*, *88*
  currant, 79–81, *79–81*
  huckleberry, 82–84, *82*, *83*
  stories about, 73, 75, 85
  strawberry, 85–86, *85*
  toyon berry, *72*
  in Wild Rice and Berry Salad, 126
  wóžapi recipe, 89
berro. *See* watercress (*Nasturtium officinale*)
Big Horseshoe Lake blackberry (*Rubus stipulatus*), 77
big house gatherings, 27
Big Sur region, Esselen people, *35*
blackberry (*Rubus* spp.), 74–77, *74*, *76*
black currant (*Ribes americanum*), 79, 80, 81
black huckleberry (*Gaylussacia baccata*), 82–84
black oak (*Quercus kelloggii*), 100–101
black walnut (*Juglans nigra*)
  profile of, 107–11, *108*, *109*
  Walnut and Watercress Pesto recipe, 110
blueberry (*Vaccinium angustifolium*, *V. corymbosum*), 78–79, *78*
blue dicks. *See* nahavita (*Dichelostemma capitatum*)
Boas, Franz, 27
book recommendations, 185
Bosin, Blackbear, 55
bracken fern (*Pteridium aquilinum*), 158, *159*, 161
British Columbia
  big house gatherings, 27
  Bulkley River bridge, *30*
  culturally significant plants, *28*
  fishing practices, 41, *41*
broad bean (*Phaseolus coccineus*), 43
broad-leaved cattail (*Typha latifolia*), 148, *148*
brodiaea. *See* nahavita (*Dichelostemma capitatum*)
Buffalo Bird Woman (Maxi'diwiac), 45–46, 58–59
buffelgrass (*Cenchrus ciliaris*), 96
Bulkley River bridge, *30*
burden baskets, *17*
butter bean (*Phaseolus coccineus*), 43
butternut (*Juglans cinerea*), 111–13, *111*, *112*, *114*

C

Cahuilla people
  mesquite use, 117
  nahavita use, 139
Cajete, Gregory, 56, 59
calabacitas, 66, *69*, 71
California bay, California laurel (*Umbellularia californica*), 105–7, *105*, *106*
California black walnut (*Juglans californica*), 113

California huckleberry (*Vaccinium ovatum*), 82–84
camas
  blooms of, *138*
  controlled burn benefits for, 20
Candied Hopniss with Maple Syrup recipe, 133
capsaicin, 62, 63
Capsicum spp. *See* chilies (*Capsicum* spp.)
Capsicum annuum 'Pequin' (pequin chili), 62–63
Capsicum annuum var. *glabriusculum*. *See* chiltepin (*Capsicum annuum* var. *glabriusculum*)
Carnegiea gigantea (saguaro), 94–97, *94–97*
cattail (*Typha* spp.), 144, 148–50, *148–50*
Cattail Pancakes recipe, 151
cedar (*Juniperus* spp.), 81
Cenchrus ciliaris (buffelgrass), 96
cha'o (Hopi word for piñon), 119
Chemehuevai people, mesquite use, 115, 117
Chenopodium spp. *See* goosefoot (*Chenopodium* spp.)
Chenopodium giganteum, 153, *154*
Chenopodium quinoa, *153*
chenopods, 147, 153
Cherokee people
  bean use, 42, 45
  blackberry use, 77
  corn use, 56
  strawberry use, 85
  watercress use, 169
  wild onion use, 172
Cheyenne people
  corn use, 52
  currant and gooseberry use, 81
  squash use, 70
chi ch'il (Apache word for acorn), 100
Chile de Diablo variety, 63
chilies (*Capsicum* spp.)
  in Aunt Vera's Salsa, 65
  cultivation of, 64
  cultural significance of, 61–63, *61*, *63*
  in Tepary Bean Soup with Fresh Greens, 155
  use as food, 63–64
chilimeyadnaye (walnut), 108
chiltepin (*Capsicum annuum* var. *glabriusculum*)
  in beans, 48
  profile of, 62–63, *63*
  in Sopa de Nopalitos, 93
Chisnedinadinave clan, 108
chuaka (Rarámuri word for goosefoot), 152
Chumash people, berry use, 73, 75
cinnamon fern (*Osmundastrum cinnamomeum*), 158, *159*
Claytonia lanceolata (spring beauty), *28*
clove currant (*Ribes aureum-villosum*), 81
coast live oak (*Quercus agrifolia*), *98*
collecting. *See* harvesting
Colorado Plateau
  corn cultivation, 18, 40, 49, 55, 57–58
  Indigenous gardens in, 25
  Sípàapu sacred site, *24*
Comanche people, mesquite use, 116, 117
comidas (traditional foods), 30–31
common bean (*Phaseolus vulgaris*), 43, 46
common blackberry (*Rubus allegheniensis*), *74*, 77
congested snake lily. *See* nahavita (*Dichelostemma capitatum*)
controlled burns
  for edible greens, 147
  in kincentric land management, 13, 15, 20–22, *21*
  of mesquite groves, 115, 117
coppicing practices, 19–20
Cora people, chili pepper legend, 64
corms. *See* tubers, roots, and corms
corn (*Zea mays*), 49–61
  in Acorn Stew, 104
  beans interplanted with, 59
  breeding of, *17*, 18
  cultivation of, 55–59, *57*
  cultural significance of, 12–13, 13, 37–41, *39*, *40*, 49–52, *49*, *55*, *57*
  goosefoot growing among, 152
  Hopi Sumiviki recipe, 60–61
  importance to Hopi people, *40*
  living knowledge of, 41
  in the three sisters, 45
  types of, 52
  use as food, 53–54, *53*, *54*
corn beer, 10–11, 13
corn husks
  dolls of, *54*
  multiple uses of, 54
  in sumiviki, 60, 61
Corn Maidens, 52, 57, *57*
Corn Mothers, 57
corn silk, 54, 59
corn smut, 54, *54*
cranberry (*Vaccinium microcarpon*, *V. macrocarpon*, *V. oxycoccos*), 86–88, *87*, *88*
creation stories, 13, 23, 119
Creek people, groundnut story, 131
Cucurbita spp. *See* squash and pumpkin (*Cucurbita* spp.)
Cucurbita maxima (winter squash, turban squash, pumpkin), 69
Cucurbita mixta (winter squash, pumpkin, cushaw), 69
Cucurbita pepo (squash, pumpkin, gourd), 66, 67, 69
cucurbitosides, 70
cuitlacoche (corn dish), *54*
culinary ash, for nixtamalization, 60
cultivation. *See also* harvesting
  beans, 45–47
  blackberry, 77
  blueberry, 79
  chilies, 64
  corn, 54–55
  cranberry, 87–88
  edible greens, 147
  huckleberry, 84
  prickly pear, 92
  strawberry, 86
currant (*Ribes* spp.), 79–81, *79–81*
cushaw squash, *68*

D

Delamar Valley, Paiute pecking at, *38*
deserts. *See* dryland farming
Dichelostemma capitatum. *See* nahavita (*Dichelostemma capitatum*)
digging sticks, 15, 57, *57*, 58
Diné people. *See* Navajo people
Dow, Judy, 77
dryland farming
  ak-chin fields, 19, *19*, 47, *47*, 56
  of corn, 19, 57
duck potato. *See* wapato (*Sagittaria cuneata*, *S. latifolia*)
Dysphania spp. *See* epazote

(*Dysphania ambrodioides*, *D. graveolens*)

E

Eastern gamagrass (*Tripsacum dactyloides*), 51, *51*
ecological knowledge. *See* kincentric ecology
ecosystems, effects of kincentric ecological practices on, 16–22
edible greens, 145–74
  cattail, *144*, 148–51, *148–50*
  Cattail Pancakes recipe, 151
  epazote, 48, 147, 156–58, *156*, *157*
  fiddleheads, 158–62, *158–60*
  goosefoot, 147, 152–55, *152–54*
  kincentric ecology of, 13, 14, 145–47, *146*
  purslane, 147, 163–65, *163*, *164*
  Sautéed Fiddleheads with Mushrooms recipe, 162
  stinging nettle, 165–68, *165–67*
  Stinging Nettle and Ginger Infusion recipe, 168, *168*
  Tepary Bean Soup with Fresh Greens recipe, 155
  watercress, 147, 169–71, *169*, *170*
  Watercress and Potato Soup recipe, *170*, 171
  wild onions, 172–74, *172*, *174*
Emory oak (*Quercus emoryi*), *102*, 103
epazote (*Dysphania ambrodioides*, *D. graveolens*)
  profile of, 156–58, *156*, *157*
  in A Simple Pot of Beans, 48
  volunteer plants of, 147, 158
Erythronium grandiflorum (glacier lily), *28*
Esselen people, ceremony on ancestral land, *35*
evening primrose (*Oenothera trilobita*), 70
evergreen huckleberry (*Vaccinium ovatum*), 82–84
Everybody's Home (*We:sic 'em ki:*) installation, *95*

F

fiddleheads (*Pteridium aquilinum*, *Matteuccia struthiopteris*, *Osmundastrum cinnamomeum*)
  profile of, 158–61, *158–60*
  Sautéed Fiddleheads with Mushrooms recipe, 162
fire management. See also controlled burns
  kincentric ecology of, 20–22, *21*
  in Rarámuri culture, 11
fish hooks, *41*
fishing
  Haida people, 41, *41*
  stinging nettle used in, 167
Fragaria spp. (strawberry), 85–86, *85*
fruits. *See* also berries
  prickly pear, 90–92, *90–92*
  saguaro, 94–97, *94–97*
  Sopa de Nopalitos recipe, 93

G

gaan dancers (Mountain Spirits), 148
Gardening at the Margins (Valle), 30
gardens. *See* Indigenous gardens
gawi wachi (place of nurturing), 22
Gay Head cliffs, *88*
Gaylussacia baccata (black huckleberry), 82–84
Gitksan people, big house gatherings, 27
glacier lily (*Erythronium grandiflorum*), 28
Glen Canyon, ancient corn seed found in, 39
glochids, 92, 93
glycosides
  in groundnuts, 132
  in wapato, 134, 136
golden currant (*Ribes aureum*), 79, 81
Goodbird, Edward, 45
gooseberry (*Ribes* spp.), 79, 80–81, *80*
goosefoot (*Chenopodium* spp.)
  native plant status, 147
  profile of, 152–54, *152–54*
  Tepary Bean Soup with Fresh Greens recipe, 155
Gosiute people, mesquite use, 117
gourds. *See* also squash and pumpkin (*Cucurbita* spp.)
  in corn beer legend, 10, 12
  vessels of, *33*
gray squash, 70
greasewood (*Sarcobatus vermiculatus*), 60
green corn, *55*, 56
green huckleberry (*Vaccinium ovatum*), 82–84
greens. *See* edible greens
groundnut (*Apios americana*)
  Candied Hopniss with Maple Syrup recipe, 133
  profile of, *130*, 131–32, *131*

H

Haida people, fishing practices, 41, 41
harvesting. *See also* cultivation
  basket-making materials, 15
  bay laurel, 107
  black walnut, 111
  butternut, 113
  cattail, 149–50
  corn, 55–56
  cranberries, 88
  edible greens, 145, 147
  epazote, 157–58
  fiddleheads, 161
  goosefoot, 154
  groundnuts, 132
  mesquite, 115, 117
  nahavita, 140
  piñon, 120, 121, 123
  prickly pear, 92
  purslane, 164–65
  saguaro, 96–97, *97*
  stinging nettle, 167
  sustainable practices for, 15, 16
  timpsila, 142
  tubers, 130
  wapato, 136
  watercress, 170
  wild onions, 174
  wild rice, 125
ha:sañ (Tohono O'odham word for saguaro), 94
Hashañi Mashad (saguaro harvest moon), 94
hasota (Rarámuri word for epazote), 156
Haulapais people, mesquite use, 117
Havasupai people
  cattail use, 149
  culturally significant plant collecting, 25
  piñon use, 119
Hesquiat people, huckleberry harvesting, 84
Hidatsa people
  bean use, 42, 45–46, *46*
  corn use, 58
highbush blueberry (*Vaccinium corymbosum*), 78–79
Himalayan blackberry (*Rubus armeniacus*), 76
Hinds' black walnut (*Juglans hindsii*), 113
Hogan, Phyllis, 25–26
honey mesquite (*Prosopis glandulosa*), 115, 116
Hopi people
  bean use, 42
  cattail use, 149
  chili pepper use, 64
  corn use, *39*, 40–41, *40*, 49–50, *50*, 51–52, *53*, 55, 57–58
  creation beliefs, 23
  culturally significant plant collecting, 25
  living knowledge of, 38
  piñon use, 119

Sípàapu sacred site, *24*
squash use, 66, 67, *67*, 69
Hopi Second Mesa, *50*
Hopi Sumiviki recipe, 60–61
hoshchoh (Apache word for saguaro), 94
hsaheʔt (Onondaga word for bean), 42
huckleberry (*Vaccinium parvifolium*, *V. ovatum*, *Gaylussacia baccata*), 82–84, *82*, *83*
huya ania (nurturing life), 22

I

Ikxareyavs (acorn people), 100–101
Indigenous gardens
multifaceted nature of, 25–31
stories about, 31–35
Indigenous peoples. *See also specific peoples*
ecosystem effects of kincentric practices, 16–22
kincentric land management by, 13–16
living knowledge of, 37–41
relationship with the natural world, 22–23
resilience of, 39–41
worldviews of, 11, 13, 22–23
interconnectedness of life (*iwígara*), 11–12
iraká (Rarámuri word for prickly pear), 90
Iroquois people
blackberry cultivation, 77
black walnut use, 109
irrigation practices, 19, *19*, 56
Ithaca blackberry (*Rubus ithacanus*), 77
iwí (rotating circle), 12
iwígara (interconnectedness of life), 11–12

J

jalapeño peppers
in beans, 48
in calabacitas, 66, 71
in salsa, 65
Johnson, Terrol Dew, *95*
Juglans californica (California black walnut), 113
Juglans cinerea (butternut), 111–13, *111*, *112*, *114*
Juglans major (Arizona walnut), 107, 109, 111, 113
Juglans microcarpa (Texas black walnut), 113
Juglans nigra. *See* black walnut (*Juglans nigra*)
juniper (*Juniperus* spp.), 60

K

kachinas (dancers or spirits)
for chili peppers, 64
for corn, *40*, *57*
for squash, *67*
Kalamazoo dewberry (*Rubus uvidus*), 77
Kanatsiohareke Mohawk Strawberry Festival, 85
Karuk people
acorn use, 100–101
huckleberry use, 84
nahavita use, 139
Kashia Pomo people, strawberry dances, 85
katniss. *See* wapato (*Sagittaria cuneata*, *S. latifolia*)
katsinam (rain and earth spirits), 42
Kawaiisu people, nahavita use, 139–40
kawi-chu-ri (Rarámuri word for piñon), 119
Kewanyama, Eldon, *57*
Ki-Aniya (The Time Before There Was Time), 10–11
kincentric ecology
defined, 11–12
effects on ecosystems, 16–22
land management practices, 13–16
oral tradition of, 38–39
relationship between humans and nature, 22–23
King, Thomas, 111
kivas, beans sprouted in, 42
Kiva Societies, 42
Klallam people, stinging nettle story, 166
Knoll Farm, 78
ko (Havasupai word for piñon), 119
kukuipad (harvesting pole), 97

L

Lakota people
bean use, 42
currant use, 81
goosefoot use, 152
timpsila legend, 140–41, 142
wild onion use, 172
lamb's quarters. *See* goosefoot (*Chenopodium* spp.)
land management
for edible greens, 13, 147, 154
Indigenous gardens, 26–27
kincentric approach to, 13–16
practices of, 16–22
leaching, of tannins, 104
legends. *See* stories
Lenape people, creation beliefs, 23
Lewis and Clark expedition, 91–92, 134
Lithocarpus densiflorus (tan oak), 100–101, 103
Litsea glaucenscens (Mexican bay), 106
Little Colorado River, *24*, 25
little hogweed. *See* purslane (*Portulaca oleracea*, *P. retusa*)
lobelia (*Lobelia cardinalis*), 70
long walnut. *See* butternut (*Juglans cinerea*)
Lookout Mountain Blackberry (*Rubus trux*), 77
lowbush blueberry (*Vaccinium angustifolium*), 78–79
Luiseno people, mesquite use, 117

M

mahis (Taíno word for corn), 51
ma'ikadicake (Hidatsa corn variety), 58
maize. *See* corn (*Zea mays*)
Malinowski, Bronislaw, 27, *27*
manoomin. *See* wild rice (*Zizania* spp.)
Maricopa people, mesquite use, 117
Matteuccia struthiopteris (ostrich fern), 158, *158*, *159*, *160*, 161
maul oak (*Quercus chrysolepis*), 100–101
Maxi'diwiac (Buffalo Bird Woman), 45–46, 58–59
Mayan people
chili pepper legend, 64
creation beliefs, 23
medicinal uses
bay laurel, 106
blackberry, 77
chilies, 64
corn, 13, 59
groundnut, 132
kincentric knowledge about, 59
mesquite, 116–17
prickly pear, 91
purslane, 163
saguaro, 96
squash and pumpkins, 70
stinging nettle, 167
strawberry, 86
traditional foods for disease prevention, 45
walnut, 109, 111, 112
wapato, 136
Menominee people
archaeological site of, 14
blackberry cultivation, 77
corn cultivation, 52
mesquite (*Prosopis* spp.)
Mesquite Flour Chocolate Chip Cookies recipe, 118
profile of, 115–19, *115–17*
Mexican parsley. *See* purslane (*Portulaca oleracea*, *P. retusa*)
Mexican tea. *See* epazote (*Dysphania ambrodioides*, *D. graveolens*)
Mexican walnut (*Juglans*

microcarpa), 113
Mexico. *See also* Sierra Madres, Mexico; Sonoran Desert; *specific peoples*
Aztec founding legend of, 90, *90*
chili pepper domestication in, 64
corn domestication in, 18, 51
milpas in, *31*
prickly pear cultural significance, 90, *90*
squash and pumpkin domestication in, 67
Micmac people, blueberry cultivation, 79
Mills, Antonia, 27
milpas (agricultural plots), 30, *31*
Minataree Green Corn Dance (lithograph), *55*
Missouri gooseberry (*Ribes missouriense*), 81, *81*
mitigomin (Ojibwe word for acorn), 100
Miwok people
basket-making practice, 41
nahavita use, 139
wild onion use, 174
Mohawk people, strawberry cultural significance, 85
Mojave people, mesquite use, 115, 117
Mono people, wild onion story, 172
moss rose. *See* purslane (*Portulaca oleracea*, *P. retusa*)
mouth of the wash (*ak-chin*), 19, 47, 56
Mt. Desert Island blackberry (*Rubus ortivus*), 77
mun (Hopi word for beans), 42
muní (Yaqui word for beans), 42
muni-ki (Rarámuri word for beans), 42

N
naavo (Yaqui word for prickly pear), 90
naayizi (Navajo word for squash), 66, 67
naayiziztossoi (Navajo word for pumpkin), 67
nahavita (*Dichelostemma capitatum*), *128*, 138–40, *138*, *139*
Na'ii'ees (Sunrise Ceremony), 100, *100*
Narama (mythological figure), 64
Narragansett people, squash use, 66, 67
narrowleaf cattail (*Typha angustifolia*), 148
Nasturtium officinale. *See* watercress (*Nasturtium officinale*)
Native peoples. *See* Indigenous peoples
Native Science, 56, 59
Navajo people
corn use, 52, 53, 55
culturally significant plant collecting, 25
currant and gooseberry use, 81
mesquite use, 117
piñon use, 119
San Francisco Peaks significance to, 26
squash use, 66, 67, 69
strawberry use, 85, 86
nawait (wine), 97
Nawait I'i (rain ceremony), 97
neesch-il (Navajo word for piñon), 119
New England
blackberry in, 77
corn cultivation, 18, 55
fiddleheads in, 161
groundnut in, 132
historical land management practices in, 20–22
New York blackberry (*Rubus noveboracus*), 77
Nez Perce people, Lewis and Clark expedition saved by, 134
nixtamalization, 48, 60
nogal. *See* black walnut (*Juglans nigra*)
nopal (Nahuatl word for prickly pear), 90
Norogachi community (Mexico), 16
nukûma (Paiute word for piñon), 119
numat'ı, 12
nuts and seeds, 99–127
acorns, *98*, 100–105, *101–3*
bay laurel, 105–7, *105*, *106*
Bean and Piñon Nut Dip recipe, 122
black walnut, 107–11, *108*, *109*
butternut, 111–13, *111*, *112*, *114*
mesquite, 115–19, *115–17*
Mesquite Flour Chocolate Chip Cookies recipe, 118
piñon, 119–23, *119–21*
Walnut and Watercress Pesto recipe, 110
wild rice, 123–27, *124*, *125*
Wild Rice and Berry Salad recipe, 126, *127*

O
oak (*Quercus* spp.), *98*, 100–105, *101–3*
oak savannahs, land management practices, 15
Oenothera trilobita (evening primrose), 70
oh-min'-nee-chah (Lakota word for bean), 42
oilnut. *See* butternut (*Juglans cinerea*)
Ojibwe (Anishinaabe) people
acorn use, 100
wild rice use, 123–24
Oneida people, corn husk dolls of, *54*
onions, wild (*Allium* spp.), 15, 172–74, *172*, *174*
Onondaga people, bean use, 42
Onorúame (the Creator), 10
O'odham people
basket-making by, *149*
bean use, 43–44, 46–47
corn use, 56–57
dryland farming, 19
saguaro use, 94, 95, 96–97, *96*, *97*
Opuntia spp. (prickly pear), 90–92, *90–92*
oral tradition, 33, 38, 39, 41
Ortiz, Seferina, 34
Osmundastrum cinnamomeum (cinnamon fern), 158, *159*
ostrich fern (*Matteuccia struthiopteris*), 158, *158*, *159*, *160*, 161
oxalates, in purslane, 164

P
Pacific blackberry (*Rubus ursinus*), 77
Pacific Northwest. *See* also British Columbia
fishing practices, 41
food plants of, *28*
Haida culture in, 41
huckleberry use in, 84
Indigenous gardening practices in, 27
nahavita in, *138*
wapato use in, 136
Paiute people
cattail use, 149
mesquite use, 115, 117
nahavita use, 138, 139
peckings of, *38*
piñon use, 119, 123
watercress use, 169
wild onion use, 172
Panamint people, mesquite use, 117
patangsivosi (Hopi word for pumpkin seeds), 67
patnga (Hopi word for squash), 66, 67
Peacock, Sandra, 27
pecking (petroglyph), Southern Paiute people, *38*
Pediomelum esculentum. *See* timpsila (*Pediomelum esculentum*)
pemmican cakes, *76*, 79, 86, 87
Penobscot people
corn breeding by, 18
cranberry use, 87
peppers, chili. *See* chilies

(*Capsicum* spp.)
pequin chili (*Capsicum annuum* 'Pequin'), 62–63
Phaseolus spp. *See* beans (*Phaseolus* spp.)
Phaseolus acutifolius (tepary bean), 43–44, 46–47, *47*
Phaseolus angustissimus (slim leaf bean), 43
Phaseolus coccineus (runner bean), 43, 46
Phaseolus maculatus, 43
Phaseolus vulgaris (common bean), 43, 46
phytochemicals
  in blackberries, 76
  in chilies, 63
  in corn silk, 59
  in cranberries, 87
  in mesquite, 116
  in squash and pumpkins, 70
pigweed. *See* goosefoot (*Chenopodium* spp.); purslane (*Portulaca oleracea*, *P. retusa*)
piki bread, *53*, 69
piki stones, 69
Pima people
  cattail use, 149, *149*
  mesquite use, 116, 117
  saguaro use, 94, 95, 96
Pinal Coyotero Apache people, 108
piñon (*Pinus edulis*, *P. monophylla*)
  Bean and Piñon Nut Dip recipe, 122
  profile of, 119–21, *119–21*, 123, 148
planting and growing. *See* cultivation
Pleiades (constellation), 173
Poaceae plant family, 52, *53*
pohohpahtoor (Paiute word for watercress), 169
pole bean (*Phaseolus coccineus*), 43, 45, 46
Pomo people
  nahavita use, 139
  seed saving, *17*
  strawberry dances, 85
  wild onion use, 174
Portulaca oleracea, *P. retusa* (purslane), 147, 163–65, *163*, *164*
post oak (*Quercus stellata*), 100–101
Potawatomi people, wapato use, 136
Powamu (bean dances), 42, *42*
powamui ceremony, *40*
Powamuya time, 42
prairie turnip. *See* timpsila (*Pediomelum esculentum*)
prickly pear (*Opuntia* spp.)
  profile of, 90–92, *90–92*
  Sopa de Nopalitos recipe, 93
Prosopis spp. *See* mesquite (*Prosopis* spp.)
Prosopis glandulosa (honey mesquite), 115, 116
Prosopis pubescens (screw-bean mesquite), 115, 116
protease inhibitors, in groundnuts, 132
proud flesh, groundnut treatment for, 132
pruning practices, 19–20
pšíŋ šičámna (Lakota term for wild onion), 172
Psoralea esculentum. *See* timpsila (*Pediomelum esculentum*)
ptaquiloside (PTA), 161
Pteridium aquilinum (bracken fern), 158, *159*, 161
Pueblo peoples
  cattail use, 149
  corn breeding, 18–19
  dryland farming, 19, *19*
  mesquite use, 117
  purslane use, 163
  squash use, 67, 69
  worldviews of, 13
Puha'gants (Paiute elders), 38
pumpkin. *See* squash and pumpkin (*Cucurbita* spp.)
pumpkin blossoms, 70
pumpkin leaves, 70
pumpkin seeds, 69, 70
purslane (*Portulaca oleracea*, *P. retusa*), 147, 163–65, *163*, *164*

Q

Qao Kachina (corn dancer), *40*
qualities. *See* purslane (*Portulaca oleracea*, *P. retusa*)
quelite (Spanish word for edible greens), 152, 154
Quercus spp. (oak), *98*, 100–105, *101–3*
Quercus agrifolia (coast live oak), *98*
Quercus chrysolepis (maul oak), 100–101
Quercus emoryi (Emory oak), *102*, 103
Quercus kelloggii (black oak), 100–101
Quercus stellata (post oak), 100–101

R

rahewaka (Rarámuri word for stinging nettle), 165
rake, of Hidatsa people, *46*
ramps (*Allium tricoccum*), 172
Rarámuri people
  bay laurel use, 106
  bean use, 42, 45
  corn beer story, 10–11
  corn use, 51
  creation beliefs, 23
  cultural legacy of, 22
  goosefoot use, 152
  gourd vessels, *33*
  piñon use, 119
  squash use, 66, 67
  stinging nettle use, 165
  views of life, 11–13, 131
  wild onion use, 172
reading recommendations, 185
recipes
  Acorn Stew, 104
  Aunt Vera's Salsa, 65
  Bean and Piñon Nut Dip, 122
  calabacitas, 71
  Candied Hopniss with Maple Syrup, 133
  Cattail Pancakes, 151
  Hopi Sumiviki, 60–61
  Mesquite Flour Chocolate Chip Cookies, 118
  Roasted Wapato, 137
  Sautéed Fiddleheads with Mushrooms, 162
  A Simple Pot of Beans, 48–49
  Sopa de Nopalitos, 93
  sprouted bean paste, 60–61
  Stinging Nettle and Ginger Infusion, 168, *168*
  Tepary Bean Soup with Fresh Greens, 155
  Timpsila Stew with Fresh Greens and Rice, 143
  Walnut and Watercress Pesto, 110
  Watercress and Potato Soup, *170*, 171
  Wild Rice and Berry Salad, 126, *127*
  wóžapi, 89
red huckleberry (*Vaccinium parvifolium*), 82–84, *82*, *83*
Ribes spp. *See* currant (*Ribes* spp.); gooseberry (*Ribes* spp.)
rincón (corner), 16
roadside blackberry (*Rubus aliceae*), 77
Roasted Wapato recipe, 137
Rodriguez Cabrillo, Juan, 103
roots. *See* tubers, roots, and corms
Rubus spp. See blackberry (*Rubus* spp.)
Rubus aculiferus (thorny dewberry), 77
Rubus aliceae (roadside blackberry), 77
Rubus allegheniensis (common blackberry), *74*, 77
Rubus andrewsianus (Andrew's blackberry), 77
Rubus armeniacus (Himalayan blackberry), 76
Rubus ithacanus (Ithaca blackberry), 77
Rubus lawrencei (Adirondack blackberry), 77

Rubus noveboracus (New York blackberry), 77
Rubus ortivus (Mt. Desert Island blackberry), 77
Rubus stipulatus (Big Horseshoe Lake blackberry), 77
Rubus trux (Lookout Mountain Blackberry), 77
Rubus ursinus (Pacific blackberry), 77
Rubus uvidus (Kalamazoo dewberry), 77
runner bean (*Phaseolus coccineus*), 43, 46

S

safety concerns
  bay laurel, 107
  chilies, 62–63
  fiddleheads, 161
  groundnut, 132
  purslane, 164
  stinging nettle, 167, *167*
Sagittaria spp. *See* wapato (*Sagittaria cuneata*, *S. latifolia*)
saguaro (*Carnegiea gigantea*), 94–97, *94–97*
saguaro boots, 97
San Francisco Peaks, Indigenous gardens at, 25, *26*
San Jose, California, gardening as resistance, 30, 31
Santa Fe raspberry (*Rubus aliceae*), 77
Sarcobatus vermiculatus (greasewood), 60
saskatoon (*Amelanchier alnifolia*), *29*
Sautéed Fiddleheads with Mushrooms recipe, 162
sauwo (Yaqui word for saguaro), 94
schumaakwe cakes, 70
screwbean mesquite (*Prosopis pubescens*), 115, 116
Secwepemc peoples, culturally significant plants, *28*
seed beaters, *17*
seed saving, 16–19, *17*, *18*
semi-domesticates, 147, 154, 163
sewa'ra (flowers), 12
Shoshone people
  mesquite use, 117
  nahavita use, 138
  piñon use, 119
sibowe (Rarámuri word for wild onion), 172
Sierra Madres, Mexico
  Basaseachi Waterfall, *8*
  chili pepper use in, 62
  controlled burns in, 20
  iwígara in, 11
  Rarámuri cultural legacy in, 22
Sierra Tarahumara, Mexico, 10, 22
A Simple Pot of Beans recipe, 48–49
Sípàapu (sacred site), *24*
sito-bachi (Rarámuri word for piñon), 119
sito-bachi (Rarámuri word for squash), 66, 67
Sium suave (water parsnip), *28*
slim leaf bean (*Phaseolus angustissimus*), 43
smoking
  corn husks for, 54
  in Rarámuri culture, 11
  at tesguinadas, 10
Sonoran Desert
  bean cultivation in, 43, 46–47
  corn cultivation in, 56–57
  mesquite in, 117
  oak in, 101
  saguaro in, 94–95, 96–97
Sopa de Nopalitos recipe, 93
southern cattail (*Typha domingensis*), 148
spiny amaranth plant (*Amaranthus spinosus*), *146*
spring beauty (*Claytonia lanceolata*), *28*
sprouted bean paste, 60–61
squalene, 70
squash and pumpkin (*Cucurbita* spp.)
  calabacitas, 66, *69*, 71
  cultivation of, 70
  cultural significance of, 66–69, *66*, *67*, *68*
  living knowledge of, 41
  in the three sisters, 45, 59
  use as food, 69–70
squash blossoms, 67, *67*, 69–70
squash leaves, 70
squash seeds, 69, 70
squash vine borers, 67
stinging nettle (*Urtica dioica*)
  profile of, 165–67, *165–67*
  Stinging Nettle and Ginger Infusion recipe, 168, *168*
stories
  acorn legends, 100–101
  about berries, 73, 75, 85
  black walnut legend, 108
  about chilies, 64
  about corn, 51–52
  corn beer legend, 10–11
  corn husk doll traditions, 54, *54*
  creation stories, 13, 23, 51–52, 119, 123
  groundnut legend, 131
  about mesquite, 119
  saguaro legends, 95, 97
  about stinging nettles, 166
  strawberry legend, 85
  timpsila legend, 140–41, 142
  values communicated through, 31–35, 111–12
  walnut cracker legend, 112
  wild onion legend, 173
  about wild rice, 123–24
storyteller figurine, *34*
strawberry (*Fragaria* spp.), 85–86, *85*
sumati okilivea (lily), 12
Sumiviki recipe, 60–61
Sunrise Ceremony (Apache people), 100, 100, 148
sv-gi (Cherokee word for wild onion), 172

T

tafvmpuce (Paiute word for wild onion), 172
tágo (Washo word for piñon), 119
Taíno people, corn use, 51
tannins, in acorns, 104
tan oak (*Lithocarpus densiflorus*), 100–101, 103
Taurus (constellation), 173
Tenochtitlan (Mexico City), 90
teosinte (*Zea luxurians*), 18, 51, *51*
tepary bean (*Phaseolus acutifolius*), 43–44, 46–47, *47*, 155
Tepary Bean Soup with Fresh Greens recipe, 155
tesguinadas (corn beer gatherings), 10–11
tesguino (corn beer), 10–11, *11*
Tesuque people, squash use, 67
Tewa people, corn use, 54, 55
Texas black walnut (*Juglans microcarpa*), 113
thorny dewberry (*Rubus aculiferus*), 77
three sisters planting method, 45, *46*, 59
thuya (Cherokee word for bean), 42
tiic'm (the land), 22
timpsila (*Pediomelum esculentum*)
  profile of, *138*, 140–42, *141*
  Timpsila Stew with Fresh Greens and Rice recipe, 143
tobacco
  controlled burn benefits for, 20
  corn beer story, 10
  in Rarámuri culture, 11
Tohono O'odham people
  bean use, 43–44, 46–47
  corn use, 56–57
  dryland farming, 19
  saguaro use, 94, 95, 96–97, *96*, *97*
toyon berry, 72
tripsacum (*Tripsacum dactyloides*), 51, *51*
tshi (Apache word for piñon), 119
tubers, roots, and corms, 129–43

Candied Hopniss with Maple Syrup recipe, 133
groundnut, *130*, 131–33, *131*
kincentric ecology of, 129–31
nahavita, *128*, 138–40, *138*, *139*
Roasted Wapato recipe, 137
timpsila, 140–43, *141*
Timpsila Stew with Fresh Greens and Rice recipe, 143
wapato, 134–37, *134–36*
tunas (prickly pear fruits), 91
Turner, Nancy, 27
Typha spp. *See* cattail (*Typha* spp.)

U

Umbellularia californica (bay laurel), 105–7, *105*, *106*
Urtica dioica. *See* stinging nettle (*Urtica dioica*)
Ute people, mesquite use, 117
Uto-Axtecan linguistic family tree, 42

V

Vaccinium angustifolium, *V. corymbosum* (blueberry), 78–79, *78*
Vaccinium microcarpon, *V. macrocarpon*, *V. oxycoccos* (cranberry), 86–88, *87*, *88*
Vaccinium ovatum (evergreen huckleberry), 82–84, *83*
Vaccinium parvifolium (red huckleberry), 82–84, *82*, *83*
Valle, Gabriel, 30
verdolagas. *See* purslane (*Portulaca oleracea*, *P. retusa*)

W

wa'a"pin (Shoshone word for piñon), 119
wah-pe to-to (Lakota word for goosefoot), 152
walnut. *See* black walnut (*Juglans nigra*); white walnut (*Juglans cinerea*)
Walnut and Watercress Pesto recipe, 110
Wampanoag people
corn husk dolls, *54*
cranberry festivals, 86, *88*
wapato (*Sagittaria cuneata*, *S. latifolia*)
importance to Secwepemc people, *29*
profile of, 134–36, *134–36*
Roasted Wapato recipe, 137
Warre, Henry, 21
Washington-Alma neighborhoods (San Jose, California), 30, 31
Washo people, piñon use, 119
watercress (*Nasturtium officinale*)
native plant status, 147, 169
profile of, 169–70, *169*, *170*
Watercress and Potato Soup recipe, *170*, 171
water management. *See* dryland farming; irrigation practices
water parsnip (*Sium suave*), *28*
We:sic 'em ki: (*Everybody's Home*) installation, *95*
Westerman, Floyd Red Crow, 171
western snakeroot (*Ageratina occidentalis*), 70
Wet'suwet'en people
big house gatherings, 27
Bulkley River bridge, 30
White Mountain Apache people, 108
White Shell Woman, 100, 148
white walnut (*Juglans cinerea*), 111–13, *111*, *112*, *114*
wild hyacinth. *See* nahavita (*Dichelostemma capitatum*)
wild onions (*Allium* spp.), 15, 172–74, *172*, *174*
wild rice (*Zizania* spp.)
profile of, 123–25, *124*, *125*
Wild Rice and Berry Salad recipe, 126, 127
wild strawberry (*Fragaria vesca*), 85–86, *85*
Willamette Valley, historical illustration of, *21*
Wilson, Gilbert L., 45, 58
woodland strawberry (*Fragaria vesca*), 85–86, *85*
wormseed. *See* epazote (*Dysphania ambrodioides*, *D. graveolens*)
wóžapi recipe, 89

X

xuntápan (Karuk word for acorn), 100

Y

Yakima people, huckleberry use, 82
Yaqui people
bean use, 42
prickly pear use, 90, 91
saguaro use, 94
Yavapai people, Arizona walnut use, 109
yellowcress. *See* watercress (*Nasturtium officinale*)
yerba zorillo. *See* epazote (*Dysphania ambrodioides*, *D. graveolens*)
Yoeme people, *huya ania* term, 22
*Yúmari (*blessing), 12

Z

Zea luxurians (teosinte), 18, 51, *51*
Zea mays. *See* corn (*Zea mays*)
Zizania spp. See wild rice (*Zizania* spp.)
Zuni people
chili pepper legend, 64
corn cultivation, 55, *57*
squash cultivation, 70

About the Author

Enrique Salmón is a Rarámuri (Tarahumara). He is head of the American Indian Studies Program at Cal State University–East Bay, in Hayward, California. He holds a BS from Western New Mexico University, an MAT in Southwest Studies from Colorado College, and a PhD in anthropology from Arizona State University. He has been a scholar in residence at the Heard Museum and has served as a board member for the Society of Ethnobiology. He has published many articles on indigenous ethnobotany, agriculture, nutrition, and traditional ecological knowledge. He has also spoken at numerous conferences and symposia on the topics of cultivating resilience, indigenous solutions to climate change, and the ethnobotany of Native North America, the ethnobotany of the Greater Southwest, poisonous plants that heal, bioculturally diverse regions as refuges of hope and resilience, and the language and library of indigenous cultural knowledge. His first book was *Iwígara: The Kinship of Plants and People: American Indian Ethnobotanical Traditions and Science* (2020).